Too Far From The Tree

Phil Sisson's Too Far from the Tree is a groundbreaking book exploring white supremacy's genesis, addressing "its incongruence with what can only be characterized as a spiritual revolution." This thought-provoking work is not just a history lesson but a spiritual journey that explores the very fabric of humanity's existence. The writing is infused with a deep sense of spirituality as the author seeks to understand the complexities of human nature and the interconnectedness of all people.

His book serves as a powerful backdrop for exploring the themes of racism, nationalism, and communism, allowing readers to connect with the material on a deeper level. The author's use of storytelling as a medium for sharing his experiences and insights is nothing short of masterful as he weaves together disparate threads to create an intimate and expansive narrative. Too Far from the Tree is a unique book on white supremacy and the color line, a reality that is as resonant today as it has been in the past.

- Reviewed by Romuald Dzemo

Too Far From the Tree by Phil Sisson is a deep, spiritual, and thought-provoking exposition into the root causes of the systemic racism manifested in the world but especially prevalent in Western society. The author examines the justifications used by the European countries to enter into the abhorrent practices of the slave trade in the fifteenth century and then to attempt to subjugate and often eradicate the native populations in the name of colonialism, greed, and civilizing the savage creatures that they found there.

This book is one of the most powerful statements I have read on the problem of systemic racism and its root causes, which many of us recognize but feel powerless to do anything about. Author Phil

Sisson has researched deeply and his extensive endnotes will show the integrity of his source information.

One of the biggest takeaways I hope readers get from this book is a phrase attributed to many over the years: "History is written by the victors." As Sisson points out succinctly, the history of colonization, slavery, and systemic racism was written by the conquerors and the enslavers.

- Reviewed by Grant Leishman

Author Phil Sisson has crafted a journey through history that will spark new perspectives for readers, leaving them pondering the enduring challenges of our contemporary world based on the trajectory of those who came before us. The narratives of historical personalities were well-paced and easy to get into, with plenty of historical context and detail so that we never feel left out or confused. The parallels to our current era are increasingly and naturally obvious as history unfolds, and Sisson draws them with resonant and memorable quotations as he compares cause and effect in complex but clear terms. The exploration of how past ideologies and ambitions continue to shape our present-day realities was both enlightening and thought-provoking, and Sisson's wise and measured approach sheds light on these contexts and prompts deep reflection on the quest for harmony and unity amidst today's global divisions.

Overall, Too Far From The Tree serves as a poignant reminder of the importance of understanding history's lessons as we navigate contemporary challenges, making it a compelling read for those interested in the intersections of history, politics, and societal harmony.

- Reviewed by K.C. Finn

Too Far From The Tree

Phil Sisson

Library of Congress Control Number: 2024909466

ISBN: 979-8-89228-097-6   (Paperback)
ISBN: 979-8-89228-098-3   (Hardcover)
ISBN: 979-8-89228-099-0   (eBook)

Printed in the United States of America

I dedicate this book to my wife who has always been my most profound inspiration; to every mother and father who believe in their children; to every teacher who lights the lamp of students' souls; and lastly (but not least), to those rare and beautiful friends who have encouraged my writing of this book every step of the way.

CONTENTS

INTRODUCTION

Why another book on white supremacy? Why? Because as novelist and poet, James Joyce wrote: *"History is a nightmare from which I am trying to awake."* However, as much as I sympathize with James Joyce, that is not the reason for my writing this book. In my seventy-four years of life on this planet, I have yet to encounter any book on the history of white supremacy that addresses its incongruence with what can only be characterized as a *spiritual revolution*; a revolution within the heart and soul of every human being be they aware or not. This spiritual revolution is destined to recast the story of humanity --- our story, in a completely new light, and its fervor is sweeping across the entire planet. This spiritual revolution began in 1844 A.D, and, in my opinion, represents the crucible of our times, and is a critical turning point in world history. For those engaged in upholding the ideology of white supremacy, this crucible is seen as the single greatest threat to its sustainability. White supremacy, materialism, and racism --- are teetering on the verge of collapse --- yet continue to be considered by most to be the three greatest impediments to human progress in the 21st century and beyond.

There is no mystery to white supremacy. It is a man-made ideology which, since its very inception, has had a single aim: to so confound the rational soul that no human being on earth will have any choice but to capitulate. White supremacy is the idea that a single European ethnic group has been preordained by God to rule over all others. To this end, all aspects of Western civilization have been constructed. The initial stage of this ideology did not begin with the transatlantic slave trade as most have been educated to believe. It began at the very creation of capitalism and world colonialism, and has been on the march ever since, seeking first to extract ancient Egypt out of Africa despite overwhelming consensus among scholars that Africa is both the Cradle of Humanity and the Cradle of Civilization. The combined efforts to extract ancient Kemet from its cradle (later renamed Egypt by the Greeks) included the desecration of its ancient religions, the ghoulish practice of excavating and then abducting sacred human remains to display them in museums throughout Europe and the Americas under the guise of educating the public --- mummified entertainment that spawned an entire genre in cinema. However, it didn't stop there. Diverse African kingdoms and cultures were subjected to contemptuous attitudes, dismissive epithets and unseemly behaviors aimed at denying its people of its worthiness of dignity and respect, disemboweling ancient kingdoms of their precious artifacts, dispossessing its people all across the entire continent of their land, their religions, and their ancient histories --- all with one intent: to erase all signs of black Africans from the human historical records. By a single Vatican decree usurpation became an unequivocal by-word unleashing European nations upon the continent to hollow out virgin lands even if it meant genocide. This was followed by the institution of the Atlantic slave trade which was brutal, unrelenting, murderous, and erected upon the lives of hundreds of millions of precious black African souls for the establishment of an all-white international system of colonialism.

This book is not intended to be a comprehensive investigation of the history of the African diaspora or what has now come to be known as "the *three false gods --- racism, nationalism and communism*." Rather, this book is but a primer, a jump-start if you will, to serve as an opening to the door of truth. It is an attempt to encourage the individual's own independent investigation of reality. It is as much a spiritual journey as it is a re-examination of historical events and the thinking that precipitated those events for it is the thinking that endures through time. For me, gaining a foothold on what actually contributed to the creation of the racist ideology of white supremacy is key to any attempt at its elimination, an ideology which has been coined "*The* Most Challenging Issue."

Family and friends say I'm a storyteller. No, not that kind of storyteller. I'm a truth-teller. I often share stories about my life experiences. This sharing reminds me of the many times prayer has unerringly shaped my thoughts and my life. I have to admit that in admitting this hasn't been easy for me because I think of prayer as a private affair between me and my Maker. It just feels self-righteous to speak it out loud. But having grown up during two of the most tumultuous decades of my lifetime --- the 60s and early 70s, by age nineteen, I had given up on religion, and had concluded that even prayer was no longer viable. Instead, I tied my ethical and moral compass to self-reliance as I had been taught by my father, and came to rely upon my own thinking, and my own reasoning, and to some extent that shift in consciousness served me well. And then reality came around and "cut me into little pieces," placing me right alongside singer Gilbert O'Sullivan as he bewailed his plight in the hit song 'Alone Again'. I knew very well the feeling of being absolutely crushed. And though being crushed had happened as a result of my own doing, hurting three people whom I had come to love; my best friend, and his girlfriend, and a wonderful young woman with whom I had fallen madly in love, I was able to muster enough self-awareness to mend my ways. The experience forced me to face up to my own egocentrism. The fact that I had been thinking only of myself with no regard for the feelings of these three wonderful souls, three people who had taken me into their hearts, had devastated me. The experience of losing these precious friendships had sent me spiraling down into a very deep depression, something I had never known before, and left me wondering who I was, why I had done what I had done, and how to atone for my selfishness. Gratefully, deep within my soul, there remained the love of family and an appreciation for the many life lessons my parents had tried to prepare me for. These lessons were my lifeline, a lifeline that I was able to hold onto as I began to reexamine my life and its purpose. Fortunately, I was able to piece myself together and started upon a new yet unchartered pathway. And so, now, whenever a brick hits me in the head, I still turn to the same Divine Source of guidance that had shepherded me throughout those difficult times in my young life. Now, as a senior adult, I feel fortunate to be able to share my personal stories. In fact, I feel privileged to be able to share these stories knowing that stories can indeed teach us how to live. I believe this strongly. And fortunately for me, I've been told that my stories have helped others to see just a bit clearer. Call it what you may, I see storytelling as a meaningful way of reaching out to others to create bonds of solidarity and friendship.

In both high school and college one of my favorite subjects was history. I love learning about the historical events of the past, but especially I love reading about ancient Kemet and other African civilizations and kingdoms, and its diverse peoples. History has so much to tell us! African history especially has much to say because it has been ignored, marginalized, and dismissed. For centuries its many important contributions to World History have been completely ignored and undermined by mainstream historians. As such, history still remains the greatest medium for the storyteller.

The story you are about to read in these pages draws attention to that marginalized history. However, it is a story told not only with the data from existing written history, but with the madness of a rapper speaking from his heart and soul, spilling his guts in the tradition of the African oral historian --- the tribal griot. This history is the stuff of life --- the who, the what, the where, the why and the how of it --- the struggles, the sufferings, the indignancy, with tales of pre-colonial Eden --- Mother Africa --- whose mortal remains intersect with the divine, to demonstrate its power to continually give it new life, a land where the inherent will to survive itself was created by the very hand of a Divine Will. You won't find this story in any past or contemporary history book. And, especially, no contemporary elementary school or university textbook can stir the blood like this! I call my book <u>Too Far from the Tree</u>. I hope this book will unleash the spirit within, informing the mind and taking the reader beyond words and syllables to the very soul of human history. For that reason alone, high school students may come to recognize the need to demand more from their history classes, their teachers and even more from their textbooks. African American kids especially are already galvanized to set out on the journey to 'know thyself' for with this spirit boredom will be a thing of the past. No longer will students go passively through chapters on American history as apathetic spectators reading uninspired chapter after chapter that contains no insight. Hopefully, existing textbooks that are bereft of insight and inspiration will soon come to be seen to be of greater service when the *caveat emptor* --- READER BEWARE --- is attached to the cover. Black students, in particular, must know that it is they and they alone who are responsible for checking the quality and suitability of the information proffered before them --- for 'they are the master of their fate and the captain of their soul'. No longer can any young mind entrust theirs to another's. And yes, the above warning should be in all caps. Black baby-boomers know exactly what I'm talking about. And if they don't, below is a brief summary of why such a warning should be stamped on the cover of any textbooks that claim to tell the true history of African Americans.

Back in the day, before cell phones with cameras, laptops, the internet and social media, the precolonial history of African peoples was never mentioned in textbooks. When it was mentioned, anglicized teachers would roll out the old audio/visual black and white television sets to show the class black and white Tarzan, African Queen or King Kong movies. It was all very entertaining. Apart from the movies, the textbook would contain a single chapter that depicted the entirety of Africa's contribution to world history as originating with the transatlantic slave trade. Of course, the *pièce de résistance* was rural black folks picking cotton accompanied by other photos, namely photographs of sharecroppers. And to drive home the supposed wretchedness of these black lives there were always the photos that showed a family with more kids than anybody could feed, standing in front of a weather-beaten wooden shack emphasizing their poverty.

These depictions were no mere insinuation, for in most cases, it was true that many black people across the country were unschooled in the prescribed and acceptable Eurocentric view of the world that was meted out under the guise of "public education". In the 1930s, this guise is what all poor people who lived off the land were fed as education. The list of American Dream wannabes included White Okie migrants from Oklahoma to Black migrants escaping the life of sharecropping in the old South, to Mexican farmworkers and Chinese immigrants. All were fed a steady diet of eurocentrism as education. But the subliminal message in the films that were shown in the 40s and 50s went far deeper than that and was constantly reinforced by the Jim Crow laws and society in which they lived. The Jim Crow era saw to that! This period saw the invention and promotion of the notion that black people were devoid of ambition. Of course, to end the two-or more days lesson on black history, attention would turn to Abraham Lincoln and the Emancipation Proclamation with a lecture on Lincoln's honesty and benevolence in wanting to free the slaves in the first place. It mentioned nothing about the fierce competitive economics between the free industrialist northern states and the slave labor agricultural southern states. The *why* of Lincoln's motive was given (at the time) that the overriding issue was that to enslave a human being was immoral. However, Lincoln's concern was far less about slavery being an affront to the dignity of a human being than it was his concern for the highly competitive economic system which was proven to be far more profitable than any pay labor system in the northern states.

In my high school class, students were assigned to memorize 'The Gettysburg Address'. However, though the Proclamation Emancipation was one of the most consequential historical documents that came out of post-Civil War America we were given no assignment to memorize _that_. These types of history narratives remain America's standard story about black Americans. Even to this day, every generation of Americans, black and white, can probably recite this prescribed narrative in their sleep; each internalizing it differently.

It's not a matter of perspective alone; it's a matter of intention. The psychological effects of intention have divided our country since long before the beginning of the nation itself, and the story has become entrenched in the minds of the American people leaving little room for sufficient awareness to allow forgiveness, correction, and any form of absolution that could elevate the human spirit's on-going quest for redemption. For both black and white alike, there is no need to wait for the outcome of the American story as long as hope is vanquished, insight is diminished, and fear lurks between the lines. Why? Because as long as the victor can tell *his* story and the disenfranchised vanquished are unable or prohibited from doing so, history is nothing more than a deafening salvo of military vengeance, family heartbreaks, destruction and devastation, and offers no insight to history at all Though perfumed with poetic odes of courage, precise dates to be memorized, speckled with blood-soaked battlefields meticulously described, with precise surnames and titles of military heroes --- men held up as being worthy of emulation, the overall narrative itself is presented with a single intent: to underscore the indebtedness of an enslaved black monolith with no acknowledged history of its own to check the white monolith view who fought and died supposedly to free them. This underlying message was targeted at a people who had rebelled against that same enslavement on foreign plantations long before their 1619 arrival in the Virginia colony. Also, the demonization of black warriors such as Harriet Tubman, Jack Sisson, Frederick Douglas, and those who had escaped the Confederate South by way of the Underground Railway were to be hated --- all of this omitted from the written textbook narrative --- but told across dinner tables from one generation to another as oral testimony: the history of African Americans. Living history is like that! Life history isn't a rigid set of dates, unsubstantiated facts, and details, or elegant literary portrayals of one-dimensional human beings dressed in military regalea perched high upon some winged white Pegasus to symbolize power, nobility, and victory. Living history is the nitty-gritty account of ordinary people --- their blood, their sacrifices. It is an ever-unfolding process of human beings becoming morally challenged along the path of their own spiritual destinies. It is a continual process of self-discovery, overcoming limitations, rectifying one's own character, having regrets, seeking forgiveness, learning, and praying for both courage and absolution. That's what history is made of, that is what it means --- to become more human. And, when experienced in this way, history, as is proven in *the Sacred Bhagavad Gita*, has the same power as *Revelation!*

The title, <u>Too Far from the Tree</u>, was inspired by a spiritual affirmation that comments on the Old Testament Genesis story about the Garden of Eden which states: "… the *Tree of Life symbolizes the prophets of God, whose guidance protects and nourishes everyone.*" [1]

Everyone? I thought. The affirmation made no judgment. There was no mention of good and evil, and it alluded to *The Tree of Life* not as garden foliage but as the prophet of God. Am I reading that right?

When I first read the above affirmation, I was reminded of an idiom a friend in my youth said when he met my father for the very first time. "An apple," he said to me, "never falls far from the tree."

At the time, I had never heard this expression but intuitively I knew exactly what it meant --- that I had a character and qualities that were similar to my dad. Years later, as I began writing this book, I realized that the theme I was addressing in this book --- the Vatican Papal Bulls and white supremacy ---was essentially that of the vile human character that has resulted from discarding the spiritual qualities that protect and enshrine the true nature of human beings which increases man's spiritual discernment. A natural transposition followed as I applied the idea of the metaphor of the *Tree of Life* as the *Divine Source* of human character and its fruits as spiritual qualities that can only be acquired by applying the teachings of *The Tree of Life* to one's own life. The knowledge and faith gained by its dependence upon that Divine Source is derived from *The Tree of Knowledge* itself. It is that faith which stands in the midst of that metaphorical garden --- the hearts of Man.

Then, an epiphany happened within me. I rethought the idiom and made it the basis of a question that occurred to me: what of an apple that falls *far* from its source? What then? Fortunately for me, Nature has a way of answering such questions metaphorically while giving tangible evidence of reality if one is paying attention. I remember looking down at the sprawling plum tree in my garden and, as if intentionally giving me tangible evidence as the answer to my question, I observed all the plums that were still clinging to the tree and those that had fallen to the ground. Most of the plums had fallen directly beneath the branches of the tree. Then I saw a ground squirrel gnawing voraciously on a plum near the base of the trunk of the tree. A few moments later, more ground squirrels appeared and began feasting on the plums nearest the base of the tree as well. After a while, I headed down into the garden to gather some of the fallen plums for myself. As mentioned, most of the plums had fallen directly beneath the branches of the tree and were still fresh and unbruised. Then I saw other plums that had fallen and had rolled far from the shade of the tree. Not even the ground squirrels were interested in these plums. These plums had fallen to the ground and once severed, had rolled down the embankment far from the tree and were now rotting --- infested with parasites and worms --- left to be consumed, without discernment, by nature's *undiscriminating* scavengers. All that remained to be seen was how long it would take for the parasites and scavengers to consume what was once a fresh, healthy, life-nurturing fruit. This is the undeniable state of the world our generation has inherited, an inheritance that has been bequeathed to humanity by the doctrines inherent in all seven Papal Bulls of the 15th and 16th centuries. These doctrines established the 'Law of Discovery' whereby any land and its peoples were deemed as "savage people and discovered lands" and were subsumed as the property of the Holy Roman empire and by association the christian monarchies of Europe. These Vatican decrees gave birth to the doctrine of scientific materialism and secured the aims of scientific racism, and the doctrine of white supremacy --- representing the man-made rancid, decayed fruits that had fallen from the *Tree of Life* --- the divine symbol of the sacred teachings of the prophets of God. It would be well for all people of good faith to ponder the following statement:

> "Those who care for the future of the human race may well ponder this advice. "If long-cherished ideals and time-honored institutions, if certain social assumptions and religious formulae have ceased to promote the welfare of the generality of mankind, if they no longer minister to the needs of a continually evolving humanity, let them be swept away and relegated to the limbo of obsolescent and forgotten doctrines. *Why should these, in a world subject to the immutable law of change and decay, be exempt from the deterioration that must needs overtake every human institution? For legal standards, political and economic theories are solely designed to safeguard the interests of humanity as a whole, and not humanity to be crucified for the preservation of the integrity of any particular law or doctrine.*" [2]

According to the Savant of our Age, Bahá'u'lláh, humanity is now slowly transitioning to the spiritual *Age of Fulfillment*, while its precursory stage, the Age of Promise, is simultaneously coming to its close. For those who remain attached and transfixed by the Age of Promise, to them, this closure is seen as "the end of the world" though the Essenes, a mystic Jewish sect of the 2nd century A.D., and Matthew in 24:3 both refer to this closure as *"the end of an Age"*. Either way, however, individuals who yearn to acquire the indivisible spiritual consciousness that spans all previous ages and specifically both the Age of Promise and the Age of Fulfillment, an individual's spiritual consciousness must be able to discern it. The age of fulfillment goes beyond personal salvation for in order to experience both Ages as necessary stages in the ever-advancement of humanity as a whole one must view humanity as a single biological unit and single human family. To achieve this glorious first new stage of humanity's spiritual evolution, Bahá'u'lláh has given humanity in this Age of Fulfillment a spiritual mandate: *"The earth is but one country and mankind its citizens."* Today, most people of good faith can feel this shift in consciousness in their guts for it is not something that's happening outside of themselves or directed at one particular group but is lodged deeply into the very essence of all humankind. We Homo sapiens have yearned to witness the fulfillment of this reality since we began our migration, out from the bowels of Africa before and during the Adamic Cycle. Throughout the many ages since that departure from Tanzania, covenants have been established between man and God with only two basic requirements --- a heart full of love and a steadfast adherence to each of the covenants progressively received during their appointed times. Both requirements complete the standard that is implicit in each one of those covenants, covenants to which humanity has agreed to honor. In <u>God Passes By</u>, written by Shoghi Effendi, the appointed Guardian of the Baha'i Faith, explains it thusly: "The Greater Covenant into which … God had, from time immemorial, entered [into] through the Prophets of each age with the whole of mankind regarding the newborn revelation, had already been fulfilled. It had now to be supplemented by a Lesser Covenant which He felt bound to make with the entire body of His followers concerning the One Whose advent He characterized as the fruit and ultimate purpose of His Dispensation. Such a Covenant had invariably been the feature of every previous religion." What this suggests is that all Lesser Covenants, that is, all the revelations of the Prophets of old were revealed to guide a humanity who had been dispersed over all four corners of the earth to embrace the Greater Covenant which was firmly established before the creation of the world.

In Gleanings from the Writings of **Bahá'u'lláh**, He writes:

> "… the Manifestations of His Divine glory and the Day
> Springs of eternal holiness have been sent down from
> time immemorial and been commissioned to summon
> mankind to the one true God. That the names of some
> of them are forgotten and the records of their lives lost
> is to be attributed to the disturbances and changes that
> have overtaken the world."

When most of us think of religion, it is the familiar Abrahamic religions. These religions were all established after the time of the prophet Adam who initiated the Adamic Cycle 6,000 years ago. However, in both primordial and ancient languages that have been lost over eons of time, every religion that preceded the Adamic Cycle and those that have appeared since the dawn of civilization has renewed the Greater Covenant and brought a new or Lesser Covenant which embodied the new teachings to address the needs of humanity for that given Age; thus the Abrahamic Age, the Mosaic Age, the Christian Age, and the Muhammadan Age. Each religion contributes to the larger, over-arching Greater Covenant with new laws from which a new civilization emerges. The Greater Covenant is the age-old connection and contract between the Creator and humanity; not one tribe or ethnic group, but the whole of humanity. That contract establishes that God will provide humanity with spiritual guidance and blessings only if we follow the terms of the agreement. And further, these covenants contain the laws which are the character and the qualities, metaphorically speaking, of the ever-ripening fruit that clings to the *Tree of Life. In the Age of Fulfillment, the Tree of Life is Bahá'u'lláh, the Manifestation of God*!

Again, my purpose in selecting the title, Too Far From the Tree, is to illustrate how the Vatican Papal Bulls of the mid-15th and early 16th centuries became the progenitor of these fallen fruits --- unfettered materialism, systemic racism, manifest destiny, and white supremacy.

These Papal Bulls are the documented evidence of man's remoteness from the *Tree of Life*. These documents remain in force and are still held in Vatican Archives to this day while millions of indigenous peoples worldwide continue to suffer unimaginable indignities and atrocities because of them.

The content of the Papal Bulls is the formal decrees that were issued by the Catholic popes on the subject of 'The Law of Discovery'. This law decreed that the lands of indigenous peoples were to be confiscated, that the indigenous peoples of those lands were to be "subdued" and "enslaved in perpetuity", and "that all their lands and possessions were to be seized." These Papal Bulls are still in force and are statutory decrees that were understood by their recipients to be upheld as religious dispensations punishable under threat of excommunication if disobeyed, as episcopal appointments, as constitutions, as canonizations, and as apostolic constitutions. Essentially, at the behest of these Papal decrees, world domination (colonialism) was established throughout the world.

What must be kept in mind, however, is that unlike the fallen plums, the freedom of choice to move away from the Tree of Life is found in the divine injunction of man's own free will. White supremacy is a choice. It is a matter of free will, and it is now rotting upon the dust heap of history --- to be forgotten. The Essenes, the writers of the 'Dead Sea Scrolls' used the term 'the end of the world' and 'the last days' to describe this period in history, though what they were addressing then was not the end of the world but the end of their own social and political order. The new cycle has already begun, and this is what every conscientious soul on planet earth is witnessing today.

CHAPTER ONE

Once on a cold winter morning in New York City, in 1978, I was put upon a platform in a dank, shadowy wet place where cold subway rails dwell. I was tired. I had recently graduated with a master's degree in fine arts from UCLA and had moved from Southern California to the 'Big Apple' eager to begin a career as a stage actor. I was making headways on this new journey in the city that had always been my life-long dream. It didn't take long though to realize that this city could easily syphone the blood of ten million distracted people. Manhattan as a city of commuters for someone coming from a small city like San Diego can often feel like an untethered tether ball. Distractions are everywhere and it seems that that is just the way it sustains itself. People come into the city by subways and busses, trains, and taxis, and then at the end of a soul crushing day they hurriedly race back to the Boroughs --- Queens, the Bronx, Brooklyn, Staten Island, abandoning the glass and concrete skyscrapers without looking back. It didn't take long for me to realize that life in the 'Big Apple' had been designed to take all it could take from the human soul in order to maintain its status as the financial hub of the world. I had to be careful; very, very careful.

On this particular day, I was rushing to an audition. It was a new play looking for a black actor who could fence. I was feeling confident. I had been fencing for three years and was teaching fencing at New York City University. I even had my own custom-made foils. I was neither warm, nor cold. I was numb. I was breathing though, and that was a good thing. The cavernous tunnel into which I had descended was eerily silent. No sound of subway wheels screeching and shooting sparks into the air; no homeless hands stretching out for coins. I was alone. Then they came ... mother and daughter ... two black-skinned beauties. The little girl rubbed sleep from her still awakening brown eyes. A look of confusion came across her face as she took in her surroundings, spotting two cat-sized rats just as I had. The rats scurried along the tracks and then disappeared into the darkness. She looked up to her mother and with sad resignation on her face said, "Mommy, how did we get to where we are *now*?" It was her Caribbean accent, the pleading in her tiny voice, and the phrasing of her question that had drawn my attention. Clearly, she was disoriented. But, in that same moment, her question had morphed into a question that I'd been mulling over for years. By then, I had seen the favellas where make-shift shelters overlooking the sea clung dangerously close to the edges of cliffs above Ipanema in Rio de Janeiro. And of course, Italy, where cobblestone streets of Rome were packed with African refugees, now street hustlers, displaying cheap brass watches and chains in their hands hoping for tourists to buy. And, in France, where the medieval holdover from the French revolution, *liberte-egalite-fraternite* had yet to be realized long after French colonialism in Algeria, Benin, Burkina Faso, Cameroon, the Central African Republic, Chad, Comoros, the Kongo, Ivory Coast, Djibouti, Gabon, Guinea, Madagascar, Mali, Mauritania, Morocco, Niger, Senegal, Togo, Tunisia had all ended by the late 1970s. There, too, I had seen the same struggle to survive in a world that had written black African peoples out of history. It all stood painfully in stark contrast to the 70,000 looted Sub-Saharan African artifacts that were held in acrylic bondage just across the street at 37 Quai Branly, in the Musee Quai Branly. It too is another irresistible Parisian tourist destination near the Eiffel Tower, not far from the Seine. By 1978, in each of those places, like that little girl in the subway, I, too, had wondered, how black people had gotten to where we were on the proverbial food chain. Hearing her young, pleading voice still rings in my ears. Her innocent but desperate plea had drowned out the screeching sound of subway car wheels and turned that single question into an obsession to find the answer.

Where were we? and how did it happen? After years of searching for that answer, this book began to take shape in my very soul.

Hopefully, the reader will approach the structure and content of my book as a historical overview, rather than simply as an academic examination of past historical events. While living in South America, I came across many library books that gave new insights into Portugal's and Spain's transatlantic slave trade. I stumbled upon goo-gobs of books strewn about like so many loose ends at Upper Eastside Manhattan flea markets. The books had been shelved randomly or taken from one shelf and then carelessly shoved among other unrelated books all balancing on rickety weather-beaten street stands. And then, there was the elderly Jewish woman from B'nai B'rith International who suddenly appeared out of nowhere. I was sitting on a stone bench that overlooked the East River wondering where I might find a specific book that for weeks I'd been hoping to find with no luck. Suddenly, the woman sat down beside me and calmly began talking to me as if I was expecting her. After a moment or two, she graciously invited me to her apartment nearby. When I entered the foyer, I saw that throughout the apartment each wall was filled with books. After a few minutes of conversation, a conversation that had nothing to do with books, she left the front room. When she returned, she handed me the very same book I'd been searching for saying, "I thought you might find this interesting." All these chance encounters soon made me aware that the *law of attraction* was real and that it was the infallible confirmation I needed to keep urging me on. These chance encounters were persistent and went far beyond reason. In fact, there was a mystical quality to them which at the time I found difficult to accept. Yet, for me, deep within, I believed it was God in action and the newfound awareness that there are no coincidences. It was all beyond anything I ever could have ever conceived on my own. I felt that I was on a mission! The mission was clear: to find answers to the questions that had pummeled my heart for years. How, I wondered, had humanity become so socially, economically, racially, and most importantly, spiritually divided? If God can so seamlessly reveal His generosity to me, why then doesn't He do so in all human affairs? The answer, I learned, lies within the reality of man himself --- it is his thoughts. However, none of my chance encounters, none of my personal research, none of the conferences or debates I had attended, none of the book-signing events held by notable scholars and activists in Manhattan and elsewhere had ever framed the discussion in a way that went beyond race or reason; none had framed it so beautifully as the introduction to me of the *most pivotal spiritual imperative of our times --- the concept of 'the Oneness of Humanity'.*

It would be impossible to peel this onion without a profusion of tears streaming down my face. When I consider all the missed opportunities to create a world of peace, justice and brotherhood, the very basis of the sacred teachings of Christ, Muhammad, Buddha, and Bahá'u'lláh, I just weep. When I consider the hundreds of millions of unknown and forgotten hearts and souls - people, who as members of the human family unknowingly lost their way or their lives in search of peace, justice, and brotherhood, it truly saddens me. I find myself infused with an indignancy that cannot be ignored. Is mankind able to sacrifice its life in service to the central and most pivotal teachings of our times --- world unity and the oneness of humanity? Can we do that? With this perhaps overlooked perspective, that is, world unity and the oneness of humanity, all who have struggled throughout these long dark nights of history for the realization of these principles, may finally reach the Age of Maturity that is now upon us. For it is an age when the acquisition of knowledge must serve justice. It is an age when faith can walk hand-in-hand with justice, enriching and uplifting words far above syllables and sounds to become a way of life --- for all. These alone are the fortifications of the soul. These alone make any efforts to put materialism and rampant commercialism --- distractions which seduce and blur the very meaning of life, in their place.

The medieval thinking and institutions that led to the financing of Europe's transatlantic slave trade, the incessant wars that have torn societies and families apart can no longer find a justifiable framework in which to continue. A new framework must be found! This we must do if for no other reason than to show that obsolete ways of being underpins everything humans experience in this demoralized state in which we find ourselves. It has the character of hypocrisy and contradicts everything Jesus Christ taught, struggling to hold on to a withering construct that no longer resonates with the body politic: to justify the mental enslavement of all peoples regardless of color. Perhaps, now, as this newfound awareness aches to attain maturity, we will be enabled to develop a more compassionate and objective perspective and view the sweep of our past common history to bring new life as it unfolded to the living, breathing people who are our common ancestors. History is not a vestige of the past and should not be forgotten. For the people it describes are with us still, waiting to be heard. To hear them, to see them, to feel them requires not only an understanding of the pre-colonial history of African, Native American, and other indigenous peoples; as well as the objectified beings who suffered beneath the trauma of the transatlantic slave trade, but more importantly, we must gain an understanding of what it is that animates both the advancement and decline of all past and future civilizations for ours is but one of many. This topic will be given much more deserved and detailed emphasis as this admittedly nuanced take on the history of the transatlantic slave trade unfolds.

Albert Einstein: Time is an Illusion

A writer wrote the following about Albert Einstein: "He would stand looking out through the window not saying a single word for hours; just looking out. It was then that Einstein would express one of his many sudden realizations. "Time is not absolute," Einstein stated firmly. "Time is an illusion." Einstein later elaborated, saying … "both the future and the past are unchangeable, and _will_ play out exactly the way _they are_ meant to." What he actually meant in saying this is still being debated; however, many physicists share this view, and some who have alternate explanations for the way things play out in the long run …" Let those words sink-in. Here's what Jaime Trosper's article, 'What Did Einstein Mean by time is an Illusion?' which appeared in an issue of Interesting Engineering.

> "When you think about it, time is an arbitrary construct — it's our way of making sense of growing up and growing old. It's only a stubborn illusion that helps make sense of the world." [3]

My own personal experience with time as an illusion is far less profound than it is simply subtle. It's a kind of whisper that evokes curiosity; changing my grasp of life from one moment to another moment which in turn influences my perception of all things and of everyone upon whom my eyes fall upon … when each of those precious moments takes on even greater meaning. I am certain that by sharing this research we will all be able to shed the old skin for something far more durable than new skin alone. My journey may not be earth-shaking to anyone except for me, and that is as it should be, for personal epiphanies are intended primarily for the individual's own personal growth. They have always been my most reliable ally though they come with no certificate of completion or trophy that I can put on display … for spiritual evolution is a continuum … *"eternal in the past … eternal in the future."*

Day-to-day reality with work, raising kids, aging and everything that happens in-between seems to confirm Einstein's statement that 'time is an illusion'. That our present 'now' is identical to a yet undisclosed moment when 'now' becomes 'then' taking form as a memory that seems too far-fetched to be of any pressing significance, some old thought or behavior that inexplicably starts to haunt the 'now', making us feel as if our lives are a series of groundhog days nestled amorphously deep within our consciousness like a dream; a frightful nightmare, and just as fleeting. It feels as detached from us as we are from it … yet it never lets go. It can feel like a stream of pure waters that rushes around our legs and feet on its way to the ocean, encircling our consciousness for a time, just long enough to make us wonder. This silky touch of water enlivens both our imaginations and our fears; entrancing or scaring us because of its potential to overwhelm and sweep us under back to a reality we were hoping to escape. So, we step lightly, staying on a familiar path, feeling the ambiguity of uncertainty and hopefulness with aching feet of clay; grateful when pain abates, giving rise to even greater hopes, yet never once asking ourselves whether or not we are even deserving leaving us with even deeper feelings of uncertainty.

I think Einstein's notion of time is deserving of reflection, meditation, and detachment. It is with these spiritual tools, perhaps, that the universe may reveal its hidden truths and just opens up to assure us that our approach is steeped in reality … humble yet fearless, expectant yet unassuming, free of bias or prejudice, filled with the spirit of readiness and a radiant heart. In this state our very being absorbs the thoughts of all who have ever dwelt upon this earth, written accounts of whisperings that some great man or woman --- unknown to us --- struggled to write down in hopes of capturing timeless memories from throughout the entire universe unrestrained by time, space, and religious beliefs, sharing what has been, what is, and what shall be --- subtle inspirations as bold as the noon day sun, giving vision to our ignorance and rebelliousness like a mystical song we can never dismiss; aiding our navigation through a continuum of time and space. Such music is the thoughts of, as **Bahá'u'lláh** states in His mystical work 'The Valley of Search', those who have "stoutly girded up the loins of service" to aid the greater good which at its purest is our purpose and who we truly are --- spiritual man. This most sublime station is the goal for which all the intermediaries or prophets of God have been made manifest. It is They Who guide our souls --- humanity's true reality; an expression of an inner comprehension of all that rekindles feelings of what our true purpose is: to arise fully as homo spiritus --- spiritual man. It's a quiet place --- indeed a very quiet place. It seeks neither reward nor applause; neither fame nor the hermit's solitude … just an exquisite quiet like the hum of busses on an empty street. It's not the passage of time that is real, but the eternal processing of reality and new insights, the loss of loved ones and our own mortality, and the confirmations and assurances that ensure that our lives have not been lived in vain. And then, suddenly, in the still of the night, a voice shatters that tranquility and shouts out loud … *nigger.*

Racism: The Most Challenging Issue

Racism is one of the greatest challenges of our age and has been characterized as _the_ Most Challenging Issue'. The ideology of white supremacy has consumed so many precious lives in ways that are still being realized, forcing us to ask many questions about its genesis in order to stay alert, and to reevaluate our notion of what constitutes social progress. Like the mistletoe, this racist ideology is a parasite. Each century in which this ideology has spread has threatened to consume the once verdant _Tree of Life_ presenting the strangest paradox of all --- religious orthodoxy --- which in essence is an human interpretation handed down by self-appointed church leaders ensconced secretly above the larger religious body of believers laying claim to honoring the original yet obsolete traditions of an ancient religious cycle. It can be likened to the process of death of a once mighty oak tree when the parasitic mistletoe takes hold of it. Unlike other plants, the mistletoe does not germinate in the soil. As a parasite, its propagation is dependent upon birds that feed on 'mistletoe seeds', and when just a few seeds drop from their mouths, they fall inside the crevices of the bark of oak trees. There, in the cracks of the branches, they remain in the cracks where they begin to germinate. In its early stages, the seeds remain completely _dependent_ upon its host. And though it only takes four embryos for the mistletoe to begin the process of populating the tree, they begin the process by gradually taking over the essence of the tree --- its sap. Next, each embryo produces stems which grow steadily into the bark of the host tree forming clumps of mistletoe. Soon, these clumps in turn produce their own seeds. These new seeds emerge with a sticky adhesive goo that begins to darken the bark of the branches enhancing its ability to spread faster. Having inserted themselves into the bark, a new stage of deterioration begins. A tiny tissue at the tip of the roots starts to penetrate deeper into the bark increasing the spread. After a year or so, the mistletoe achieves a more stable level of self-reliance because it is now able to produce its own photosynthesis; yet it remains moderately dependent upon the host tree. However, when the tissue of the mistletoe's root reaches the host's conductive tissue, that is, the water and nutrition transport system that nurtures the branches, the leaves and any budding fruit, and is now fully dependent upon the host for its nutritional needs. As time passes, the mistletoe penetrates further into the host tissue and continues to drain the tree of its sap which, again, is the very essence, soul, and life of the once mighty oak.

Over the centuries, white supremacy has had many variants as it applied the Law of Discovery as was decreed by the Vatican Papal Bulls of 1452 to 1514 AD. Its mandate: to subdue non-Christian indigenous populations all around the world. The many issues that have resulted include the tuning-out and loss of faith, or worse, giving up and accepting white supremacy as if it is an inherent attribute, quality, and character of Christianity and therefore the supposed divine will of an omnipotent and all-loving God. Yet, the drive to eliminate this disease of ethnic self-worship which holds that 'whiteness of skin', a superficial human variant, makes one race superior to all other human beings has not been completely abated. To destroy and eliminate this false god from the current social order ... though it has come to dominate every aspect of it ... it would do well for people of conscience to consider the historical evidence of when a society refuses to open its eyes and take action. One such example is Belshazzar, the King of the Babylonian empire. In Daniel 5:1-5:28 of the Old Testament, Belshazzar is described as a rebellious monarch. His defiance against God took form in the worship of *idols and materialism*. It was idol worship that brought upon him the wrath of God ending in the destruction of his kingdom by the Persians and Medes. Daniel describes this failure to illustrate the eternal presence and proof of God --- for be it a 'golden calf' worshipped at the foot of Mt. Sinai by the Hebrews, a wood or stone image worshipped by Babylonians, or an idol in human form, it is man's *defiance* that heralds such condemnation; a condemnation that comes from the same eternal God who demands obedience and fealty to His Covenant. It is this obedience that was, that is, and will forever be at the core of His many Covenants with humanity. To destroy and eliminate racism from the current social order --- even though it dominates every aspect of it, one must open one's eyes to be reminded that the persistent evils it has engendered not only has corrupted its perpetrators but violates the Greater Covenant upon which all religions and civilizations have been erected. Essentially, white supremacy is the same idol worship that Daniel describes in the Old Testament. It is the same spiritual test that Belshazzar and his Babylonian court faced when they saw the handwriting on the wall; men who chose to praise their own manmade idols rather than obey the commandments of Yahweh, the creator of all human beings.

The Handwriting on The Wall

Shoghi Effendi, Guardian of the Baha'i Faith and its worldwide community, observed that what we are witnessing today is the death throes of the Old-World Order. The premise of this book is that white supremacy is the rancid fruit of that old order, the fruit that has fallen too far from the *Tree of Life*. The violent movements and daily political intrigues that the people of the world are now experiencing as reported daily in numerous media outlets is the fearsome, tormenting convulsions of a defunct and obsolete world order. Biblically, Daniel's narrative of the fall of Babylon in Chapter 5:2-4 establishes a historical precedence to be ignored at one's own peril. It is a warning to all world leaders, all nations, and to all generations that follow:

> "Belshazzar, the son of King Nabonidus, began to co-reign over the Babylonian empire with his father starting in 553 B.C. Fourteen years later, Belshazzar decides to hold a great feast for one thousand of his nobles (Daniel 5:1) in Babylon. No expense is spared in carrying out this lavish banquet! During the revelry Belshazzar, now drunk from wine, commands that the holy vessels that Nebuchadnezzar took from Jerusalem's temple be brought to the festivities. He then proceeds to have himself and his honored guests drink from these gold and silver goblets. In contempt against God, the guests soon begin to use the vessels to celebrate and praise their own pagan deities (Daniel 5:2 - 4). [4]

The Meaning of the Handwriting

As those attendees seated at Belshazzar's massive banquet continued to indulge in drunkenness and idolatry, the fingers of a man's hand mysteriously appeared near one of the walls in the hall. The supernatural manifestation then began to write on the wall the now well-known words, "Mene, Mene, Tekel, Peres." (Daniel 5:25). In Verses *26-28, Daniel interprets each word: 'MENE', 'MENE' as "God hath numbered thy kingdom and finished it." 'TEKEL' as "Thou art weighed in the balances, and art found wanting," and lastly, 'PERES' as "Thy kingdom is divided, and given to the Medes and Persians."* [4]

I am convinced that we must stop "chasing our tails" and "gnashing our teeth" and begin to pay attention to the same writing on the wall facing humankind today. For, just as Belshazzar was called upon to choose between the worship of God over the worship of idols, the people of the world are now being called upon to choose between the frivolity of excess materialism and racism and the courage to bury the man-made ideology of white supremacy once and for all. To do that, a global convocation of world leaders, scholars, legislators, social scientists, educators, social activists, and religious leaders of diverse major Faiths must be established to acknowledge the devastating harm that the ideology of white supremacy has inflicted upon humanity and provide legal remedies to eradicate it. In recognizing the need for such a summit, the call is for the best minds on the planet to participate. Finally, it is imperative for all participants to keep in mind that there is no difference between Belshazzar's idol worship of gold and clay and race self-worship. For the only difference between them is that the material idol being worshipped is one's own ethnic group. This is the crucible of our times. This is the legacy of race supremacy. It in itself is a response to the most profound spiritual principle ever enunciated by a prophet of God, a spiritual principle that was stated unequivocally at the end of the 19th century and is *the* pivotal message addressed specifically to *our* generation --- *the Oneness of Humankind.* However, this single principle is a two-edged sword. And by its introduction into the body politic, both radiant acquiescence and terror have been engendered in the hearts of men. For it is not an ideology, it is divinely inspired and therefore inevitable!

In 1938, Shoghi Effendi, the great-grandson of the Prophet Founder of the Baha'i Faith wrote in *The World Order of Bahá'u'lláh*: "The disquieting influence of over thirty million souls living under minority conditions throughout the continent of Europe; the vast and ever-swelling army of the unemployed with its crushing burden and demoralizing influence on governments and peoples; the wicked, unbridled race of armaments swallowing an ever-increasing share of the substance of already impoverished nations; the utter demoralization from which the international financial markets are now increasingly suffering; the onslaught of secularism invading what has hitherto been regarded as the impregnable strongholds of Christian and Muslim orthodoxy— these stand out as the gravest symptoms that bode ill for the future stability of the structure of modern civilization. Little wonder if one of

Europe's preeminent thinkers, honored for his wisdom and restraint, should have been forced to make so bold an assertion: "The world is passing through the gravest crisis in the history of civilization." "We stand," writes another, "before either a world catastrophe, or perhaps before the dawn of a greater era of truth and wisdom." "It is in such times," he adds, "that religions have perished and are born."

Why 'Spiritual Principle' is Essential to the Implementation of Practical Measures to Eliminate the Scourge of White Supremacy and Racism

In 1985, the Universal House of Justice released *The Promise of World Peace: to the people of the world.* Among its many pages are the following passages: "The essential merit of spiritual principle is that it not only presents a perspective which harmonizes with that which is immanent in human nature, it also induces an attitude, a dynamic, a will, an aspiration, which facilitate the discovery and implementation of practical measures" to achieve any goal." [5]

> "The Divine Messengers have been sent down, and their Books were revealed, for the purpose of promoting the knowledge of God, and of furthering unity and fellowship amongst men. But now behold, how they have made the Law of God a cause and pretext for perversity and hatred. How pitiful, how regrettable, that most men are cleaving fast to, and have busied themselves with, the things they possess, and are unaware of, and shut out as by a veil from, the things God possesseth!" [6]

Therefore, if mankind's aims are sincere in achieving the goal of eliminating white supremacy and its love child, racism, the application of the principle of the oneness of humankind is where leaders of thought, legislators, heads of state, as well as ordinary people, are encouraged to begin. However, there are many who will view this principle and this advice as the *dream of poets* and will choose to remain fixed and dependent upon its ideology; preferring to preserve the material benefits derived rather than the spiritual courage and magnanimity it demands to enable humanity to extract itself from its all-consuming, all-pervasive ubiquitous grip upon the levers of governments.

The implementation of these far-reaching measures was indicated by Bahá'u'lláh: *"The time must come when the imperative necessity for the holding of a vast, an all-embracing assemblage of men will be universally realized. The rulers and kings of the earth must needs attend it, and participating in its deliberations, must consider such ways and means as will lay the foundations of the world's Great Peace amongst men"* [7]

CHAPTER TWO

The Transatlantic Slave Trade

North American
Chieftain

Arab Muslim
Saracen

Pope Nicholas V
Head of Christendom

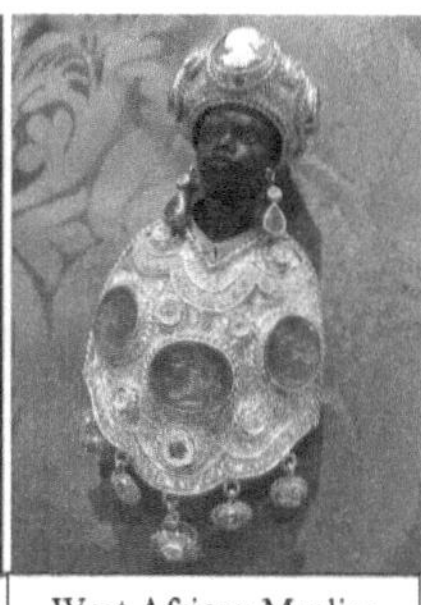

West African Muslim
Moor

The transatlantic slave trade did not happen in a vacuum. No, no, no, no! Its goals stretched far beyond the enslavement of African and other indigenous peoples. It was the strategic outcome of several Vatican decrees called Papal Bulls. The spiritual mission of 15th century papal authority was no longer to just 'spread the gospel of Jesus Christ to every people on earth' but was inexorably seeded in fifteen centuries of medieval pagan rebellions and wars between European tribes against papal authority. And, by mid-15th century, threats to its power had exponentially increased due to a number of developments which included astronomer Nicolaus Copernicus' revolutionary theory that the earth revolved around the sun and not the other way around; and Johann Gutenberg's invention of the printing press making the Bible accessible to everyone. These new developments in both science and technology changed everything! Reading the Bible was no longer the exclusive domain of religious clerics, but was now made available to ordinary people as well. As a result, the ensuing firestorm that erupted across Europe, eradicated the very idea of Papal Authority. What once were naive and ignorant believers clinging to superstitious beliefs, were now being transformed, protesting and reducing to ashes those same beliefs. Furthermore, Gutenberg's new invention had democratized the reading of the Bible, which as a consequence put monarchies across Europe into a panic. All this spiritual fermentation galvanized Martin Luther's religious movement and changed it into a spiritual revolution known as the Protestant Reformation, an often violent *'protest'* against the supremacy of the Catholic Church. These developments brought down upon him the wrath of both the monarchies and the Vatican. Perhaps more threatening to papal authority was the encroachment of the newly formed Islamic Ottoman empire with its own religious revelation which had obliterated the Christian Byzantium Empire; itself having emerged from the ruins of the ancient Roman Empire. European pagan kingdoms were continuously at each other's throats and were always engaged in religious disputes and battles over land. By the 16th century, all these contentious, spiritually immature kingdoms unknowledgeable about non-European cultures and ancient kingdoms were now turning their sights to dominating the world.

Martin Luther was a humble German theologian. It was he who initiated the Protestant Reformation. This reformation began to stir Martin Luther's conscience when he came face-to-face with the Vatican's corruption of the Faith of Jesus Christ. Upon his return home from pilgrimage to the Vatican (Rome), he was struck by the utter poverty of the masses of German serfs and peasants in contrast to the extravagant lifestyle of Catholic church leaders in Rome. Typically, poor Catholics have been taught as an article of faith that they could pay indulgences to the church to avoid eternal damnation. And after having witnessed the material excesses in Rome, he felt compelled to publish the famous document, 'Disputation on the Power of Indulgences'. Catholic Indulgences were payments made by believers which initially began during the Crusades. Indulgences served to not only allow monarchs and wealthy landowners to escape "eternal damnation in hell" for sins committed in life, but it also provided the Vatican with a tremendous source of income and political control over them. This document was also known as

Ninety-five Theses, and when Luther posted this document outside and on a church door in Wittenberg, Germany for all to see he was threatened with excommunication from the Church by Pope Leo X. However, Martin Luther persisted not only in his denunciation of the Church, but the Pope as well. Pope Leo then promulgated a Papal Bull condemning Luther's unrepentant indictment of the Catholic Church in June 1520, and an official copy finally reached Luther at Wittenberg in October. Commonly known by the Latin phrase in its opening lines, *Exsurge, Domine* (Arise, O Lord), the Papal Bull accuses Luther of heresy and issues an ultimatum: recant the heretical statements in the *Ninety-five Theses* and other writings within sixty days or face excommunication and authorized Luther's works to be burned in public, adding that all Christians who owned, read, or published them faced automatic excommunication. Luther now had reason to fear for his life: the punishment for heresy was burning at the stake. However, the critical split from the Catholic Church occurred over Luther's struggle to translate the Holy Bible from Latin to German which would make it accessible to even the lowest class of people in the realm. This struggle led to an intense power struggle between Martin Luther and his growing allegiance with the common people against both the German monarchy and aristocracy who supported the Pope. It also underscored the many disagreements over the meanings of Christ's sayings and His teachings. The real confusion was due to the yet to be resolved tribal polytheistic beliefs within the realm, the Catholic religion, the political, and the social structures all of which had been firmly established in Europe by mid-15th century. Like all gentiles, the Roman elite viewed these German tribes as crude, illiterate, superstitious and uncouth people. This Hebrew term *gentile* had no other meaning than barbaric. If that weren't enough, Islam, under the umbrella of the newly found Ottoman Empire, had already become an imminent threat in Eastern Europe and were viewed likewise by both Christians and Jews. With the conquering of Constantinople by the Muslims, the same were knocking at the door of the Vatican itself, threatening, from their perspective, the whole of European Christendom.

The Ottoman Empire was the Seat of the Islamic Caliphate. Even after its followers were able to dispense with its warring swords and to rely upon the Word of God to attract adherents to its Cause without violence, most continued their zealous pursuit of world domination as an essential feature of *their* faith. In the 7th century, this, unfortunately, became the Christian Church's most convincing characterization of the religion of Islam. In spite of Muhammad's teachings regarding "holy war", a phrase which referred not to violence against others but to the individual's responsibility to overcome his own spiritual battles, the term *Jihad* became one of the most convoluted concepts within and outside the Faith of Islam. To be fair, in order to gain a better understanding of the phrase 'Islamic jihad' one must examine and contextualize the pre-Islamic environment in which the Prophet Muhammad taught.

Pre-Islamic Arabia was predominantly a nomadic society. Like most areas of the Levant, Arabia was inhabited by warring tribes. However, unlike in those other areas, Arabs were constantly on the move. These nomadic tribes had been the most significant political units of the Arabian Peninsula constantly changing their alliances with never ending anarchy and warfare which, if not their *raison d'être*, was the only way to survive a hostile environment drenched in many superstitions. Therefore, the emphasis in such a life was on kinship and family ties. Organized territories and realms were extremely rare and centralized statehood was non-existent. Violent clans roamed through the desert landscape either maintaining their livestock which consisted primarily of camels, sheep, and goat while always being vigilant for violent marauding tribes. These nomadic tribes lived in tents, and it was the tribal leaders who enforced the unwritten and unique rules of their particular tribe. For instance, a woman could not inherit property and had no human rights. Living in a state of perpetual conflicts, tribal Arab women were considered to be liabilities for they could be seized as spoils of war, allowing captors to marry as many of their captives as they wanted who would give birth to mixed-blood children with conflicting or no loyalties to either tribe.

In Maxime Rodinson's 'Life of Muhammad', the French historian gives perhaps the most unbiased secular biography of the Prophet of Islam. He writes: *"The free Arabs were bound by no written code of law, and no state existed to enforce its statutes with the backing of a police force. The only protection for a man's life was the certainty established by custom, that it would be dearly bought. Blood for blood and a life for a life. The vendetta ... is just one of the pillars of a Bedouin society.* The prophet of Islam, Muhammad, and some of his future companions belonged to the Hanifi religion. The Hanifi rejected the idolatry and paganism of the majority of Arabs, thus sharing some of the features of other Abrahamic religions which included the prohibition of eating pork. According to Rodinson, "The scope of expansion of the Hanifi people is unclear, but according to some Islamic sources, the Arabic term, jihad, which has become very familiar to most Westerner's understanding in recent times as *holy war.* However, that meaning is a gross misunderstanding, and Muhammad's purpose in speaking on this topic has often been misrepresented in the West with devastating effects, distorting and even dismissing His divine station as a prophet. The phrase *internal jihad* or *greater jihad* refers not to an external war but to the internal war --- *the efforts expended by believers to live according to the teachings and laws of Islam to the best of their ability.* Most true believers of any Faith strive to live a life that is pleasing to God. Muslims are no different. Their focus is on making great efforts to live as God has instructed: obeying the spiritual laws of the Quran, being devoted to God, and doing all one can to be of service to others. For most people, no matter how much they love God, living according to His statutes is indeed the real war. And because the standards of God are so high, believers must fight with their own selfish desires to live up to them. H.M. Balyuzi, in his book, Muhammad and the

Course of Islam, puts it succinctly: "Over and above everything else, Muhammad taught the oneness and transcendence of God." [8]

Muhammad's teachings brought to His follower's the awareness of the knowledge that there is but one God. He taught them to promulgate social and economic justice, to denounce the worship of idols, and He made it clear that His Mission was to remove the misguiding beliefs, propositions and dogmas that had no basis in reality but had been put into place, and to correct the ideas spread by people who were not living according to the clearly expressed teachings of Jesus Christ. This last is a telling one. And it is to this point that this book is directed.

Muhammad's mission was the furtherance and clarification of Christ's revelation that had suffered from the insertion of human interpretations of the Word of God, otherwise known as progressive revelation. However, the same unfortunate schism happened almost immediately within the Faith of Islam. Soon after Muhammad's death in 632 A.D., even while His body was still warm, Islam fell into two irreconcilable sects --- Shia and Sunni. Reconciliation was impossible because of a single fact: Muhammad had not written a Will to specify His successor. And although Muhammad had mentioned orally that Ali, who was both the Prophet's cousin and son-in-law, should succeed Him. However, the greatest threat to his successorship was his youthful age.

> "Much older prominent and well-tested men in the ranks of the Muslims, believed that their age coupled with their experience gave them a valid and indisputable claim. There were many leading tribal figures among the Muslims who for a variety of reasons were hostile towards 'Ali. Thus, it was that at the gathering assembled on the very day of the Prophet's death, whatever rights 'Ali did possess were, with no warrant of authority, entirely ignored." [8]

This single fact is what caused the immediate sectarian split of the religion of Muhammad. With this initial split, the leadership of the now Sunni sect set the course of Islam. And, just as in many other religions, over time, seventy-three different Islamic sects emerged each with its own unique interpretations of the Quran, and its own beliefs and customs.

According to Sunan Tirmizi and Mishkaatul Masaabeeh, the Prophet of Allah Sallallahu Alahi Wasalam said: "My Ummah (Community) will be divided into 73 sects. All of them will be in the fire except one." The people asked him, "And which one will that be?" He replied, "The one that follows what I and my companions are upon right now." [9]

Out of the seventy-three which include Ibadi, Ahmadiyya, and Sufiism, eight emerged as the main Islamic groups: Mutazilah, Shia, Khawarij, Murjiyah, Najariyah, Jabariyah, Mushabiha and Naajiya. Each of these eight main Islamic groups are split further into multiple branches: the Mutazilah have 20 branches, the Shia sect has 22, the Khawarij have 20, the Murjiyah have 5, the Najariyah have 3, the Jabariyah, Mushabihah and Najiyaah each have one, and Sufism has one with each of the eight sects.

As their north star blazoned before them, untempered, undisciplined, and still ensnared by tribal loyalties, fanatical Muslims erupted out of Arabia like a swarm of locust, swept into the Christian Byzantine Empire, and across Egypt and North Africa forcing conversions often at the tip of the sword. And by 1453, Islam was now rapidly closing in and securing long-established European borders. In that same year, Sultan Mehmet II finally vanquished the Christian Byzantine Empire by capturing the heavily fortified Christian city of Constantinople which later became known as Istanbul. The Muslims quickly destroyed and replaced all Christian symbols, idols and icons believing they had an overarching and profound religious mandate: "Submission to the Will of God". Up until this time, the Holy Roman Empire had held sway over these lands, and the beliefs of the common people, the aristocracy, and monarchs were all dictated by the papacy. All had been subsumed beneath the banner of Christendom which later came to be known as Western Europe, distinguishing it from the fallen Byzantine Empire of Eastern Europe. As the faith of Muhammad began its slow climb from Barbarism to civilization, the now fracturing religion of Christ, characterized by growing sectarianism, reinterpretations of canonical biblical texts, the Church was now threatened both from within and without. Having been liberated by the printing press, peasants and serfs were now able to read the bible for themselves. Rebel rulers were now challenging Papal authority, claiming the divine right of kingship for themselves and blatantly ignoring Papal decrees. The divine source that had once been the impetus for Europe's relative peace and prosperity, that had dragged conflicting kingdoms out from under the darkness of conflicting polytheistic beliefs for over a thousand years was now under siege by self-doubt, fear, revenge and hatred of Islam and its revolutionary spiritual concepts.

In 1452, a year before the fall of Constantinople, Pope Nicholas V issued the first Vatican Papal Bull decree. This decree represented his fervid anti-Muslim response to the newly established Caliphate of the Ottoman Empire. This Papal Bull was the first documentary evidence of the Vatican's call for "the destruction, subduing and enslavement in perpetuity of Muslim Arabs and both Muslim and non-Christian peoples throughout the African continent." In addition, it specifically called for the confiscation of land, ancient artifacts and other cultural possessions, goldmines, and salt-rich West African kingdoms. These were African kingdoms namely, Niger, Mali, Kongo, and Benin, ancient kingdoms whose origins date back to over 100,000 to 40,000 BCE.

The Vatican's Papal Bull was the signature document of its time. It was sent as a directive to King Alfonso of Portugal which initiated what came to be called "the Doctrine of Discovery". This doctrine" was no mere pipe dream. It established a clear Christian imperative that would secure its place in a global system of conquest and land seizure which would be used as a future model for all European Christian monarchs with no regard to language, tribal loyalties, and religious belief which translated as all of Christendom aka the Holy Roman Empire.

Pope Nicholas V's directive was as follows: King Alfonso was directed to travel to West Africa and to "invade, capture, vanquish and subdue all Saracens (Muslims) and pagans (people who followed a religion other than Christianity) who were considered to be 'enemies of Christ'... 'to reduce their persons to perpetual slavery' and to take all their possessions, properties, and lands." [10]

This instruction to King Alfonso to dominate indigenous peoples of Africa did not happen because the populations were black but because they were not Christians. It followed after nearly two centuries of reports given by Venetian merchant, Marco Polo, where he described his journey across Asia at the height of the Mongol Empire between 1271 and 1295 AD. But the most urgent and worrisome matter that weighed upon the thinking of the Vatican was the conquest of Constantinople by the Muslim Sultan, Mehmed II. Mehmed II's first reign witnessed the defeat of Christian Crusaders. Later, in 1451, at the age of twenty-one, Mehmed II was the first to ascend the Ottoman throne. His first act as Sultan was to strengthen the Ottoman Naval Fleet and to prepare for his attacks on Constantinople. By conquering what was considered to be 'the impregnable capital of the Byzantine Empire', the Muslim Sultan was now unimpeded in erecting a completely Islamic civilization which came to be known as the Ottoman Empire. Constantinople was captured on May 29, 1453. The siege lasted fifty-three days. This sudden and unexpected turn of events fueled a fire that had been raging within the very heart of all Christendom headed by the Vatican, obligating, and impelling all subsequent popes to issue even more Papal Bulls. Under the very real threat of losing numerous of Christian kingdoms to the Ottomans, Pope Nicholas V issued a second Papal Bull in 1455. This second decree added zeal to an already frenzied religious campaign to stop the advance of Islam in Europe and was completely devoid of Christ's mandate to his twelve disciples to spread the teachings of Christ. <u>Mark 16:15</u> states: "And he said unto them, go ye into all the world, and preach the gospel to every creature." According to Matthew 28:19 stated: "Go ye therefore, and teach all nations, baptizing them in the name of the Father, and of the Son, and of the Holy Spirit."

This second Papal Bull unleashed a torrent of religious fanaticism the like of which had not been experienced since the 'Holy Crusades' of 1095 and 1291 AD. With this edict, Pope Nicholas V triggered a wave of ambitious zealots and young earnest explorers, believing they were fulfilling their religious obligation to obey the pope, which by 1492 included the iconic figures of Christopher Columbus, Hernan Cortes, Ferdinand Magellan. In no uncertain terms, this Papal Bull urged them to conquer all the lands and peoples of North, Central and South America, the Philippines, the Pacific Islands, both Asia and Asia Minor, India, and the entire continent of Africa, dubbing this period in world history as the 'Age of Exploration'.

Over time, this tsunami of religious and racial bigotry began to take shape around a single all-consuming idea: colonialism. To ensure its sustainability, a wave of race-based institutions was erected to express their overriding goal of world colonialism --- the doctrines of white supremacy, scientific and systemic racism. This man-made ideological trinity quickly matched and supplanted the Church's doctrine of the 'Holy Trinity' which had been established by Roman Emperor, Constantine at the Council of Nicaea in 325 AD, gaining adherents almost immediately; surgically implanted as the new nervous system of the now defunct and obsolete Holy Roman Empire --- the Royal Heads of State of all European Christendom eagerly consumed and destroyed any vying ideology, belief, rebellion, or socio-political and economic movement that dared to threaten its dominance. Additionally, this edict was raised to the level of principle by basing them upon the words of Christ Himself: "And he said unto them, go ye into all the world, and preach the gospel to every creature." In Matthew 28:19, it is written that Christ counseled his twelve apostles, each of them drawn from the ever-contentious in-fighting between the twelve tribes of Israel, "Go ye therefore, and teach all nations, baptizing them in the name of the Father, and of the Son, and of the Holy Spirit."

In all, there were seven of these specific Papal Bulls issued (1452, 1455, 1456, 1481, 1493, 1506 and 1514) which, over time, became racialized edicts. One hundred and ninety-two Papal Bulls had been decreed between 1059 A.D to 1451 A.D, and one-hundred and eight were decreed between 1515 A.D and 2015 A.D, totaling 307 Papal Bulls. Essentially, they are the documented thoughts, plans, strategies, and human interpretations of what Christ meant in spreading Christianity. The consensus, however, was clear. According to the institution of the 'Vicar of Christ', that is, the successive lines of Vatican Popes, Catholic doctrine was the exclusive domain of the Vicar of Christ. He alone is the "representative of Christ on earth", who, as successive Heads of the Holy Roman Empire in Europe (aka Christendom – the domain of Christianity), expressed these thoughts under the premise that only he knew God's Will and that all Christian Catholics (be they peasants or Kings) were obliged to obey him. In effect, all successive Popes wielded supreme power even above that of Kings.

Necessarily, the reader must be prepared to participate not as passive readers but as active witnesses to the historical records. The information contained throughout the following pages requires a mature adult comprehension of the devastating effects of the Papal Bulls which were, by any other name, the progenitor of white supremacy and institutional racism because it was from these Vatican decrees the inspiration for the colonization of indigenous lands was erected. Embedded within these Papal Bulls was an economic, socio-political system, and a religious attitude toward non-white peoples that was based upon differences of religious beliefs as well as superficial differences such as color of skin, levels of material accumulation, titles, and other fleeting aspects of material existence. Therefore, the visual images presented herein are necessarily painful to witness. Without them, words alone are powerless to convey the human degradation experienced in the past and which continues to exist right now, in the present time, the bitterest of fallen fruits --- the 'Scramble for Africa'.

To successfully navigate the present, it helps to know where we've been and to where we are going. In this way, it is hoped that humanity can *extract* itself from the matrix which is none other than the bitter fruit of the Papal Bulls --- white supremacy ideology --- the very foundation of racism. The first step is for all to acknowledge that white supremacy and racism are the most grievous and challenging issues of our times.

In 1985, the Universal House of Justice published 'The Promise of World Peace. In it, they wrote: "Racism, one of the most baneful and persistent evils, is a major barrier to peace. Its practice perpetrates too outrageous a violation of the dignity of human beings to be countenanced under any pretext. Racism retards the unfoldment of the boundless potentialities of its victims, corrupts its perpetrators, and blights human progress. Recognition of the oneness of mankind, implemented by appropriate legal measures, must be universally upheld if this problem is to be overcome." [11]

The Papal Bull of 1452 initiated the 'Law of Discovery'. It called for the "'Domination' and the enslavement of people termed "indigenous peoples." Most know this historical period as 'the Age of Exploration'. Few know it as the 'Law of Discovery'. There were numerous explorers who responded to this call from the Vatican with Christopher Columbus being the most iconic. This 'Age of Exploration' unleashed a wave of race-based campaigns which culminated with the Berlin Conference held at the end of the 19th century and came to be known as the 'Scramble for Africa'.

The intentions expressed in the Papal Bulls is unequivocal. It leads us to conclude that the reality of the thoughts of the popes who decreed them had nothing to do with the command of Jesus to carry His teachings to every land. He had made no mention of the confiscation of indigenous lands or enslavement in perpetuity. For centuries thereafter, the Papal Bulls condoned European colonialism which was carried out in lock step as consistent with the spread of Christianity. To this day these Papal Bulls underlie the "Law of Discovery" by both European and governments in the Americas in respect to the treatment of indigenous peoples and their lands. These *decrees* were Papal mandates specifically addressed to the monarchs of Portugal and Spain, were later appropriated by other European monarchs, and, by 1530, after King Henry VIII had firmly established the English Reformation in England, the formation of the Anglican, Church of England irrevocably and decisively severed ties with the Roman Catholic Church --- forever. Three years later, Elizabeth I ascended the British throne, and after a devastating defeat of the powerful Spanish Armada, the race to become the most powerful nation in the world was on. By the 18th century, the British Empire controlled lands across the globe and became known as the empire upon which the sun never sets --- North, Central and South America, the Caribbean, Australia, New Zealand, Hawaii, India, Africa, Asia, and throughout the indigenous non-Christian world.

CHAPTER THREE

Papal Bulls: The Foundation of the 'Law of Discovery'

The Papal Bull of 1452, also known as *Dum Diversas*, was issued **by** Pope Nicholas V on June 18, 1452. It authorized King Alfonso V of Portugal to reduce any Muslims and pagans (any non-Christians) and any other "unbelievers" to perpetual slavery. This Vatican document initiated the Portuguese slave trade from West Africa and was quickly followed by a frenzy of human exploitation by Protestant European powers as well. On January 5, 1455, Pope Nicholas V then followed this initial gambit with the document known as the Romanus Pontifex Bull. It too was addressed to King Alfonso of Portugal. The intent of this second papal bull served to extend dominion over all discovered lands during the Age of Discovery to all Catholic nations of Europe, and, by divine papal right, essentially obligated the king of all seizures of non-Christian lands to the official domain of the Pontificate and authorized the enslavement of non-Christian indigenous peoples in Africa, the Pacific Islands, Asia, and the New World. The following is the wording of the *Dum Diversas:*

> *"We weighing all and singular the premises with due*
> *meditation, and noting that since we had formerly by*
> *other letters of ours granted among other things free and*

ample faculty to the aforesaid King Alfonso – to invade, search out, capture, vanquish, and subdue all Saracens and pagans whatsoever, and other enemies of Christ wheresoever placed, and the kingdoms, dukedoms, principalities, dominions, possessions, and all movable and immovable goods whatsoever held and possessed by them and to reduce their persons to perpetual slavery, and to apply and appropriate to himself and his successors the kingdoms, dukedoms, counties, principalities, dominions, possessions, and goods, and to convert them to his and their use and profit – by having secured the said faculty, the said King Alfonso, or, by his authority, the aforesaid infante, justly and lawfully has acquired and possessed, and doth possess, these islands, lands, harbors, and seas, and they do of right belong and pertain to the said King Alfonso and his successors.''[12]

The Old World Order: Christendom and The Holy Roman Empire

Emperor Otto, the Great

Codex Vaticanus of the
Holy Roman Empire

Emperor Charlemagne

Bahá'u'lláh's great-grandson, Shoghi Effendi, the appointed Guardian of the Baha'i Faith, introduced and often used the phrase "old world order" in many of his letters to believers but never specifically identified exactly what timespan he deemed as the *Old World Order*. As a young and very religiously naïve person, I, like many of my generation, assumed that the period he was referring to was the social and political world order of the 1960s, a time of tremendous social and political turmoil. I admit, I was very naïve about such matters, and generally felt that religion had nothing to do with what Shoghi Effendi was alluding to. However, after a lot of painful research and fruitless inquiries, I found myself digging deeper and deeper until I realized that I was digging my own unique rabbit hole. It was unlike the rabbit hole that Alice found herself in. It was filled with hints that had been tacked against the walls of this hole and had been affixed there right in plain sight for centuries. I just had never thought of them as related to religion. This rabbit hole suddenly grew brighter as the light of knowledge began to slowly illumine my thinking --- the notion of 1,000 years religious cycles.

Since the inception of the Adamic Cycle 6,000 years ago, historically, religious cycles have occurred every 500 to 1,000 years each bringing with it a new spiritual world order. A spiritual world order operates as the spiritual foundation upon which the establishment of subsequent political world orders that come into being are administered based upon the needs and advances of an ever-changing world and operates according to the spiritual principles enunciated by its Divine Founder (prophet) to ensure the world's spiritual and material stability simultaneously. At its most basic function, all past "world orders" have one thing in common: they have been the cause for the creation of all of the ancient civilizations that dot the planet today --- from the ancient Kingdom of Aksum (Ethiopia) to ancient Kemet (Egypt) and the ancient Sumerian civilizations; from the Inca civilization to the Azteca and Maya civilizations, etc. Briefly, a world order is established in history with the spiritual renewal that occurs from the implementation of the sacred teachings of a divine revelation and is enshrined in the hearts of men as a renewal of the *religion of*

God; a single entity that by virtue of an All-Perceiving, All-Knowing Creative Force (i.e., God) is manifested in innumerable expressions of the virtues of its Founders, that is, the prophets or Manifestations of God who make their appearance every 500 to 1,000 years. This range of appearances can be seen in the following brief timeline between the ministry of Moses which began circa 1445 B.C, followed by Buddha's ministry circa 500 B.C., and Jesus Christ's three- year ministry beginning circa 27-29 A.D. It shows that the years between the ministry of Moses and Buddha was 945, and 527 to 529 years between Buddha and Jesus Christ. By being faithfully aware of this timeline, men like the *three wise men* --- one from Elam (ancient Persia), one from Ethiopia (East Africa), and the other from India, all of whom, according to many biblical scholars, were Zoroastrians, were able to calculate astrologically precisely when and where the appearance of the Messiah would occur.

The Old World Order, spoken of by Shoghi Effendi, can be said to have begun with the inception of the Christian cycle, circa 1st century A.D. Figuratively speaking, like spiritual runners in a relay race, the baton of the Word of God carried by Christ was carried forward and passed to Muhammad who, continuing the race of sacred revelation, established the efficacy of the religion of God with a new name, Islam. The formal ministry of Muhammad was inaugurated when He received revelation on Mount Hira circa 630 A.D. Again, the timeline between the revelation of Jesus Christ and Muhammad was about 651 years, well within the 500 to 1,000 years religious timespan. What many Christians have failed to acknowledge is that Muhammad's ministry occurred at a time in history when nomadic Arab tribes were still enmeshed in obsolete social and political structures that no longer met the spiritual needs of a people. Just as the nascent Christian world order had successfully evolved from tribes to chiefdoms to kingdoms to city-states and then to empires, each inevitably in turn became subsumed beneath the umbrella of the national state, each with its own sovereignty while Islam underwent its own process of social evolution characterized by continual tribal feuds fought to avenge with no legal structures to protect. By establishing the Ottoman Empire, Islam started the long climb to civilization. Each of these stages was characterized by literate and illiterate royal classes, literate priestly classes, a military class, and indistinct lesser classes. All stages were characterized by some form of loyalty to family and clan, yet it was Islam that established the system of nationalism. And when it proved to be a more efficient way to organize societies militaries were raised more often to seize, expand, and protect confiscated territories; to maintain both domestic and transnational political power, as well as to maintain economic stability and social order by force.

The Christian World Order, under the name Christendom (literally, Christian dominion), is traditionally believed to have been established by Charlemagne who was crowned emperor of the Holy Roman Empire by Pope Leo III in 800 A.D (about 190 years after the birth of Islam). Subsequently, Emperor Otto, the Great of Germany, replaced Francis II and reigned until 973 AD. He later revived the imperial title after the Carolingian decline which is regarded as the beginning of the empire. The Holy Roman Empire lasted until 1806 A.D (about 1,000 years) during the Napoleonic Wars when Francis II renounced the imperial title. The name Holy Roman Empire was adopted in the mid-12th century during the reign of Frederick I (Barbarossa) who agreed that Charlemagne's claim that his empire was the successor to the Roman Empire and that this temporal power held a greater status as God's principal vicar in the temporal realm which he made to be parallel with the Pope's position in the religious realm.

What does all this mean For Us today?

Good question. What this means is that humanity has reached the end of one age and is now suffering the birth pangs of a new age. This 'end of a religious cycle' is as organic to the advancement of civilization as the end of one season harbors the beginning of another --- Spring, Summer, Fall to Winter. As we've learned, a religious cycle can range anywhere from about 500 to 1,000 years. However, human beings can only estimate this timeline because ultimately divine dispensations appear at the bidding of God alone. This is what is implied in Matthew 24:42 when Christ's disciples asked regarding His return, saying, "Watch therefore, for you do not know what hour your Lord is coming." He repeats this statement again in Matthew 25:13. And in Revelation 16:15 in answer to the same question He offered these words saying, "Blessed is he who watches ... because the return of the Spirit of Truth will happen unexpectedly --- *"like a thief in the night."*

As per the foregoing passages, the long decline of the Christian era began around the year 1,000 A.D. It took time to completely reach the point when many having had begun, questioning or abandoning their faith entirely, believing that religion was no longer a viable medium for the advancement of civilization. How then can we be assured that divine revelation is not a random occurrence? Taking an unbiased look at history indeed shows that the rise and decline of civilizations are integral components to the Plan of God, which assures humanity of its continuance as a specie and that it is the core purpose to its fulfillment. That assurance comes by heeding the beginnings and endings of religious cycles that have followed one after another throughout the many millennia of human existence.

It was Muhammad's intermediary cycle which quickly followed in 622 A.D. We can therefore literally calculate the years between 1,000 A.D (the end of the Christian cycle) and 622 A.D (the beginning of the Islamic cycle) to establish Muhammad's divine authority as the 'Seal of the Prophets' at the close of the Age of Promise. There were 378 years between the end of the Christian era and the beginning of the Islamic 1,000-year cycle which itself ended a thousand years after its inception. This brings us to the 17th century to the year 1622 A.D. If religious cycles have any predictability, it will reveal itself in the historical record and that record would demonstrate that the spiritual influence of Christianity as a unifying force in the world would have, by the early 7th century, begun to show signs that it was waning, albeit initially imperceptible to the majority of its followers. When considering the irrefutable law of change and decay as mentioned earlier, the signs of a religion, spiritual influence and decline would be observable. Pews would go empty, memberships would drop precipitously, conflicting beliefs, and interpretations would arise marriages would falter, family unity would be frayed, youth would lose interest and fall away, Desperate attempts to stabilize the foundations of society and the status quo would be made, yet would disrupt even further the very feeling of peace and security, until, alas, the religion itself becomes a mere ... spiritual sanctuary. This is exactly what happened during the period known as the Reformation, a period riddled by efforts to reform the religion of Christ. And such has been the state of religion to this day --- teetering and squabbling over inane dogmas, punctuated with dramatic but empty rituals, with new conflicting human interpretations and non-sensical commentaries arising every day, all hastening to replace the original authoritative text. What had once been the very Source of its ascendancy was now rising on a New Horizon, a new Faith --- gone. More than this, the essential spirit, the Divine Source that had once inspired its followers, disassociates from the former cycle of revelation, gradually rendering it incapable of sustaining its original spiritual potency and moral constancy, and, like the proverbial "new wine", infuses the new cycle with a revelation that fulfills the spiritual needs of a sorely tried humanity for generations to come with such irresistible spiritual power that the former falls prey to numerous unauthoritative human interpretations and dogmas, infighting, schisms, confused and disaffected congregants, manmade secular ideologies, and disputing substitute religious sects. Ultimately, it succumbs to the "immutable law of change and decay" further devolving to become a hollow, empty shell with its followers with nowhere to turn but to religious leaders who can offer nothing more than outworn rituals, ancient traditions, irrational beliefs, racism, xenophobia, and religious intolerance with a plethora of various forms of militant religious fanaticism. Hearts hardened, and with faith having been reduced to mere ritual, and spiritual teachings now falling upon deaf ears, the move to replace religion with pure reason for commercial profits propelled the ascendancy of pure science thus leveling the final death blow to any form of godliness. Under these circumstances, in His Book of Laws, Bahá'u'lláh poses the question:

> "What 'oppression' is more grievous than that a soul seeking the truth, and wishing to attain unto the knowledge of God, should know not where to go for it and from whom to seek it?"

The conclusive evidence for this decline lies in the fall of the Holy Roman Empire itself and its surrogate replacement --- scientific materialism --- in 1806. This was the clarion call so vociferously expressed most by philosophers, economists, social thinkers, revolutionaries, scientists, and scholars --- men who themselves had lived and benefited from, and who had once believed in its spiritual ascendency but were now witnessing its decline within the very precincts of the Seat of the Holy Roman Empire --- Germany.

By 1806, the Holy Roman Empire's core constituents --- Germany, Austria, Bohemia, and Moravia. Switzerland, the Netherlands, and northern Italy sometimes formed part of it; France, Poland, Hungary, and Denmark were initially included, and Spain was viewed as a nominal component *while Britain was ignored completely.*

The Holy Roman Empire was formed in 800 A.D when Charlemagne of Germany was crowned by Pope Leo III. It was established in Germany with the express purpose of spreading Christianity throughout the whole of Central to Northern Europe, a region filled with barbarous tribes clinging to their own ancient polytheistic beliefs. Rome's goal was to bring all throughout this broad region under the shelter of a single religious Faith --- Christianity. The Middle Ages in Europe was as violent a region as pre-Islamic Arabia. The rise of Christianity and Europe, therefore, can be attributed to the impact of the spiritual teachings of Christ's 1000-year dispensation and upon Europe and the success of the newly formed Holy Roman Empire in Germany at the beginning of the ninth century. However, considering the rise of Islam in Europe during the same period, one must consider the impact of this rise in the light of the nature of divine revelation; that is, its recurrent appearance every thousand years or so. A good question to ask at this juncture is why a new revelation is necessary? Spiritually speaking, reason would suggest that something had gone terribly wrong in human affairs as Christianity's spiritual influence began to decline. It is exactly at this point that the proverbial "Plan of God" is renewed. This renewal is not only necessary but crucial to upholding the very purpose of religion for the well-being of humanity, that is, the greater covenant of God.. By the 11th century, militarism in the form of the crusades was established to reinforce the goals of the Holy Roman Empire, firmly establishing it as the European World Order. As new secular ideologies emerged to challenge Papal Authority, desperate worlds of thought within and without collided. The religious militarism of the Crusades eventually morphed into a new banking system reinforcing and reshaping the European World Order, and fostering the notion that Europe was the center of the world (if not the universe) while kingdoms clashed, tribes battled, religious sects multiplied --- all taking place as secularism and scientists of the time strove to replace God himself. All of this reflects both the literal and intellectual proof of the very words of Jesus Christ Himself where He says: "Think not that I am come to send peace on earth: I came not to send peace, but a sword. For I am come to set a man at variance against his father, and the daughter against her mother, and the daughter-in-law against her mother-in-law. And a man's foes *shall be* they of his own household." [13]

If there was ever a clear description of Europe in the mid-12th century and its impact upon non-European lands during this twelve-hundred-year period, the above citation from Luke 12:49-53 is the quintessential evidence of the type of world order world leaders envisioned at the time. During this period, Bahá'u'lláh three signature spiritual principles, the 'Oneness of Mankind', 'World Peace' and

'Progressive Revelation', had yet to be proclaimed which reflects the nature of divine revelation, that is, that it is not imposed upon humanity but rather it is proffered to humanity as a fulfillment of God's Covenant that they espouse --- that is, that mankind has free will to either accept it or reject it when it *is* publicly proclaimed.

Timeline of Scientific Racism

There is a plethora of articles on scientific racism online. The timeline below can be found under the title 'Confronting Anti-Black Racism Resource - Scientific Racism' and is located online at *https://library.harvard.edu/confronting-anti-black-racism/scientific-racism.* It gives an overview of scientific racism throughout Europe, placing Social Darwinism and the Eugenics Record Office right in its center. The timeline below demonstrates the broad historical framework that extends from the Enlightenment Era in Europe to present-day social thought throughout the world. This timeline is a factual illustration of the increasing urgency that was given to scientifically justify racism. And further, it shows how science, and the reinterpretation of biblical text were combined to justify the transatlantic slave trade and the marginalization and extermination of entire indigenous tribes, as well as the land grabs that were the objects of their primary agenda:

1. Dutch naturalist Petrus Camper begins developing his "facial angle" formula, <u>basing his scientific conclusions on his ideal of the angularity depicted on Grecian statues.</u>

2. 1791: Isaac Collins and Isaiah Thomas Respectively Produce the First Family Bible and First Illustrated Bible Printed in America. Both were King James Versions, with All 80 Books.

3. 1795: Anthropologist Johann Friedrich Blumenbach names the *five races of man.*

4. 1828: George Combe publishes The Constitution of Man Considered in Relation to External Objects, linking phrenology and racial comparison.

5. 1830s: Orson Fowler opens his Phrenological Cabinet in the heart of downtown Manhattan.

6. 1832: Johann Gaspar Spurzheim invigorates the American phrenology movement with his series of lectures in Boston.

7. 1839: Samuel George Morton introduces his theory of craniometry in <u>Crania Americana</u>.

8. 1844: Scottish publisher Robert Chambers releases his <u>Vestiges of the Natural History of Mankind</u>, the most popular work of natural history prior to Darwin's <u>Origin of Species</u>. Chambers argues that each race represents a different stage of human evolution with whites being the most evolved.

It is important to note here that the public proclamation of Bahá'u'lláh occurred in Baghdad in 1863. The following timeline demonstrates the *response* to His proclamation of the pivotal teaching as enshrined in the principle of the *Oneness of Mankind:*

<u>Timeline of Scientific Racism from 1853 to 1892</u>

1853: French thinker Arthur Comte Gobineau publishes An Essay on the Inequality of the Human Race, arguing for the primacy of the Aryan race.

1859: Charles Darwin releases the first edition of On the Origin of Species.

1863: In Iraq, Bahá'u'lláh announces his claim to a Divine Revelation from *God in the Garden of Ridvan (Iraq).*

1868: Baha'ullah is exiled once again from Iraq to the Ottoman prison in Akka (the Holy Land).

1877: Richard Dugdale publishes The Jukes, which links crime and heredity.

1882: The Chinese Exclusion Act is passed, excluding Chinese laborers from immigration for ten years.

1883: Galton coins the term eugenics.

1886: Chief of the New York City Detective Bureau Thomas F. Byrnes publishes Professional Criminals of America in which he collects the mug shots of notable criminals.

1892: The Chinese Exclusion Act is renewed for ten more years under the Geary Act.

1892: The Ascension of **Bahá'u'lláh** on May 29, 1892.

The Origin of Everything

With all the foregoing in mind, let us consider why 17th Century monarchs, aristocrats, ecclesiastics, scientists, philosophers, and merchants funded, colonized, and enslaved, conceived and created an entire social, political and economic system to justify the enslavement of more than 29.5 million African human beings.

Follow the Money

When considering how the ideology of white supremacy originated, it would be intellectually simplistic to attribute it to the superficial metric of skin color alone. There is a far more profound reason for its conception and can be summed up in the 'Seven deadly Sins: envy, gluttony, greed, lust, pride, sloth, and wrath. However, for the purpose of this discussion, I will address only the deadly sin of envy. The 'seven deadly sins' were formulated by a Catholic monk, Evagrius Ponticus, in the 4th century C.E, and are considered by him and most Christians to be 'sins' because they lead to even more horrendous vices. The 17th century saw the emergence of a movement called 'The Enlightenment. The motivation of its adherents was to demonstrate the superiority of human reason over religious and spiritual beliefs. Many would say that 'the Enlightenment' freed human beings from the degradation of superstition and dogma and set the stage for the development and clamor for egalitarianism as demonstrated by the French and American revolutions. Since the 17th century, the Enlightenment has continued to develop politically giving rise to the Civil Rights Movement of the 1960's and protests around the world including China and Iran. However, what was not anticipated was that when religious faith in God was replaced by scientific materialism coupled with pure reason, the separation from God's grace was complete. Therefore, the ideology of white supremacy was now unrestrained, and a new notion of human thought emerged --- racial superiority.

The bedrock of white supremacy and racism has little to do with biblical misunderstandings, bad translations of biblical texts, God, faith in Him, or divine religion. Those components of white supremacy came later. It would be misleading to view envy as a vestige of the medieval past which led to the establishment of the Crusades or colonialism, for to envy and to covet are one and the same things. Humanity was introduced to the condemnation of this 'sin' in the Ten Commandments --- *thou shalt not covet thy neighbor's goods and wife,* thus preceding ancient periods and is still condemned to this day. And, no, it is not an outworn remnant of something that once was and that has vanished. It continues to be a reality to this day.

As we have learned, the long-storied history of civilizations is the account of nomadic migrations moving from one simple stage of social organization to increasingly more complex social organizations. At a minimum, these groups living in relative peace encounter a change that drives tensions over previous tribal agreements, natural resources, the need for land expansion for a growing population, etc.. If unsettled by these skirmishes, war becomes inevitable. This, however, leads to formations of even more complex social organizations in the hope of averting any future war. Mankind's story is just that. Africa, the Americas, Asia, and Europe all are stories of family units becoming tribes that often vied for territory and control of trade by force which led to bloodier conflicts even as spiritual evolution demanded the emergence of villages that later became fiefdoms kingdoms, city-states, and as the continuum of the political order evolved becoming nation-states. This political stage is where we are today. Yet, today's innovative technologies have contracted the world into a single entity. A new world order is now apparent.

By the 16th century, Europe had historically developed and evolved from a bartering system to feudalism and mercantilism to capitalism. Capitalism dramatically expanded industrialization and the large-scale production of mass-market consumer goods; with an ever-growing need for a much larger labor force than any one European country could ever provide on their own.

Considering all of the above one has to ask --- what then was the underlying thinking of 16th, 17th, 18th, 19th, and 20th century heads of state. And now in the 21th century we ask what is the underlying thinking of heads of state, scholars, philosophers, scientists, religious leaders and titans of industry? and now 21st century heads of state, scholars, philosophers, scientists, religious clerics, and mercantilists? With the new-found scientific discoveries that also promises to eradicate diseases, increase food production, supplies and new inventions --- why was the extraction of Egypt from the African continent and the enslavement of black Africans preferred over liberty and coexistence? To glean some understanding of the European mindset during and after the Enlightenment, let us turn to the English language itself to see how words and phrases shine a light on the motives for establishing the existing social structure. Here are just a few words and phrases that have been used when it came to peaceful co-existence: land expansion to provide living spaces for a growing population and to increase crop production, to provide grazing for farm animals, to exploit natural resources in the homeland, of annexing new territories; to establish housing for the poor in slums, reserves, preserves and sanctuaries. We'll stop right there just to keep this simple and manageable. Now, let's turn to contemporary language which essentially describes the same needs but in the context of contemporary suburban and city dwelling: community, gated community, association, commune, settlement, reservation, quarter, district, section, ghetto, slum, hood. Notice any similarities? What do these terms reveal about the thinking of those who created and used these specific terms to describe how to engineer living spaces, establish social structures and societies and to care for the needs of people? For me, although the terms used are different, the essence of the thinking behind the use of these terms is identical --- division, separation, control, disenfranchisement, and social, political and economic hierarchy. The idea of living together in peace and unity as members of a unified society is non-existent. Language is the codified expression of thought, and thought, not flesh, is the inner reality of all human beings. In Proverbs 23:7, we are given insight into this in the phrase "As a man thinks, so is he." Should one underestimate the power of this insight, the proverb further elucidates stating "For as he thinketh in his heart, so is he: eat and drink, saith he to thee, but his heart is not with thee." The import is not simply an allusion to the cunningness of humans but is a spiritual warning against the dangers of greed and dishonesty and its long term impact upon the very soul of man.

Now let's consider the following. After writing numerous Tablets to the crown heads of state in Europe, in the Americas, in Persia (Iran), and in the Ottoman Empire, in the early hours of *29 May 1892*, across the bay from Haifa, Israel in the Holy Land, the Blessed Beauty, **Bahá'u'lláh**, passed away at the Mansion of Bahjí. Nine days later His Will was unsealed. It designated 'Abdu'l-Bahá as His successor, the Sole Interpreter of His Writings, and the head of the Bahá'í Faith. *It is the first time in religious history that the founder of a world religion had made explicitly clear whom people should follow after His death.* This declaration of a successor is the pivotal provision of what is known to Bahá'ís as the "Covenant of **Bahá'u'lláh**." It has enabled the Bahá'í Faith to remain united around one central authority for more than a century and a half up to this very day.

The tablets which Bahá'u'lláh addressed to these crown heads of state of Europe called for the establishment of the 'Most Great Peace.' This was Bahá'u'lláh's divine vision for humankind at the end of the 19th century. He envisioned a future when the peoples of the world will live together in peace and unity as members of one faith. Universal justice would be established and would be based on obedience to the law of God. In His Tablets to the kings, Bahá'u'lláh wrote:

> "O kings of the earth! We see you increasing every year your expenditures and laying the burden thereof on your subjects. This, verily, is wholly and grossly unjust. Fear the sighs and tears of this Wronged One and lay not excessive burdens on your peoples. Do not rob them to rear palaces for yourselves; nay rather choose for them that which ye choose for yourselves. Thus, we unfold to your eyes that which profiteth you, if ye but perceive. Your people are your treasures. Beware lest your rule violate the commandments of God, and ye deliver your wards to the hands of the robber. By them ye rule, by their means ye subsist, by their aid ye conquer. Yet, how disdainfully ye look upon them! How strange, how very strange!" [14]

In effect, His Message was a call for the *renewal of civilization*. And unlike previous civilizations of ancient times, His civilization would emerge not by conquering foreign lands but would be based upon eternal spiritual values and referred to this period in history as the Golden Age of the Baha'i Dispensation --- the Most Great Peace. Unfortunately, His call to the crown heads of state was ignored. Bahá'u'lláh, the Tree of Life, wrote to them again:

> "Now that ye have refused the Most Great Peace, hold ye fast unto this, the Lesser Peace, that haply ye may in some degree better your own condition and that of your dependents." [14]

In response to this message to the kings of Europe at the end of the 19th century, materialism and militarism steadily increased accompanied by the erection of luxurious palaces, colonial expansion and to pay for all of these expenses the burden upon the people grew exponentially harsh. And in response to Bahá'u'lláh's divine claim to be the Mouthpiece of God and to his call to establish the most great peace and the oneness of humanity, thus calling for the abandonment of all emerging racist ideologies in Europe, the same kings and rulers turned their backs and unleashed a calculated campaign known as the Scramble for Africa. And to support the claim of a racial superiority, scientific racism was put in place. Both responses were a clear refutation of his claim to be the manifestation of God of all ages.

Timeline of Scientific Racism 1893 to 1912

1893: A year after the ascension of Bahá'u'lláh, The World's Columbian Exposition opens in Chicago featuring pavilions that represented different countries from around the world. The pavilions were organized according to scientific theories of race. It is at this time that the first mention of Bahá'u'lláh and the Baha'i Faith were mentioned in the United States.

1864: Herbert Spencer coins the phrase "survival of the fittest" in developing his theories of social Darwinism.

1865: French anthropologist Paul Broca develops his "table chromatique" for classifying skin color.

1866: Physician John Downs defines "Mongolian idiocy" which he argues is a regression to the "Oriental stage" of human development.

1869: Francis Galton publishes Hereditary Genius, outlining his theories on human breeding.

1876: Italian psychiatrist Cesare Lombroso releases Criminal Man, which outlines his theory of criminal anthropology.

1889: Andrew Carnegie pens "The Gospel of Wealth," justifying the extreme wealth of the robber barons.

1900: Gregor Mendel's theories of inheritance are "rediscovered."

1902: The Chinese Exclusion Act is made permanent.

1904: Curator of physical anthropology at the Smithsonian Institute Ales Hrdlicka publishes Broca's "table chromatique" in the U.S.

1905: The German Society for Racial Hygiene is founded. The term racial hygiene was used to describe an approach to eugenics in the early 20th century, which found its most extensive implementation in Nazi Germany (Nazi eugenics). It was marked by efforts to avoid interracial sexual relations (aka) miscegenation, analogous to an animal breeder seeking purebred animals. This was often motivated by the belief in the existence of a racial hierarchy and the related fear that "lower races" would "contaminate" a "higher" one. As with most eugenicists at the time, racial hygienists believed that the lack of eugenics would lead to rapid social degeneration, the decline of civilization by the spread of inferior characteristics.

1905: Alfred Binet invents the IQ test for measuring intelligence.

1907: The Eugenics Education Society is founded in Britain.

1907: The first American compulsory sterilization law goes into effect in 1907 in Indiana with dozens of states following suit.

1910: Zoologist Charles Davenport founds the Eugenics Record Office at the Cold Spring Harbor Laboratory with a grant from Mrs. E.H. Harriman.

1911: The Joint-Congressional Dillingham Commission recommends reading and writing tests to slow "undesirable" immigration.

1911: Franz Boas publishes The Mind of Primitive Man arguing for the role of environmental factors in the apparent differences between races.

1912: The First International Conference of Eugenics is held in London, presided over by Charles Darwin's son Leonard.

White Supremacist's Reaction to Abdu'l-Baha's Monumental visit to Western Europe, Canada and the United States of America.

In 1912, after a lifetime of imprisonment and persecution, 'Abdu'l-Bahá, the son of **Bahá'u'lláh** (the Prophet-Founder of the Bahá'í Faith), traveled from coast to coast for 239 days by train across the United States. During his travels, he met with Andrew Carnegie and conversed with him at Carnegie's request. He also met with President Theodore Roosevelt, Attorney Louis Gregory, and, although he was scheduled to meet with President Woodrow Wilson and to speak to a joint session of the U.S. Congress, neither of those meetings took place; however, we know that Wilson's eldest daughter, Margaret Wilson, was one of the early Baha'is in Washington, D.C. Abdu'l-Baha also met with other prominent industry, political and religious American figures during his travels, and gave talks throughout from the east to the west coast at numerous Christian churches, Jewish Synagogues, Muslim Mosques as well as both Howard and Stanford Universities. These talks attracted thousands, rich and poor, Southern Segregationists (Democrats) and New England Abolitionists (Republicans), Asian, black, and white which due to the diversity of races among the attendees garnered the attention of both the local and the national press.

| Theodore Roosevelt | Louis Gregory | Woodrow Wilson | Andrew Carnegie |

| Phoebe Hearst | Margaret Wilson | Abdu'l-Baha (seated) |

Timeline of Scientific Racism 1913 to 1965

1913: Eugenicist Henry Goddard introduces the IQ test at Ellis Island.

1916: Madison Grant publishes The Passing of the Great Race, splitting Europe into three racial groups: Nordic, Alpine, and Mediterranean.

1917: The Immigration Act of 1917 includes the Asiatic Barred Zone, which excludes nearly all immigrants from Asia.

1920: Lothrop Stoddard writes The Rising Tide of Color Against White World-Supremacy.

In 1921, nine years after Abdu'l-Baha's travels and his talks which he gave across the United States, including Washington, D.C. --- the citadel of American democracy, the Ku Klux Klan paraded down Washington D. C's Pennsylvania Avenue in a show of force and recruitment. Later that same year, Abdu'l-Baha passed away in the

Holy Land, after having appointed his grandson, Shoghi Effendi, the Guardian of the Baha'i Faith and its fledgling world-wide community.

President Woodrow Wilson - Advocate for White Supremacy in the United States

Woodrow Wilson was the 28th president of the United States and is known among other things as the First World War president. As President, Wilson earned a Nobel Peace Prize for his efforts to establish the League of Nations, and as a progressive reformer he fought against monopolies and child labor. Wilson served two terms, 1913 to 1921, and was a member of the Democratic Party (not to be confused with the Democratic Party of today). At that time, the Democratic Party was *the* party of white southerners; bitter white supremacists who had fought and lost the American Civil War. Originally from Virginia, Wilson was the first southerner to become president since the Reconstruction and was a rabid segregationist.

Prior to being elected to the Presidency, Wilson served as president of Princeton University from 1902 to 1910, and was elected governor of New Jersey, in 1910. With what can only be considered by all standards, an illustrious career, as President of the United States, however, he promoted a racist agenda which oversaw "the resegregation of the federal workforce which helped to erase the many gains that African Americans had made since the start of Reconstruction." [15]

On June 26, 2020, the Princeton University Board of Trustees voted to change the names of both the School of Public and International Affairs and Wilson College both of which had been named for him. The trustees had concluded that Wilson's racist thinking and policies made him an inappropriate namesake for a school or college whose scholars, students, and alumni must stand firmly against racism in all its forms.

It is both confounding and notable that as President of the United States, Wilson was also responsible for the formation of the League of Nations, which formation stands as confirmation of the influence Abdu'l-Baha's visit and many public talks he had given in Washington, D.C. as well as other urban centers during his travels across the nation. One can only speculate about who or what actually influenced Wilson's decision to form the League of Nations; however, it is widely known that Margaret Wilson, his eldest daughter, was a member of the nascent Baha'i community in Washington, D.C., and spoke often of Abdu'l-Baha's message of world peace and the pressing need for unity among nations. Today, the United Nations stands as his effort to form an assembly to build global consensus for the establishment of world peace and to forestall a second world war. However, scientific racism persisted.

Timeline of Scientific Racism 1921 to 1965

1921: The Emergency Quota Act is signed into law, heavily restricting immigration from Eastern & Southern Europe.

1921: The Second International Congress of Eugenics is held at the American Museum of Natural History in New York City.

1921: The Ascension of Abdu'l-Baha in the Holy Land.

1923: Carl Bringham publishes A Study of American Intelligence, which uses the IQ testing done by Robert Yerkes to support differences in intelligence between races.

1924: The Immigration Act of 1924 becomes law imposing a quota system that favored Northern & Western Europe and excluding immigration from all of Asia.

1924: U.S. Congressman from New York Emanuel Celler gives his first major speech on the House floor against the Immigration Act of 1924.

1927: The Supreme Court upholds compulsory sterilization in Buck v. Bell.

1932: The Third International Eugenics Conference is held at the American Museum of Natural History in New York City. <u>Eugenics Record Office</u> Director Charles B. Davenport presides.

1932: The Encyclopedia of the Social Sciences is released with many of the anthropology articles written by Boasian, not Grantian.

1933: The Third Reich enacts the first German compulsory sterilization law.

1935: The Carnegie Institution of Washington orders an external scientific review of the <u>Eugenics Record Office</u> and finds its records "unsatisfactory for the scientific study of human genetics."

1937: Madison Grant dies.

1937: The Pioneer Fund is founded by Wickliffe Draper to support racial research. ERO superintendent Harry Laughlin serves as its first president.

1939: The Eugenics Record Office shuts down. (*)

1943: Chinese Exclusion is repealed, and a quota is given of 105 immigrants per year.

1952: The McCarran-Walter bill is passed, revising but not eliminating the quota system of immigration.

1963: The first Baha'i Congress meets in London to elect the first nine members of the Universal House of Justice, exactly 100 years after the Declaration of Bahá'u'lláh.

1965: The Hart-Celler Act repeals the immigration quota system and establishes a new system based on skills and family relations

Eugenics and Scientific Racism

The National Human Genome Research Institute describes Eugenics as the unscientific theory that human beings can be genetically improved through selective breeding of entire populations. Those who upheld eugenics as a science believed that genetics determined intelligence and social behaviors to be a function of genetic inheritance, though such human qualities as intelligence are abstract and are unable to be passed genetically to one's offspring.

This theory has been completely debunked and is scientifically inaccurate as the 1999 letter to Arthur L. Caplan shows below. It is a reply to the question: "What is immoral about eugenics?" Caplan served as the director of the Center for Bioethics at the University of Pennsylvania Health System:

> "It is a "given" in discussions of genetic engineering that no sensible person can be in favour of eugenics. The main reason for this presumption is that so much horror, misery, and mayhem have been carried out in the name of eugenics in the 20th century that no person with any moral sense could think otherwise. In fact, the abysmal history of murder and sterilization undertaken in the name of race hygiene and the "improvement" of the human species again and again in this century is so overpowering that the risk of reoccurrence, sliding down what has proved time and time again to be an extremely slick, slippery slope, does seem enough to bring all ethical argument in favour of eugenics to an end." [16]

Considering the long historical timeline of the development of scientific racism going as far back as the year 1770 A.D, it becomes clear that the efforts to establish a *rational* basis for the notion that there is a superior race to which all other races are subordinate and therefore inferior implies an urgency to respond to Abdu'l-Baha's message of the Oneness of Humankind. It also raises a simple question --- why? For what purpose was so much money poured into genomic studies? Why all the coordinated and complex cranial studies done over centuries of research? Why the obsessive interest in proving such a ... what ... theory? Why the obsession? To what end could this heavily funded pseudoscience --- eugenics --- serve humanity? And who would be the beneficiaries of this pursuit? As I consider these questions, an excerpt from 'The Tablet of Ahmad', a prayer penned by Bahá'u'lláh comes to my mind:

> "Say: O people be obedient to the ordinances of God, which have been enjoined in the Bayán by the Glorious, the Wise One. Verily He is the King of the Messengers and His book is the Mother Book did ye but know. Thus doth the Nightingale utter His call unto you from this prison. He hath but to deliver this clear message. Whosoever desireth, let him turn aside from this counsel and whosoever desireth let him choose the path to his Lord. O people, if ye deny these verses, by what proof have ye believed in God? Produce it, O assemblage of false ones! Nay, by the One in Whose hand is my soul, they are not, and never shall be able to do this, *even should they combine to assist one another.* [17]

The answer to the above questions speaks volumes. To my mind, the obsession to expand so much time, attention, and money to scientifically prove the superiority of one race over all others was in gendered by the vitriolic outcome of a single document and can only be attributed to those centuries-old documents previously referred to as *the Vatican Papal Bulls.*

Edwin Black is the author of 'IBM and the Holocaust' and 'War Against the Weak: Eugenics and America's Campaign to Create a Master Race'. His article of September 2003 is entitled 'The Horrifying American Roots of Nazi Eugenics'. It can be found on the History News Network and is supported by the University of

Richmond (Virginia). And, although the article focusses on the Nazi Holocaust of the European Jews specifically with no mention of Jews still living in Palestine, it serves as a clarion call to all people of good will but especially to all people of African descent and indigenous peoples throughout the world.

The eugenics movement was established under the canopy of a social and scientific campaign funded by the United States government. The movement also received extensive financing from a variety of leading corporations under the guise of philanthropy. In addition, such euphemisms were commonly used to shield major private U.S. corporations such as the Carnegie Institution, the Rockefeller Foundation, the Harriman Railroad fortune, and the Ford Foundation. According to the proponents of the eugenics movement their aim was "to improve the genetic quality of the human population by eliminating the *'unfit'* and by enhancing the *'fit.'* However, ListVerse.com describe the movement in far clearer terms:

> "The American eugenics movement formed the basis for the Third Reich's belief in a Master Race and their attempts to create one. There was a bizarre sort of mutual respect that went on between American eugenics supporters and the Nazi party. In 1937, the American Eugenics Society issued statements of praise for the work that the Nazis were doing to cleanse the gene pool. For them, the scale on which the Nazis were carrying out their mass sterilization was what they had wanted for America. Original writings of eugenic supporters spoke of cleansing the American population by methods ranging from gas chambers to simply leaving the lower classes to the mercy of the elements or to disease; they went on to lament that American society wasn't ready for such a widespread, sweeping cleanse and saluted the Nazis for doing

exactly what they had wanted for their own country. Hitler's fondness for the theories and science behind American eugenics was clear; he would not only quote American texts but use them as evidence to support his madness and to recruit others to his cause." [18]

In 2020, Sanjana Manjeshwar was a senior majoring in Legal Studies and Sociology at Berkeley. Her research interests include workers' rights and access to justice. On November 4, 2020, her article 'America's Forgotten History of Forced Sterilization' appeared in the Berkeley Political Review. Manjeshwar stunned her readers with the following report: "California's "Asexualization Acts in the 1910s and 1920s led to the sterilization of 20,000 disproportionately Black and Mexican people who were deemed to be mentally ill. Throughout the 20th century, *nearly 70,0000 people* (overwhelmingly working-class women of color) were sterilized in over 30 states. Black women, Latina women, and Native American women were specifically targeted. From the 1930s to the 1970s, <u>nearly one-third of the women in Puerto Rico</u>, a U.S. territory, were coerced into sterilization when government officials claimed that Puerto Rico's economy would benefit from a reduced population. Sterilization was so common that it became known as *"La Operación* (The Operation)" among Puerto Ricans."[19]

In the 1930s, one of the main goals of the Third Reich was to create a German master race. It is reported that Hitler was inspired by California's laws when it came to formulating their own genocidal eugenics. Hitler wrote about the 'Asexualization Acts' of California saying: "There is today one state in which at least weak beginnings toward a better conception [of citizenship] are noticeable. Of course, it is not our model German Republic, but the United States." This statement shows that the Third Reich didn't invent the idea of a Master Race, or of eugenics —America did. Several decades before the movement caught on in Germany, Americans were flaunting their Caucasian genes and the "Better Babies" they would bear, and sterilizing those deemed less worthy of a family. [20]

Back to the Future: How the Papal Bulls, Eugenics and Scientific Racism Combined to Devastate the Kingdom of Kongo in the 1900s

Congolese laborer's tap rubber near Lusambo in Kasai

King of Belgium, Leopold II

One clear historical illustration that the Christian cycle had ended, that is, that its spiritual light had faded, comes from the Catholic nation of Belgium. In devastating clarity, the horrendous effects that nation's barbaric racist policies had upon the Kingdom of Kongo and its peoples is illustrative of the effects of European colonialism throughout the world.

From 1885 to 1908, under the absolute rule of King Leopold II of Belgium, untold atrocities were committed in the Kingdom of Kongo which he renamed the 'Congo _Free_ State'. The heinous atrocities that were inflicted upon the Congolese people were exclusively associated with the labor policies that were put into place by Leopold's racist regime not only to seize the abundant natural rubber resource for export, but to do so without any expenditure to Congolese laborers. Epidemic disease, famine, and a decline in the birth rate further disrupted and caused even more suffering which resulted in a sharp decline in the overall Congolese population of some thirteen million human souls.

The Berlin Conference of 1884–1885

The Berlin Conference of 1884–1885 was a series of negotiations among thirteen European powers and the United States. The purpose of the conference was to literally slice up the African continent with impunity and to distribute these ancient lands and kingdoms among themselves. As representatives of sovereign nations all nations would therefore be held exempt from punishment for any injurious consequences of their actions. Why was/is this the case?

John Mearsheimer, author of *The Tragedy of Great Power Politics*, explains it in very simple terms: "In the international system there is no higher authority than national sovereignty. "Power," Mearsheimer says, "is the currency of our current international relations system." The author further explains that essentially State sovereignty in the international political arena is anarchy and is the opposite of hierarchy. In effect, "nationalism is an anarchic system ... whereas a world state is hierarchal." In other words, a world hierarchal system would have power above that of national sovereignty; however, such a system was not in place at the time of the Berlin Conference of 1884-85 which is why the conferees at the Berlin Conference were able to deliberate from their relative positions of power with impunity. The conferees ultimately agreed to allocate the vast basin region of the Kingdom of Kongo to King Leopold II of Belgium, the least powerful nation seated at the table which came to be known as 'The Scramble for Africa'.

The first action taken by Leopold was to officially rename the Kingdom of Kongo to the 'Congo *Free* State' (changing even the spelling from <u>K</u>ongo to <u>C</u>ongo; which, in effect, erased the thousand-year cultural history of the Kingdom of Kongo from future human consciousness by a race-conscious, dismissive, materialistic colonial power uninformed and dismissive of the Congolese people, their culture and ancient history). This name change from 'Kingdom of Kongo' to "The Congo *Free* State" was executed by Leopold to impress upon the more powerful and wealthier Western nations that his was a *philanthropic organization* which was to be administered by Leopold himself. At best, however, it was a political and economic chimera for the kingdom under his control was anything but *free*. The choice of name was a smoke screen hoisted to obscure the real intent, and was calculated to gain advantage in what became the imposition of colonialism and domination by European powers throughout the African continent.

Leopold had long held ambitions to participate in European colonial expansion and now it was given to him. The territory under Leopold's control exceeded a million square miles, and this land grab took place amid financial problems that the king was facing. Initially the quasi-colony state was always close to bankruptcy. Then things turned in the king's favor. The boom in demand for natural rubber skyrocketed due to the demand for rubber for automobile, airplane and bicycle tires. Given the abundant Kongo territory, a radical shift occurred in the 1890s, and to accelerate the extraction and export of rubber, Leopold decreed that all vacant land in the kingdom was to be nationalized, distributing the majority of the land to private European and American companies as concessions, and kept the rest for Belgium and himself. Between 1891 and 1906, the companies were allowed free rein to exploit the concessions using forced unpaid labor and violent coercion to cheaply tap the rubber to maximize profit. It was the Force Publique (the Free State's military force) that enforced the labor policies which included chopping off of hands of laborers and their children's hands who were forced to scale towering and dangerous rubber trees, killing individual laborers who refused to collect rubber, as well as completely destroying entire villages by fire.

Before the Berlin Conference, Belgium was considered a small insignificant European country, and Leopold was considered just as insignificant, an even petty European monarch. Leopold wanted to gain entrance and a seat at the conference table, and desperately needed to impress his European rivals and American government leaders to gain their endorsements. His colonial ambitions depended upon it! He believed that to relieve the anxieties of American financial investors, he had to assure them that his intentions were honorable and philanthropic. Once convinced of this, both the United States and Britain sanctioned the name change. After the Catholic king's non-altruistic intent became known he wasted no time in officially making the kingdom of Kongo his own colonial private property; an act which was firmly grounded in the historical Papal Bulls of the 15th-16th centuries' 'Law of Discovery' decrees. In effect, the sanction given to King Leopold gave him sole ownership of the Kongo and not to the administrative government of Belgium though after the atrocities against the Congolese was revealed this colonial arrangement ended after a mercilessly gruesome and brutal period of 23 years. Yet, within that relatively short period, the King's rule and his policies in pursuit of personal profit resulted in the rapacious confiscations of natural resources, human mutilations, murders, brutal slavery, and diseases that killed ten million of the 30 million people under His dominion. There are an abundance of narratives and documentary videos that describe the litany of crimes committed by the Belgian king whose sole goal was to reap unimaginable wealth for himself, a king who --- with neither remorse nor conscience --- had never set foot in the country among the Congolese children, women, and men whom he so mercilessly brutalized.

Belgian Chocolate Anyone?

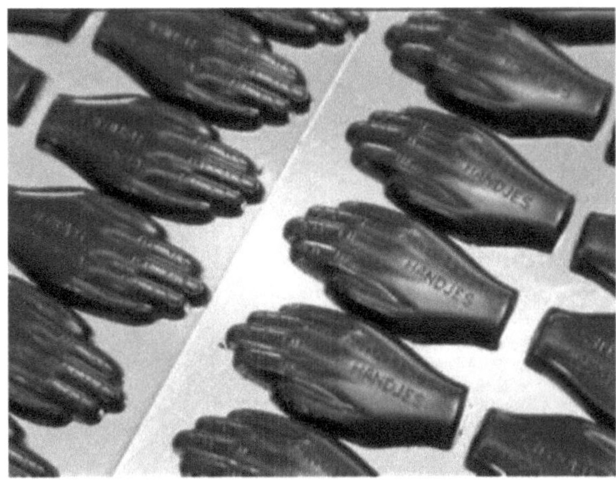

Today Belgian chocolate is one of the most important, prosperous, and readily identifiable part of Belgium's cultural identity and national Gross Domestic Product (GDP). And to immortalize this prosperity, chocolate candy hands were created as tributes to Belgium's financial success. However, these hands were not some random inspirations of a *Belgian* chocolatier, it reflected the tens of thousands of Congolese hands that were severed during the reign of King Léopold II. Between 1885 to 1908, Leopold ruled the Congo after renaming it the Free State of Congo. In the 23 years ten million Congolese were massacred by cutting off their hands and genitals, flogging them to death, starving them into forced labor, holding children ransom, and burning villages.

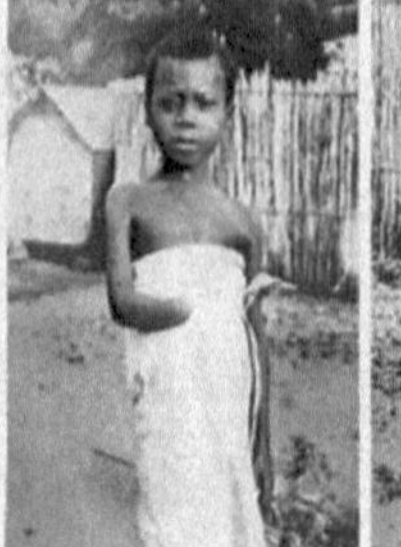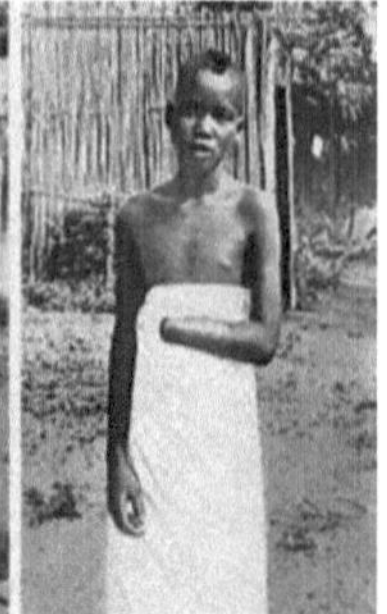

Colonel George Washington Williams, 1889

(1890) GEORGE WASHINGTON WILLIAMS'S OPEN LETTER TO KING LEOPOLD ON THE CONGO, https://www.blackpast.org/global-african-history/primary-documents-global-african-history/george-washington-williams-open-letter-king-leopold-congo-1890/.

George Washington Williams was far more than an historian. He was a published author, a lawyer and a United States minister. His work *History of Negro Troops in the War of Rebellion* was published 1887 which turned his interests to international affairs. His appointment in 1885 as United States minister to Haiti was brought to an end when President Benjamin Harrison refused him a commission. Williams then decided to go abroad, and in 1889 he participated in what was dubbed "the antislavery conference" in Brussels. The following year he traveled to the Congo Free State to see for himself the good works he had learned about during the antislavery conference in Belgium only to find the conditions so abhorrent that he published what is known as "An Open Letter to His Serene Majesty, Leopold II, King of the Belgians." This letter was circulated in both England and the United States and was the first criticism of King Leopold's regime. As a result, other letters of condemnation by independent sources followed echoing Williams strong condemnation of the king for his cruelty and oppression, and for his brutal exploitation of the people of the Congo. Frustrated at the moral, political, and social catastrophe that he had witnessed in the Congo, his view of Belgian philanthropy was permanently altered for what he had witnessed was far greater than slavery but the pursuit of global imperialism, a barbaric inhumanity he had thought eliminated with the abolition of slavery. When Williams left the Congo, he did not return to the United States but traveled extensively in South and East Africa instead. In 1891, he moved to England, and in that same year he died in the English coastal town of Blackpool.

Williams writes further that "The "free state" of Congo was put to work for King Leopold II of Belgium. Children and old men had their hands cut off for the slightest infractions, an indigenous force founded by the king (the notorious *Force Publique*) could, without reservation, destroy whole villages if they refused to work. All subjects of the Free State of Congo were forced to extract rubber from rubber figs. Only free in name, every Congolese citizen was effectively still a slave. Everybody was forced, with a labor tax by Leopold."

To this day, chocolate remains a major industry in Belgium and has been so since the 19th century. However, the raw materials used in the production of chocolate did not originate in Belgium. Most cocoa is produced in Africa, Central and South America, all lands populated by indigenous peoples. Nonetheless, Belgium has an association with the product that dates to the early 17th century. The industry expanded massively in the 19th century, gaining an international reputation and, together with the Swiss, Belgium became one of the commodity's most important producers in Europe. Although the industry has been regulated by law since 1894, there is no universal standard for the chocolate to be labelled "Belgian" but the most commonly accepted standard dictates that the actual production of the chocolate must take place inside Belgium. However, In the mid-1880s, the major legacy King Leopold of Belgium left behind in Africa was neither candy, Catholicism, trade alliance, industry, education nor democracy … it was plunder under a brutal dictatorship, a depleted rainforest, political and social instability, generational trauma, physical and sexual abuse against women, girls and boys, and mass genocide --- all of which redounds to all who must have Belgian chocolate down to our present time.

To illustrate the utter inhumanity of the effects of the 15th and 16th century Vatican Papal Bulls upon the Congolese people, the above photographs show what Belgian colonialism did as punishment for not meeting rubber quotas: "Extreme violence was employed to impose King Leopold's dominion. The right hand of those who failed to meet rubber quotas was severed. Even young children were not spared."

Yet, ask anyone today what small European nation is most famous for its chocolate candies and you'll probably receive a resounding "Belgium." Today, in Belgium, this act of extreme violence against the people of the Kongo is rarely mentioned and has been minimalized in its efforts to increase its production of "dark chocolate candy hands." The general Belgian citizen's unawareness continues as their consciousness has been purposefully programmed to believe that their government's presence in the Kongo was "to educate a savage people." Only now are responsible members of Leopold's own family helping Belgian citizens to make the connection between the brutality of King Leopold's regime and the sweet chocolate they consume so fancifully.

<u>Kingdom of Kongo, Sacrificial Lambs on the Altar of the 'Oneness of Humanity'</u>

For me, the African Kingdom of the Kongo under Belgian rule represents the sacrificial lamb on the altar of the Oneness of Humanity, a spiritual principle enunciated in 1868 by Bahá'u'lláh while imprisoned in the Most Great Prison, in Akka, Palestine. During this same period the powers of Europe had established and were expanding colonialism as the means of world domination and spreading Christianity as a means to justify it. Despite having evolved from diverse indigenous African tribal groups, the so-called Belgian Congo was promoted as a "spoil of war" though no war was ever declared or fought. Centuries before, in 1390 A.D, the Kingdom of the Kongo had come into being out of the mutual need of diverse tribes in the region to survive, forming a single kingdom during the Adamic Cycle. This cycle of many thousand-years of religious cycles *began some 4,610 ago and ended in 1844 AD;* an end that coincided with the brutal colonization of the Kingdom of the Kongo and the birth of Twin spiritual processes initiated by a new spiritual cycle and a new world religion --- the Baha'i Faith, thus initiating the "rolling up" --- as Bahá'u'lláh stated unequivocally --- of the 2,000-year Old World Order that had been established by the Revelation of prophet, Adam, and followed by successive monotheistic revelations by Abraham and Moses; and built upon by the sacred teachings of Jesus Christ who singularly introduced the concept of the "Kingdom of God", a concept that in the annals of religions had never been framed as such. This pivot away from localized revelations specific to a particular tribe was accompanied by or followed every five hundred to a thousand years by the Prophets Buddha, Zoroaster, and Muhammad (the Seal of the Prophets) and represent the Word of God Himself distilled by different Voices to carry out an Ever-Progressive Divine Will. However, this concept was of no concern to the monarchs of Europe prior to and during the 19th century.

The Kongo had become an organized region throughout the span of the Adamic Cycle. This religious cycle which *began some 4,610 years ago* was like the birth of a newborn infant. Its birth was one of Africa's greatest pre-colonial political and sociological achievements for it had united different tribal groups beneath a single kingdom. Founded in 1390 A.D, the Kingdom of the Kongo was based upon alliances between four different tribes in the region, and within 100 years, had grown to rule over three million subjects. In 1490, the King of Kongo *converted to Christianity.* Many of his elites did the same. Why this happened, no one knows. What is known is that most of his subjects did not follow the king immediately. For most people, both Christianity and Islam were just two religions among many, and traditional African beliefs persisted. This demonstrates just how strong traditional religions were at the end of the fifteenth century. The fact that the Kongo was an organized, prosperous and well-recognized kingdom completely flies in the face of 19th century colonizers' characterization of the Congolese as uncivilized pagans, and reveals the underlying motive and interest in the region had little to do with spreading the teachings of Jesus Christ, for in a purely religious context, the very term "pagan" signifies *"a person holding religious beliefs other than those of the main or recognized religions."* So, contrary to popular belief, the term does not mean uncivilized or without any belief in God, it means a practitioner of a religion other than that practiced by the general population --- the mainstream.

The Kingdom of Kongo had a powerful army and a sophisticated political structure. Congolese society was organized into villages. Each village was made up of big families called 'kanda', united by a common ancestor. Social status and wealth were passed on through women, not men. Property and royal status were dependent on the mother, not the father. Usually, the head of the kanda was male, but in the 16th and 17th centuries it was also common for women to be in charge.

So, whose philanthropic idea was it to enslave the indigenous people of West Africa? Was it merely because of the differences in skin color or was it differences in religious beliefs and practices? Certainly, we can now dispense with speculation and name the individual. It was the Vatican's Pope Nicholas V, head of the Holy Roman Empire (aka Christendom, the domain of Christianity, Europe). However, we cannot overlook the Papal Bulls which authorized Spain and Portugal to colonize and enslave the people in the Americas, nor the impact of the Muslim conquest of Constantinople upon the papacy and its religious authority; and, for added clarity, the papal bull that annulled the Magna Carta in 1215 AD. All of these papal bulls predated Pope Nicholas V's Papal Bull of 1452 each having an undeniable historical impact upon various kingdoms and realms throughout the world.

CHAPTER FOUR

Roderic, King of
the Visigoths

General Tariq Ibn
Ziyad, the Moor

Ferdinand and Isabela,
King and Queen of Spain

Ancient Africa, Arab Saracens, and the Influence and Conquest of Portugal and Spain in the Middle Ages by the Black Moors of West Africa

What took place in the Kingdom of the Kongo under King Leopold of Belgium in the late 19th century did not happen in a void, rather, it was an extension of the long historical march of mankind's resistance to change. Since time immemorial, this resistance to change has been rooted in the cyclical rise and fall of civilizations and the religious teachings that inspired them. It would do well to pause and reflect upon the question posed in the introduction to this book for it serves to remind us why our presence in the universe even matters:

> "If long-cherished ideals and time-honored institutions, if certain social assumptions and religious formulae have ceased to promote the welfare of the generality of mankind, if they no longer minister to the needs of a continually evolving humanity, let them be swept away and relegated to the limbo of obsolescent and forgotten doctrines. Why should these, in a world subject to the immutable law of change and decay, be exempt from the deterioration that must needs overtake every human institution? For legal standards, political and economic theories are solely designed to safeguard the interests of humanity as a whole, and not humanity to be crucified for the preservation of the integrity of any particular law or doctrine."(2)

A careful reading of the above statement clearly places humanity at the heart of creation on planet earth, suggesting that the basis of all human conflicts, anxieties and oppressions arise from all That humanity will never fully understand without guidance. A profound shift in consciousness is required for an even higher degree of consciousness to take root. This requires a divine educator who sows the seeds of revelation which are the teachings of a new religious cycle. This science cannot do. What exactly were our ancestors' social assumptions? What were the different religious formulae created throughout the millennia? And why was it necessary to create multiple formulae? Certainly, we can all agree that throughout the millions of years there must have been a necessity for all the changes made to those assumptions and religious formulae. However, reactionary resistance (especially in the face of social decay) has always accompanied these changes for as certain as change and decay is an immutable law, uncertainty and unpredictability are just two of its inevitable consequences. In essence, this struggle is the age-old struggle between man's will and the Divine Will. In the West, we can trace this age-long, gut-wrenching evolutionary process to numerous sacred texts. Written history goes as far back as 5,153 years ago when the first sacred text, the Bhagavad Gita, was written (Hinduism). It was followed by numerous other texts such as the 'Pyramid Texts' (The religion of ancient Kemet [aka Egypt] currently undetermined), the 'Kinzeraba' (the Sabaean religion of ancient Yemen), the 'Torah' [among others] (Judaism), the 'New Testament'(Christianity), the 'Quran' (Islam), and more recently, the 'Holy Bayan' (Bab'i Faith) and the 'Kitab-I-Aqdas' (Baha'i Faith). From age-to-age, all human struggles eventually explode in visceral form --- war. Struggle results either in radiant acquisition or violent resistance. If the human response to revelation results in radiant acquisition, saintliness is the result; violent resistance is the effort to preserve that which is familiar. Regardless of the Age in which Divine Revelation occurs, the same rejection takes place against that same divine authority no matter the name of the Deliverer or the Messenger; or the geographical location where it is delivered.

Among the many chapters of this single but long human saga includes the story of Genesis with Adam and Eve as both protagonists and antagonists, and later, in other accounts that describe the same rejection of Divine Authority by both Pharaoh and the twelve contentious nomadic Hebrew tribes as they waited at the foot of Mt. Sinai full of anxiety for their Lord. Their trek out of Egypt and through the desert lasted 40-years, time enough to humble their hearts before finally being worthy of entering the "Promised land" of Canaan.

In medieval times, the Spanish monarchy's rejection of Muhammad as a divine prophet was targeted at the Moors who had reached the Iberian Peninsula in the 8th century A.D. to spread the Sacred Teachings of Islam. They were, after all, the living, breathing embodiments of Islam and had inhabited and literally changed the entire landscape of the Iberian Peninsula by neither sword nor forced conversion.

Typically, western history divides these seemingly unrelated cultural epic narratives into two separate historical categories. The one, Genesis, has been placed in the context of the rise of the Judaic religion and the twelve tribes of Jacob. The second, the expulsion of the Muslim Moors from Spain, has been placed in the context of political and social science. Having done so, the impact of Islam upon the continent is therefore deemphasized and makes it easier to ignore the spiritual influence Islam has had on a vast range of cultural, scientific and social transformations in Europe (otherwise known as 'the Enlightenment'). This appears to have been a willful choice intended to deny Islam's revolutionary influence upon Spain in particular, and the rest of Europe in general. It seems that this was a strategy devised by Queen Isabela of Spain and the Vatican for two reasons: first, because for Christian theologians and historians to acknowledge Muhammad as a Prophet of God it would put all Christendom in an existential pickle (so to speak). Both the monarchy of Spain and the Vatican refused to acknowledge that Islam is to Christianity what Christianity is to Judaism, and that Judaism is to the Hebrew religion what Buddhism is to Hinduism, the oldest religion in the world, all the way back to our primordial beginnings; each representing the *Spring Equinoxes* of different religious cycles since time immemorial. The second reason is that *'battles and wars'* are typically categorized as *observable* socio-political phenomena. This categorization is far easier to comprehend, manage and explain to ordinary people and is to be expected since the sciences in general are captives of the Enlightenment's 'scientific method' which is exclusively concerned with observable phenomena and not supernatural forces though they are the central focus in every religion. Simply put, in order to determine *if,* in fact, divine intervention is a reality *<u>then</u>* scientists would necessarily be obligated to strictly adhere to the tenets of the scientific method. Using this method one must first objectively assess the worthiness of the proposition, then form an hypothesis, and then devise experimentations whereby direct observation and inductive reasoning rule rather than feelings and emotions. It's a left-brain kinda thing! The left hemisphere is often identified as the 'masculine' hemisphere, and right hemisphere is identified as the 'feminine' hemisphere.

As an aside, researchers have determined that the left hemisphere is generally responsible for reasoning, logic, aggression, dominance and language, while the right is responsible for emotions, intuition, passivity, cooperation, imagination, and creativity.

This suggests that these traits influenced Francis Bacon's coinage of the phrase 'the scientific method'. Given the chauvinistic structure of British society in the early 17th century and the goals of the scientific revolution against religious orthodoxy, if his gender played a role in the formulation of the scientific method, it is no wonder that the scientific method avoids at all cost the traits associated with the feminine hemisphere of the brain. The right hemisphere of the brain which scientists have found includes among its extrasensory traits intuition and emotions which could, if given more research and attention, be the generative factor for other marginalized extrasensory perceptions and psychic phenomena such as precognition, clairvoyance, telepathy, revelation, meditation, and other feminine attributes that both male and female exhibit. It is not conceivable that had such feminine attributes been recognized during the lifetime of Joan of Arc's unprecedented mystical role in the leadership of the French Army during the 100-years War against the English that the role of women in human affairs would be considered the height of civilization. Instead, she was declared a heretic by the male dominated Catholic Church and burned alive at the stake as a witch because of her right brain gifts. By ignoring intuition and imagination as sister approaches in our search for truth, this omission seems more an act of self-shackling, chaining itself to its own rubric, which in effect is a useful form of self-discipline to produce material results; and thus the status quo. This seems to be a contradiction of sort --- which overlooks the subtleties that a less aggressive approach may have to offer. After all, science is an investigative tool, and not a tool to be used to dismiss other possibilities. Reason does serve as a stabilizing force which is critical. It stabilizes the intuitive feminine traits of the right hemisphere thereby preventing dogma, superstitions, and irrational beliefs from contaminating the scientific method. At the same time, it can be said that the left hemisphere of the brain receives *insights* that might otherwise be deemed irrational. A balance must be struck between the spiritual and the material. Pre-modern (male) scientists who dominated the field were therefore forced to confine their investigations to the investigation of matter and the observable natural world which omits the possibility that there are other means by which knowledge is conveyed to the mind, the heart and the soul by spiritual means (meditation) rather than by material means alone; simultaneously conveying the activities of both the left and right hemispheres of the brain in a perfectly organic, and symbiotic way that is in harmony with both the natural and supernatural worlds.

Back From the Future

Both rebellions which occurred against Moses in Sinai on the one hand, and the expulsion of Muslims from Spain on the other, serve as classic reminders of man's continual fear of and resistance to change. Spain's hatred of the Muslim Moors was not due to skin color but rather it was against the Moors' spiritual prowess. It was this prowess which had ushered in Spain's 'golden era'. However dismissed, be it envy or religious fanaticism, the Moor's contributions to the advancement of world civilization has been forever etched into the annals of history. Islam's spiritual prowess is best illustrated not only in terms of its revolutionizing influence upon the hearts, the minds and the souls of people but also in what resulted in their technological advancements during their 800 years presence throughout Europe.

Multiple advances in technology were made as a result of this presence, and this 'golden age' was when learning increased, where libraries, colleges, public baths were established, where literature and poetry soared, and where architecture flourished. This period also included exponential advancements in astronomy, medicine, surgery, agriculture, art, and engineering --- gifts brought to Spain by a people once isolated and known only to medieval Europe as barbaric desert nomads --- the Arabs; and black African Muslims. Yet, it was these two distinct peoples who demonstrated the transformational power of the sacred teachings of Muhammad and changed medieval Christianity forever. Some six centuries later, this same spiritual prowess came to be seen as a threat to Catholic orthodoxy. Rather than seeing it as a blessing to humanity, and especially Spain (its primary beneficiary), after gaining such ascendancy throughout Europe, transforming Spain into a beacon of light for the entire continent, the light of Islam began to fade in Europe.

However, since the 8th century A.D., Islam's rising influence in West Africa and the Levant radiated in stark juxtaposition to Christian Spain's eventual stagnation, while the light of Islam had steadily increased on the African continent. In our own times, in order for us to grasp the gravity and the historical and spiritual significance of what has been dubbed *'the Reconquista'* (the battle between Spain and the Moors in Granada), it is important to note that this conflict of cultures was essentially a battle of religious intolerance on the one hand and spiritual efficacy on the other. It is this fact which has too often been obscured by the vitriolic debates over Islam. However, this rift between religious intolerance and decline and spiritual efficacy and ascendency lies at the heart of all religious and secular conflicts. These plagues are still with us and must be openly addressed for the discourse is too important to ignore. It also underscores the desperation felt, the fanaticism that has ensued, and the horrendous acts of genocide and starvation committed in the name of religious beliefs.

Once again, I am compelled to reiterate that my purpose in writing this book is to shed light, however dim it may be judged to be, on any discourse on religious, racial or ideas of national or racial supremacy. I personally eschew anything that keeps humanity from loving one another. When we keep in mind the 1,000-years cycle of all religions, perhaps that dim light will grow ever more radiant. The knowledge of the 1,000-years cycle is nothing short of the recognition of the never-ending cycle of decline and renewal, the rise and fall of civilizations, and the spiritual impetus of divine intervention in the affairs of humanity. It is what all religions have come to understand as "the Plan of God", which has been repeating its spring time spiritual renewal over and over from the beginning of time --- "progressive revelation." Despite the religious biases and often skewed historical accounts of this religious phenomenon that ironically ushered in the Spanish Inquisition, the Age of Reason and the Renaissance we must gird up our loins and have the courage to face what is rational and true, yet heart wrenching and instructive. We revisit history in hopes of gaining more insight beyond mere bravado or the licking of wounds. For either "progressive revelation" is an indispensable component of human spiritual and social evolution or it is not. The setting began in 8th century Iberia when the African Moors ended Germanic Visigoth rule on the Iberian Peninsula and brought Islam to Europe. It ended in late-15th century with Spain reconstituting its Catholic sovereignty imbuing it with genocide, reactionary medieval Catholic doctrines and by employing the now infamous *Spanish Inquisition against all non-Catholic religions. This all took place* in the year *of our Lord,* Christ, 1478 A.D.

Food for Thought:

I'd like to briefly summarize the left-brain, right-brain discussion that was presented earlier. It seems that contemporary researchers and scientists have learned something new --- that in reality, both hemispheres of the brain work together, and that stronger skills result when the two hemispheres <u>do</u> work together. However, the myth of "opposing hemispheres" persists, but the contemporary prevailing opinion is that *that* notion only "satisfies the need to keep order" in a left-brain-logic driven-uncreative-emotionless male conception of reality and one of perhaps infinite multi-verses.

Now, let's meet the Black African Moors, the conquerors of the Iberian Peninsula (Spain).

The Visigoths were described by Romans as a motley collection of barbaric migratory Germanic tribes. They had dominated Spain since the 6th century. At the beginning of the 8th century, the peninsula was invaded and conquered again by an African general named Tariq, a convert to Islam during the Arab invasion of Morocco, thus ending Visigoth rule over Spain. Tariq's Muslim army was known as the Moors. The Muslim Moors ruled Spain for nearly 800 years from 711 AD to 1492 AD, when within forty years after Pope Nicholas V had decreed his first Papal Bull inaugurating both the 'Age of Discovery' and the 'Law of Discovery', Christopher Columbus set sail westward across the Atlantic Ocean in search of new lands for the Crown. The Columbus expedition was financed entirely by King Ferdinand and Queen Isabela, the Catholic monarchs of Europe who gained to reap unimaginable wealth if successful. Spain itself was already viewed by the Vatican as being in line to become the supreme power in Europe, and with the promise of the financial gains nipping at its heels, the exploitations of New World natural resources, said to be found in abundance in these lands, they would secure not only the power that all European nations craved, but the blessings of the

Vatican. That same year, the Muslim Moors lost a series of bloody battles against the Spanish and were summarily expelled in 1492. But, what of this "conquest of Spain by the Moors?" What does it have to do with the ideology of white supremacy? Everything!

Mansa Musa and his army, Muslim King of Mali

Before the Moors conquered Spain, the history of the Iberian Peninsula dates to the pre-Roman peoples known as the Tartessos of the Mediterranean. In antiquity, Spain was the site of multiple and successive colonizations by the Greeks, the mixed-ethnic (Black and Semitic) north African kingdom of Carthage, and ultimately by the Vatican, the Seat of The Holy Roman Empire in Rome. These native peoples of the peninsula intermingled with the colonizers to create a uniquely Iberian culture. The Romans referred to the entire peninsula as Hispania and this is where the modern name of Spain originated. After the collapse of the Holy Roman Empire in 476 AD multitudes of white warring tribes from the Caucasus were pushed into Western Europe by the invading Huns who were pastoral nomads from Central Asia.

With the Moors invasion of Spain in 711 AD, African Muslims literally civilized the wild, barbaric tribes from the Caucus, and Spain eventually became the envy of the European world.

Despite what many would have us believe, the Moors had made an indelible impact upon human consciousness throughout the European continent with the Sacred Teachings from Muhammad, changing their diverse cultures through mathematics, their sciences and engineering prowess, which included indoor plumbing, water fountains, agricultural irrigation systems, etc. These and other Islamic contributions to the flowering of Europe which came to be known as "the Enlightenment" still remains a testimony of the Moors' impact upon the Spanish civilization. However, the sacred teachings of the Quran were completely demonized and the Moors were unceremoniously ousted from Spain.

Exquisite Moorish Architecture in Andalucía, Spain

CHAPTER FIVE

How the Papal Bulls Invoked the Myth of 'The Curse of Ham'

The Table of Nations is a compilation of the patriarchal founders of the seventy nations which, according to the Table, is a list of the descendants of Noah through his three sons, Shem, Ham, and Japheth and was written by Flavius Josephus, a Roman-Jewish historian and military leader. The Table can be found in Genesis, Chapter 10. According to the Table of Nations, twenty-six of the seventy descended from Shem, thirty from Ham, and fourteen from Japheth. In Genesis 10:32, the chapter reads as follows: "These are the families of the sons of Noah, according to their genealogies, by their nations; and out of these the nations were separated on the earth after the flood." Chapter 11 goes on to describe the division of the descendants of Noah at Babel.

Italian Catholic Dominican priest, Joannes Annius Viterbo was famously known for his fabrications of religious texts. He claimed to be skilled in "Semitic languages", and his expertise, which had once been celebrated even by 'sober' ecclesiastical historians, was later determined to be "entirely imaginary".

Viterbo frequently used the term Saracen when he wrote of the "superiority of Christians over the Arab Muslims." Saracen was a term he used at first to describe tribal Arabs, but later was applied to all Muslims, including those of African descent. He claimed that due to "a curse imposed upon black people" they would inevitably remain permanently subjugated by Arabs and Christians and would not rebel. Viterbo invoked what he dubbed the 'Curse of Ham' to explain the differences between Europeans and Africans in his writings and wrote that the fact that so many Africans had been enslaved by Muslim heretics was, according to him, "proof of their inferiority."

The historian David Whitford writes of a "curse matrix" which was derived from the vague wording of Genesis 9 and interpreted by racialists to mean that "it mattered not who was cursed or which specific group of people the curse originated with, all that [mattered was] that there was the vague reference to a generational curse that could be exploited by those seeking to justify their actions against black people, such as Southern slaveowners [in the United States]. Pro-slavery intellectuals were hard-pressed to find any justification for slavery and racism in Christian theology, which taught that all human beings were descendants of Adam (and therefore one race), possessed equal salvation potential and were deserving to be treated as kin. However, in spite of this acknowledgment of the Oneness of Humanity, the curse of Ham was used to drive a wedge in the biblical teaching that humanity is a single race by intellectual elites who were able to convince the masses of people that the three sons of Noah represented three categories of human beings and their respective hierarchy of different fates. Leading intellectuals in the south, like Benjamin M. Palmer, claimed that white Europeans were descended from Japhet who was prophesied by Noah to cultivate civilization and the powers of the intellect, while Africans, being descendants of the cursed Ham, were destined to be possessed by a slavish nature ruled by base appetites."

Papal Bull – Spanish Bull

The Spanish Royal Court of King Ferdinand and Queen Isabella, 1493.

The biblical *curse matrix* was the foundation that gave the Papal Bull decrees their allure, and during the reign of King Ferdinand and Queen Isabela of Spain its call for the domination and genocide of indigenous peoples and the confiscation of their lands was put into full force long before the English Reformation had been firmly established, signaling its complete break with Rome. Upon Columbus' return to Spain in 1493, and upon receiving his vivid accounts of the people, the natural resources, the land and promises of vast gold deposits --- confirming nearly two centuries of murmurings about Mansa Musa, the black African-Muslim King of the Mali Empire, and his multiple attempts to reach *a new world* (Mesoamerica) that lay on the other side of the Atlantic. At a time when Europe was still wrestling with the idea that the world was round and not flat, these murmurings were nothing short of awe and disbelief. Mansa Musa's final voyage to Mesoamerica was fatal, and by 1493, his explorations came to an end and were now being hailed as Christopher Columbus' "discovery of the New World." These riveting stories had reached the ears of European monarchs and were told unceasingly throughout the 14th through 16th centuries. There were many stories told about Mansa Musa. For two hundred years, European monarchs sat riveted around elaborate banquet tables as numerous accounts of Mansa Musa, the King of the Mali Empire, were repeated. The King of Mali was considered to be the wealthiest monarch on earth, and among the many impressive accounts of his reign was the pilgrimage he made from Mali to Mecca. When crossing the Sahara to Cairo, his caravan carried so much gold that his generosity to ordinary people caused a devastating inflation throughout Egypt. Aware of these murmurings and based solely upon her family connections to the Vatican, Queen Isabela was eager to comply with all seven Papal Bulls (1452 through 1514), and immediately wrote to Nicolas Ovando authorizing and establishing his role as "overseer of the transatlantic slave trade."

Nicolas Ovando

Again, Queen Isabela's letters clearly endorsed the enslavement of African peoples (in particular) as unpaid laborers to work the sugar plantations in the Caribbean where sugar cane grew in abundance. Sugar was fast becoming a booming global commodity throughout Europe whose sale was quickly outpacing that of cotton and coffee. Needless to say, the queen's letter was in perfect alignment with and obeisance to the Papal Bull of 1452 and reemphasized the urgency of the enslavement of Black African peoples. And, to pour salt into the wound, the letter stipulated that the descendants of these peoples would be enslaved in perpetuity as both retributive justice for the Moor's invasion of Spain some 800 years earlier, and as a war strategy against the swiftly growing expansion of the Islamic Caliphate's reach into Europe --- now the preeminent threat to their own Catholic Spanish Kingdom. The desperation to fend off the Muslims was becoming increasingly urgent with the Arabs having already conquered nearby Constantinople, Turkey. Constantinople was and still is the most strategic city on the Bosporus Strait. To this day it remains an internationally significant trade waterway connecting the Black Sea to the Sea of Marmara and forms part of the continental boundary between Asia and Europe. Funds were desperately needed to cut off any potential incursion by the Muslims upon Spain. Constantinople had already fallen some 40 years earlier to the Ottomans on May 29, 1453, which had culminated after a 53-day siege led personally by Sultan Mehmet II the Conqueror, the Caliph of Sunni Islam, giving urgency to the commitment to write and to circulate the subsequent six Papal Bulls. The Fall of Constantinople signaled the death knell of the capital of the Christian Byzantine Empire (Constantinople) which was now in the hands of Sultan Mehmet II marking the rise and threat of the Ottoman Empire to European Christendom.

Digging Deeper into the Old Testament Version of 'The CURSE OF HAM'

As described in the Book of Genesis, Ham's curse was imposed by Noah upon Canaan, Ham's son. It occurs in the context of Noah's drunkenness and is provoked when Ham sees the "nakedness of his father" and asks his two brothers to help cover Him against the cold and wet after the proverbial "flood" had abated. Since this story appears in the Old Testament, its original purpose may have been to justify the biblical subjection of the Canaanites to the Israelites. At what point did the biblical Hebrews of the Exodus take upon themselves the new name Israelites? This, unfortunately, remains obscure. However, we know that the tribe of Joseph was not the only tribe of the Hebrews who were brought out of Egypt by Moses. It seems reasonable to assume that the term 'Hebrew' referred to all twelve tribes and not just to the tribe of Joseph. Many questions surround the name Hebrew. Is it a religion? An ethnic group? If it is a religion who is its Founder? If it is a single ethnic group what is their place of origin? What say about Black Africans who claim to be Hebrew? According to Josephus and others, Ham's descendants are to have populated Africa and adjoining parts of Asia. And in Psalms 78:51; 105:23, 27; 106:22; and 1 Chronicles 4:40 of the Old Testament, all these beg further analysis for after examining the DNA of ninety-three bodies recovered from archaeological sites around the southern Levant (the biblical land of Canaan), researchers have concluded that modern populations of the region are descendants of the ancient Canaanites (descendants of Canaan) who were not Hebrews. Most modern Jewish groups and Arabic-speaking groups from the region show at least half of their ancestry as Canaanite.

The Canaanites' religious practice was *monolatrist* which means they recognized the existence of many gods (prophets?), but consistently worshipped only one supreme deity (God), thus, monotheists. This distinction is very important to our understanding of the purpose and nature of religion itself (that is, that it is progressive and not static), and alludes to God's Greater Covenant and the reason why (according to the Biblical texts) Joshua instructed the newly freed Hebrews to destroy the Canaanites in the first place. By the 15th century, the narrative was conveniently re-interpreted by Jews, Christians, and Arab Muslims alike to explain why some people had dark skin attributing it to the now infamous *Curse of Ham* which had no other purpose than to justify a contrived pseudo religious concept used solely to attract wealthy investors to allay any moral concerns they had in order to secure their financial interests in the enslavement of Black African peoples. Nevertheless, most religious scholars now discredit this interpretation, reasoning that in the biblical text, Ham himself is not cursed, and that neither race nor skin color are ever mentioned. Yet, racism continues. Perhaps we need to look at the underlying, invisible (if you allow me) driving force behind the Hebrews' determination to subdue the land of Canaan. Perhaps history can show the way.

Considering the time-span of the spread of Christianity in Europe (1500 years), and later the spread of Islam in Africa and Asia, it is reasonable to conclude that the motive behind the conquest of Canaan was the same as in most Faiths of the Adamic Cycle --- the propagation of their own religion by any necessary. The Christian Crusades were executed to defend Christendom against the spread of Islam both factions did so even if at the point of a sword.

Certainly, if Moses was prohibited by God from entering the 'Promised Land' for disobeying God's command *to speak* to a rock to produce water for His thirsty followers instead of striking the rock with his staff as God had directed him to do, an act that in the eyes of God was considered disobedience to His divine command. In the Torah, we learned the reason He gave Moses this specifically worded command. It was given as such to show honor to Him by acknowledging that it was He, God, who was the provider of the water and that it was not to be attributed to Moses. Therefore the seriousness of Moses disobeying the command of

God should be clear to any fair-minded person. Here, I defer to Christopher R. Smith's *Good Question blog* where he addresses this subject. Smith sums up the issue between God and Moses referring to this passage in the Old Testament: "Because you did not believe in me, to uphold me as holy in the eyes of the people of Israel, therefore you shall not bring this assembly into the land that I have given them." Another translation puts it this way: "You did not trust me enough to honor me and show the people that I am holy. You did not show the Israelites that the power to make the water came from *me*. So, you will not lead the people into the land that I have given them." [21]

In other words, according to the Torah which the majority of modern scholars say was written during the Babylonian captivity in the 6th century BCE, Moses was not allowed to enter Canaan because He did not follow God's command to the letter. Why was that so important? Because it illustrates the importance of acknowledging God above all beings and above all things. For even after having been liberated from Egypt as promised by God, the Hebrews continued to argue and contend with Moses, even begging to return to slavery in the land of the Pharaohs. God's command to Moses was given as such to show unequivocally that the water came from the All-Powerful, Invisible God and not from His Servant, Moses. You may be asking, why is that so important to our discussion on white supremacy and racism? Because white supremacy and racism are akin to Moses' disobedience to God's clear instruction to "uphold Me as holy in the eyes of the people of Israel by "speaking" to the rock instead of "striking" the rock to bring forth the water. In effect his disobedience suggested to the people that it was him and not God who had performed what would have been understood as proof of God's power and sovereignty or a miracle; an act that was tantamount to claiming partnership with God. As Smith points out, "God had told Moses to gather all the Hebrews together *in front of the rock*, and God had given him specific instructions to speak on His behalf, and to say:

"Speak to that rock before their eyes and it will pour out its water."
But instead of carrying out these instructions to the letter, Moses
had gathered the Israelites together and, speaking for himself and
his fellow leader Aaron *rather than on God's behalf,* said to them,
"Listen you rebels, must we bring you water out of this rock?"
Then he struck the rock twice, and water came out, thus omitting
Who had provided the water to a rebellious and contentious people.
In the bible when Jacob was in his nineties God changed his name
to Israel. In Hebrew, the meaning of the name Israel has various
meanings: "May God prevail", "He who wrestles, struggles,
contends, and fights with God" and "God perseveres". This is why
it was essential for Moses to obey God's command to the letter.
He didn't, and he was punished. You now may be asking yourself,
why is all this relevant to any discussion on white supremacy and
racism? Fasten your seat belt.

CHAPTER SIX

As we have learned the Table of Nations identifies Ham as the second son of Noah and the father of Cush, Mizraim, Phut and Canaan. Mizraim is a name that generally refers to both the land of Egypt in the Bible and people descended from the son of Noah, Ham; also known as Hamites. This came about as a result of the interpretations of Flavius Josephus and others stating that it was these black-skinned people who populated the African continent and Southern Arabia. However, according to a contemporary modern study that includes Professor Israel Finkelstein of the Department of Archaeology and Ancient Near Eastern Cultures conducted by an international team of archaeologists and geneticists, their study shows that most "modern-day Jewish and Arabic-speaking populations share a clear and strong genetic link to the ancient Canaanites" This study has even gone so far as to conclude that "modern-day groups in Lebanon, Israel and Jordan share more than half of their ancestry with the people who lived in Canaan over 3,000 years ago.

Some Eurocentric researchers have determined that the Canaanites themselves were descendants from a mix of an "earlier Levantine population as well as tribal groups who had migrated from the *Caucasus region* and *ancient Persia*; however, this theory is fraught with biblical contradictions and is thus easy to debunk yet remains controversial but is outright misleading. For even a superficial reading of the Old Testament by upholders of the 'curse of Ham narrative, would recognize its incongruity. For according to that same biblical narrative Canaan, the son of Ham, was the progenitor of all Black African peoples, and were identified by the name Mizraim (the ancient Aramaic and Hebrew name for the land of Egypt and black Africans in general). The obvious intellectual incongruity that arises is that this theory on the racial makeup of the population of the land of Canaan is that the geographic location of the Levant is in the Eastern Mediterranean region of West Asia. It includes Syria, Israel, Jordan, Lebanon, Turkey, Greece, Cyrenaica, and Eastern Libya in north Africa. In other words, these are the supposed biblical lands bequeathed to the descendants of Japheth, and not Ham, the father of Canaan. Researchers can't have it both ways. Either the Canaanites were from the Levant, or they were the descendants of Canaan, the supposed 'cursed son of Ham, the heir to the lands of Mizraim (Egypt), and father of Black people throughout the African continent, and elsewhere.

And so, here is where the rubber meets the road. Given the historical data and the study mentioned earlier, why then did the Jews, Christians and Arab Muslims use this story to identify dark African peoples as the descendants of Canaan, son of Ham, grandson of Noah? *It becomes self-evident that this deceptive* interpretation by Flavius Josephus (the Jewish Historian) had tremendous influence upon the Jews, and later, Protestant Christians and Arab Muslims. In a sweeping stroke of a pen Flavius Josephus presented the religious foundation for the seven Papal Bulls that were decreed in 1452 and included it in the Old Testament. By identifying the descendants of Ham as "cursed" … which marginalized an entire group of people throughout the entire African continent proved to be the elusive, long sought-after religious justification for the enslavement of dark-skinned African peoples. It was the religious green-light signaling 'all systems go', granting permission and endorsement of the systemic institution of the transatlantic slave trade, the ideology of white supremacy and racism replacing one obsolete world order with an even more warped version of its own medieval ideas with the colonization of the entire continent of Africa. This replacement was done with the intent to justify a convoluted and racialized human interpretation of the sacred ministry of Noah, using His three sons, Ham, Japheth, and Shem to create what has come to be called 'the Curse of Ham'. This corruption of the sacred text has thundered down from synagogues to cathedrals to mosques for over 4,000 years. It has stained the hearts and hardened the minds of toddlers and children in our primary schools and universities, in our literature and films, in our politics and health care systems, and has continued to ravage the human soul ever since.

Biblical Translations, Revisions, Interpretations, Re-interpretations, and 'The Curse of Ham' in the Minds of the Common Man and Woman

What could possibly go wrong?

Just to put things into perspective, there have been over 30,000 changes made to the Bible, of which more than 5,000 represent differences between the Greek text used for the Revised Version which was also used as the basis of the King James Version revisions that are still in use today. There are approximately 150 different *versions* of the Bible with twelve main versions none of which are "authoritative" texts but are still in circulation today. As relates to religion, the actual meaning of the term "authoritative" means that Jesus Christ Himself wrote, endorsed, and reviewed any text that expressed His revelation. None of these happened. Jesus Christ neither authorized nor made provisions for any additions or deletions of what is referred to as the 'Sacred text' which necessarily would have to be either what *He actually said or wrote.*

The text of the New Testament was compiled from a variety of writings that were circulating throughout Emperor Constantine's East Roman Empire known as Byzantium. Constantine was the first Christian Roman Emperor and founded the city of Constantinople. The Council of Nicaea was held to convene the diverse Christian bishops from throughout the empire. They were called to Nicaea (Turkey) in AD 325 to settle a number of thorny issues including the divinity of Christ. The New Testament is the result and represents selected narratives of Jesus' life and sayings by only four of the twelve disciples of Jesus Christ — Matthew, Luke, Mark and John.

The Geneva Bible is unique among all other Bibles. It was the first Bible to use chapters and numbered verses and became the most popular version during medieval times because of the extensive marginal notes. These notes, written by Reformation leaders such as John Calvin, John Knox, Miles Coverdale, William Whittingham, Anthony Gilby, and others, were included to explain and interpret the scriptures for the common people --- us. King James I was unsettled by some of these notes, as it related to the tyranny of leaders, adultery, and other thorny religious differences of opinion.

In an effort to censor these scriptural explanations and to establish himself as the authority on what Scripture intended, he demanded that a government "authorized" version be created — omitting the notes with which he disagreed. Of course, this disagreement and omission was never made public.

Another consideration is that the language of Jesus Christ was Aramaic and not Hebrew. All of Jesus' teachings and sayings were first translated from Aramaic to Greek. According to religious scholars, the first manuscript of the Bible was called the '_Mt. Sinai Arabic Codex 151_'. Although it is a large, bound book, it contains the Book of Acts and the Epistles only, all translated from Aramaic (Syriac). Familiarizing ourselves with its contents may shed light on why there have been so many 'versions' published since the inception of Jewish and Christian thought. That's a very ... long ... time ...

In addition, Jesus did not write any of His Teachings or sayings; nor did he assign scribes to record them. In AD 325, the _First Council of Christian bishops_ was convened by the Roman Emperor Constantine in the Bithynian city of Nicaea (now Turkey). By convening the Council, Constantine sought to save his empire. It became known as the Council of Nicaea and was the first effort to attain consensus on the varying narratives among the diverse Christian bishops from Arabia, Armenia, Coptic Egypt, Ethiopia, Georgia (Russia), Greece, Libya, Palestine, Persia, Syria and Thrace, each representing their own tribal, ethnic and racial groups within the empire. This ecumenical Council was Emperor Constantine's first effort to attain consensus in the church through an assembly representing all Christendom. From this Council a single narrative was produced: the Christian Bible as opposed to the singular writings found in the Jewish Torah and numerous New Testament scrolls scattered throughout the Empire. This original compilation included both the Old Testament (the Torah) and the New Testament of Jesus Christ. It was the first Judeo-Christian Bible composed in the language of the Romans (Latin).

In 1604, England's King James I commissioned and authorized a new translation of the original Geneva Bible. This bible is known today as the King James Version, and that is exactly what it is --- a version. This version of the bible was aimed at settling some thorny religious differences in his own kingdom and to solidify his own power over land barons and other members of the aristocracy. But in seeking to prove his own supremacy the king inadvertently ended up democratizing the Bible (that is, to make it accessible to everyone) which was absolutely counter to his autocratic ambitions, which is why you and I are able to read the bible for ourselves, a luxury that thousands of years ago the unlettered Hebrew and Jew were neither capable nor even permitted to do.

Clearly, King James I commissioned to have the Geneva Bible retranslated into English in order to establish the authority of the newly established 'Church of England' founded by his patriarch and heretic king, Henry VIII. Pope Clement VII had excommunicated him from the Catholic Church for essentially political reasons, ushering in the concept of the 'divine right of kings' which was in opposition to papal supremacy over kingship. King James' purpose in establishing both his own church and "version" of the Bible was identical to that of both King Henry VIII of England and Emperor Constantine: to unite the powerful and influential contending religious factions — and his people — under one nationally accepted text. The idea was proposed at a conference of scholars at Hampton Court by a Puritan, John Rainolds, the seventh President of Corpus Christi College. Rainolds hoped that James would turn his face against the Bishops' Bible (another version of the Bible), but his plan backfired when the King insisted that the new translation be based on it and condemned what he considered to be "the partial, untrue, seditious" notes of the Geneva translation. Jewish tradition says there were seventy scribes who between 285 B.C. and 247 B.C. translated the Hebrew Bible into Greek. Today the Jews call the Old Testament the Tanakh. All of the books of the Christian Greek Scriptures which were written during the 1st century CE do not recognize the Catholic Papacy. These scriptures remain under the authority of the Greek Orthodox Church to this day. Later, these same Greek Scriptures were translated into Latin and then into Spanish but do recognize the Catholic Papacy. In addition to these translations, two hundred years after the Arab conquest of the Middle East in 636 AD., *Bishr ibn Siri, a Nestorian Arab Christian, performed a separate translation.* Who was this Arabic translator? He was a Nestorian Christian living in Damascus. Nestorian belief *denied the Incarnation of God as a human being (Jesus Christ) and represented Him instead as only a God-inspired man.*

Names and Timeline of the Old and New Testament Versions of the Bible from 240 BC up to 1560 A.D.

- Septuagint or LXX – about 240-150 BC
- Aquila's version – 130 AD
- Symmachus's revision – 170 AD
- Theodotion's revision – 180-190 AD
- Origen's Hexapla – sometime after 200 AD
- Dead Sea Scrolls (21 BC – 60 AD)
- John Wycliffe Bible (1380's)
- Gutenberg Bible (1452-1453)
- Tyndale's Bible (1523)
- Matthew's Bible (1537)
- The Great Bible: *The First **"Authorized Version"*** (1539)
- Taverner's Bible (1539)
- The Geneva Bible (1560)

History of the Timeline of re-translations of the New Testament up to 1782

In the interest of brevity, the timeline below includes only the eighteen most consequential re-translations of the Bible that have occurred since the 1st century AD and its first compilation by conferees at the Council of Nicaea in 325 AD.

1.) 1st Century AD: Completion of All Original Greek Manuscripts (translated from the Aramaic, the language in which Christ taught) which make up the 27 Books of the New Testament.

2.) 315 AD: Athenasius, the Bishop of Alexandria, identifies the 27 books of the New Testament which are today recognized as the canon of scripture.

3.) 382 AD: Jerome's Latin Vulgate Manuscripts Produced which contain All 80 Books (39 Old Test. + 14 Apocrypha + 27 New Test).

4.) 500 AD: Scriptures have been Translated into Over 500 Languages. 600 AD: LATIN was the Only Language Allowed for Scripture.

5.) 995 AD: Anglo-Saxon (Early Roots of English Language) Translations of The New Testament Produced.

6.) 1384 AD: Wycliffe is the First Person to Produce a (Hand-Written) manuscript Copy of the Complete Bible; All 80 Books.

7.) 1455 AD: Gutenberg Invents the Printing Press; Books May Now be mass-Produced instead of individually hand-written. The First Book Ever Printed is the Gutenberg Bible in Latin.

8.) 1516 AD: Erasmus Produces a Greek/Latin Parallel New Testament. 1522 AD: Martin Luther's German New Testament.

9.) 1526 AD: William Tyndale's New Testament; The First New Testament printed in the English Language.

10.) 1534 AD: The Anglican Church originates when King Henry VIII breaks from the Roman Catholic Church after the pope refuses to grant him an annulment.

11.) 1535 AD: Myles Coverdale's Bible; The First Complete Bible printed in the English Language (80 Books: O.T. & N.T. & Apocrypha).

12.) 1537 AD: Tyndale-Matthews Bible; The Second Complete Bible printed in English. Done by John "Thomas Matthew" Rogers (80 Books).

13.) 1539 AD: The "Great Bible" Printed; The First English Language Bible Authorized for Public Use (80 Books).

14.) 1560 AD: The Geneva Bible Printed; The First English Language Bible to add Numbered Verses to Each Chapter (80 Books).

15.) 1568 AD: The Bishops Bible Printed; The Bible of which the King James was a Revision (80 Books).

16.) 1609 AD: The Douay Old Testament is added to the Rheims New Testament (of 1582) Making the First Complete English Catholic Bible; Translated from the Latin Vulgate (80 Books).

17.) 1611 AD: The King James Bible; Printed originally with all 80 Books. The Apocrypha was officially removed in 1885 leaving only 66 Books. Apocrypha are works, usually written, of unknown authorship or of doubtful origin. The word apocryphal was first applied to writings which were kept secret because they were the vehicles of esoteric knowledge considered too profound or too sacred to be disclosed to anyone other than the initiated, and especially the common man.

18.) 1782 AD: Robert Aitken's Bible; The First English Language Bible (KJV) Printed in America.

Note: Since 1782, there have been numerous re-translations of the King James Version alone.

CHAPTER SEVEN

Elizabeth, the Virgin Queen and the Church of England

After the Moors were forced out of Spain and following 'the Enlightenment', which had been ushered in by the Moors, introducing new social norms, a revolutionary numeral system, new architectural designs, new lifestyles, the use of Arabic linguistic terms into the Spanish language, and many more cultural innovations, medieval Spain became the envy of Europe. And with this newfound fame, status, and intellectual prowess, wealth soon followed, innovations in the arts surged, science and technological advancements emerged and accelerated outcompeting anything that was happening in other European kingdoms. However, all these advancements were being attributed not to the Moors, but to Spain. By the 15th century, Spain had become the most powerful nation in all of medieval Europe and was considered to be the greatest ally of the Vatican. By 1492, it was Spain that was carrying out all seven Papal Bull Decrees with a vengeance, unleashing a wave of new discoveries as the mandates of the Law of Discovery were enforced, dominating indigenous people and taking their lands became equivalent to carrying out the *Will of God*. By 1492, Columbus had claimed the Caribbean islands for the Crown, and Hernan Cortez had done the same in the land of the Aztecs, the Mayans and the diverse indigenous tribes and kingdoms of Central and South America. Meanwhile, Portuguese navigator and explorer Ferdinand Magellan had set sail for southeast Asia and "discovered" the Philippines, an archipelago then known as Malay. These islands were declared a colony of Spain and Spanish rule was imposed. Apart from the southwest islands of the archipelago the people who lived there remained Muslim while a majority of Filipinos became Catholics. Colonial administration assured the Catholic Church's primary purpose for the Papal Bull decrees: wealth and power. King Philip II of Spain was the inspiration for the change of name to Las Filipinas (the Philippines) and finalized the claim for the Spanish Crown. Clearly, Spain and Portugal were well ahead of England in the scramble to fulfill the Vatican Papal Bulls' 'Law of Discovery' which in no uncertain terms was a decree for the conquest of indigenous lands around the globe. This religious mandate put the two powers on a fierce competitive course for dominance in what for them was termed the *'new' world*.

Both Spain and England viewed one another as each other's greatest enemy. With that in mind, it is absolutely critical to understand how the British Protestant Reformation, the Vatican Papal Bulls and the expulsion of the Moors from Spain in 1492 all coalesced in England replacing Spain as the superpower of the medieval world. What was the thinking, we should ask, that led Elizabeth I to make the decisions to take the bold actions which paved the way for England's rise to world dominance? Clearly, just by the fact that she was not only a young, beautiful, and fiercely intelligent woman, she was also under intense pressures from within and outside of the kingdom. Fortunately for her, Elizabeth was fluent in nine languages. And, it is reported that she not only spoke these languages but was able to read them so thoroughly that each appeared to be her native tongue. Of the nine languages, five of these were languages spoken by people considered to be savages in the lands she reigned over in the British Isles --- English, Welsh, Cornish, Scottish and Irish. Unlike French, Spanish, German and English, each of the aforementioned languages was entirely different from the others so much so that it was impossible for speakers of one language to understand any of the others. In spite of this, she had mastered the intricacies of speaking with the accents of French, Latin, and Italian with flawless precision and ease. With all of that going for her, it isn't much of a leap to consider that she was well aware that Spain had begun colonizing most of the lands in the New World and its peoples. This savvy was perhaps the singular determining factor in what soon became her fascination for world imperialism. Whatever moral compass she may have had that would have conceivably led her to either object to the authority and goals of the Vatican Papal Bulls or to participate in achieving them, knowing that they specifically called for the vanquishing of, the domination of, and the enslavement of indigenous peoples, was obviously compromised given the choice that she ultimately made. In 1533, at age twenty-five, this very young, beautiful, yet admittedly naïve Elizabeth I was crowned Queen of England. Her coronation was neither welcomed nor inwardly celebrated by the male population of her realm. England had always been a male dominated, chauvinistic, patriarchal society that upheld a medieval caste-system on par with that of India. Political intrigues and power plots had been swirling like a violent vortex above, below, in front and behind, to the right and to the left of the young Elizabeth even before it had been formally announced that she was heir to the throne. This state of affairs steadily intensified even after her coronation. Above all, she was considered a *persona non grata* for the reason that she was a woman, and above that, she was dubbed the bastard child of King Henry VIII by the pope.

During the year of Elizabeth's coronation, all the Jewish traditions in the 3rd Century BC Hebrew Bible (the Tanakh or Old Testament); and all the Greek, Latin and Spanish translations were translated into the first English translation known as _the Geneva Bible_. It was this bible that nurtured Queen Elizabeth's early childhood _Catholic_ beliefs. It's important to any discourse about Elizabeth I to understand that just twenty-five years earlier, in 1534, Elizabeth's father, King Henry VIII, had broken with the _1500-year-old_ Roman Catholic Church and in that same year had passed a law called the "Acts of Supremacy" making him the _Supreme Head of the 'Church of England'. This act ignited the fire which blazed forth as the English Reformation'_ and terminated England's connection to the Roman Catholic Church. Henry proceeded to set up his new _Protestant Church of England_, known today as _The Church of England_ and _The Anglican Church_. This term, 'Anglo', was intentionally applied as a reminder to all that King Henry VIII was determined to break from the holy Roman Empire, Rome, and the Vatican's power over the monarchy.

The catalyst to King Henry's break with the Roman Catholic Church was Pope Clement VII's refusal to annul his marriage to Catherine of Aragon, the daughter of King Ferdinand and Queen Isabela, monarchs of Spain. Henry's request to annul his marriage was due to Catherine's inability to provide him with a male heir. At the time, Charles V of Spain, nephew of Catherine of Aragon, was Emperor of the Holy Roman Empire. This familial connection included Pope Clement VII who as a matter of political control over other European monarchs had no choice but to remain in good standing with this most powerful ruler in Europe at the time. In spite of this, Henry declared his marriage to Catherine invalid and banished her from his realm. But Henry went further than that, he dissolved Catholic nunneries and monasteries and married Anne Boleyn without making any formal notification or request for permission to remarry from the Pope. According to Papal law, royal marriages were granted at the permission by _papal dispensation. For royals in good standing, this requirement was both a 'moral'_ obligation and an affirmation of the supremacy of the Pope over kingship. In addition to disobeying the Pope's refusal to annul the marriage and by not informing the Pope of his marriage to Anne Boleyn, it was not only a blatant 'spit in the eye' of Papal supremacy, it also guaranteed that any child born to the marriage would be declared a 'bastard child' and would be banned from the line of succession according to Papal decree. Clearly, it was a reaffirmation of Henry's determination to break with protocol, and to ignore both the canonical laws and the station of the Pope as supreme head of all Christendom.

Anne Boleyn gave birth to a daughter, Elizabeth. Sixteen months after the marriage to Henry as his second wife, Henry had her beheaded. Officially, the beheading did not cite the beheading as punishment for not producing a male heir but as the result of the machinations of the royal court which accused Anne of committing multiple adulteries.

As the young Elizabeth grew, intrigues and plots swirled all around her. After her father's death in 1547, Elizabeth lived with her stepmother, Katherine Parr, who had married Thomas Seymour, the Lord Admiral and King Edward's uncle. As the half-sister of boy-King Edward, Elizabeth found herself the object of Thomas' ambition to replace his brother as Lord Protector to the young king. His marriage to Katherine had put him into direct contact with the young Elizabeth who now was becoming an attractive young woman, exposing her to harsh sexual contact with this same step uncle. All this was combined with never-ending political schemes by numerous courtiers in the royal court who sought to uphold Mary Tudor's right of succession after Edward's death, for in the eyes of the Vatican, she was by Papal decree the Catholic heiress to the throne. Mary Tudor and Elizabeth's relationship had been scarred from its very beginning.

Mary Tudor was the only surviving child of Henry VIII by his first wife, Catherine of Aragon. Henry had declared her to be illegitimate, and following the annulment of her parents' marriage, she was barred from the line of succession in 1533. However, Mary was restored to the line of succession in 1543. Her younger half-brother, Edward VI, son of Jane Seymour, third wife of King Henry who replaced Anne Boleyn after her death, succeeded their father in 1547 at the age of nine. When Edward became terminally ill with cancer in 1553, he attempted to remove Mary from the line of succession because he correctly believed that she would reverse the Protestant reforms that had taken place during his reign. Upon his death, leading politicians proclaimed Edward's Protestant cousin, Lady Jane Grey queen instead. Mary deposed Jane, who too was beheaded, making Mary the first *female* queen in English history. In July 1554, Mary wed Prince Philip of Spain making her "queen consort" of Spain in 1556.

In spite of Mary's rancor and suspicions of Elizabeth, after her death, in 1558, Elizabeth became Queen of England. She restored Protestantism which Queen Mary I had fought her entire life to eliminate as *the* national religion. Elizabeth never married, and ruled her kingdom as the "Virgin Queen, the singular female monarch who led England to its Golden Age.

After the death of Edward VI, Mary had been crowned Queen of England despite a distressed English aristocracy's constant fear of placing a woman on the throne. Their fear was that England's wealth would be foolishly used to aid Spain by funding Spanish ambitions in the newly 'discovered' Americas. In addition, a rising level of popular discontent with Mary's political and religious choices were breaking out throughout the kingdom with rebels siding with Elizabeth's attempt to continue her father's Reformation. The rebellious were ultimately quashed but their support had demonstrated that Elizabeth represented a younger and better educated generation with no fear of Catholic orthodoxy especially after a more informed and aggressive sense of nationalism that had been developing in England since the start of the Reformation. Mary, suspected that Elizabeth was at a minimum involved in the rebellion against the old order though she had made no public statements on either the Reformation or her half-sister's marriage to Philip II of Spain. This marriage made Mary the first female monarch in England to hold the same rank as a king. The marriage had been suggested by the Holy Roman Emperor Charles V, whose aim was to create an Anglo-Spanish alliance against France and to restore England to the flock of Rome as a Catholic kingdom. Regardless of this very consequential marriage which had the potential to weld England back to Papal influence, Elizabeth was jailed for two months inside the notorious Tower of London, and then later moved and kept under house arrest. Over the next year, the two half-sisters did reconcile with Mary giving Elizabeth her freedom; however, intrigues and betrayals by both opportunistic and real lovers continued to hound her.

In the mid-to-late-16th century England, the deep Catholic-Protestant divide that had been fostered by the Reformation had grown deeper and wider. While Mary was a devout and zealous Catholic and ruled as such, Elizabeth was a voracious reader fluent in French, Italian, Latin, and Greek, as well as an avid student of theology, history, music, moral philosophy, and rhetoric. Following in her father's footsteps, she embraced Protestantism and attempted to convert her entire country. This act resulted in the Vatican formally excommunicating her from the Catholic Church in 1570. However, her excommunication, instead of dampening her resolve, inflamed her commitment to rekindle the English Reformation. Having been reunited briefly with Rome during the reign of Queen Mary I, under Elizabeth I, the separation between the Church of Rome was finalized by the Elizabethan Religious Settlement which established the Church of England as a conservative Protestant church. During this time, Queen Elizabeth authorized the Book of Common Prayer as the Church of England's official liturgy along with the Thirty-nine Articles which became its doctrinal statement. Subsequently, the Book of Common Prayer underwent several changes but fundamentally continue to be the very foundation of Anglicanism (White Anglo-Saxon Protestantism).

The Rival for World Dominance - Protestant England vs Catholic Spain

Although in a far less obvious form, the rivalry between Protestant England and Roman Catholicism has been bequeathed to modern Americans and shows up in Latin American Catholic immigration and border relations to this day. In the late 1580s, English raids against Spanish commerce and Queen Elizabeth I's support of the Dutch rebels in the Spanish Netherlands led King Philip II of Spain to plan the conquest of England. Pope Sixtus V gave his blessing to what was called "The Enterprise of England" with the expectation that it would bring the Protestant Church of England back under the influence of the Vatican. By 1587, a massive Spanish invasion fleet called the Spanish Armada, was completed, but was delayed until May 1588. On May 19 of that year, the *Invincible Spanish Armada* set sail from Lisbon to secure control of the English Channel. A Spanish army contingent was sent to the British isle. The Spanish fleet, under the command of the Duke of Medina-Sidonia, had 130 ships with 2,500 guns aboard, 8,000 seamen, and nearly 20,000 soldiers. Despite this manpower, the Spanish ships were slower and less well armed than the English fleet. And, eager to adhere to conventional warfare, the Spaniards had planned to accept force actions in which the two opposing infantries would board each other's ships to do battle in accordance with this wartime convention. If so, seeing themselves as the superior infantry, the Spanish expected to prevail. However, mother nature seemed to have had different plans for the conclusion of the sea battle. A fury of storms delayed the armada temporarily forcing it back to Spain, giving the British two months to fortify their military readiness.

"On July 21, the English navy began bombarding the seven-mile-long line of Spanish ships from a safe distance, taking full advantage of their long-range heavy guns. The Spanish Armada continued to advance during the next few days, but its ranks were thinned by the English assault. On July 27, the Armada anchored in exposed position off Calais, France, and the Spanish army prepared to embark from Flanders. Without control of the Channel, however, their passage to England would be impossible. Just after midnight on July 29, the English sent eight burning ships into the crowded harbor at Calais. The panicked Spanish ships were forced to cut their anchors and sail out to sea to avoid catching fire. The disorganized fleet, completely out of formation, was attacked by the English off Gravelines at dawn. In a decisive battle, the superior English guns won the day, and the devastated Armada was forced to retreat north to Scotland. The English navy pursued the Spanish as far as Scotland and then turned back for want of supplies. Battered by storms and suffering from a dire lack of supplies, the Armada sailed on a hard journey back to Spain around Scotland and Ireland. Some of the damaged ships foundered in the sea while others were driven onto the coast of Ireland and wrecked. By the time the last of the surviving fleet reached Spain in October, half of the original Armada was lost with some 15,000 men perishing." [22]

Queen Elizabeth's decisive defeat of what was feared as the *Invincible Spanish Armada* reversed England's fortunes and transformed it into a world-class power overnight, when long-range weapons were introduced by the British into naval warfare for the first time and proved far superior to conventional warfare of which the Spanish had become accustomed, thus ending the era of boarding and close-quarter fighting. With this decisive blow to the Spanish Armada, England was now put on course to vigorously exploit their victory over Spain, and to compete for and to claim their share of the lands of the New World. And, despite its severance from the Church of Rome which had decreed the Papal Bulls, the 'Law of Discovery' became England's gateway to imperialism, and the initiation of her own global campaign of colonization. The English Reformation had liberated Britain from her encumbrance and fealty to the Vatican and changed the direction and destiny of all mankind. However, whether one celebrates or condemns this turn of monumental events, the underlying principle of the 'Law of Discovery' was a two-edged sword, for its motive was not based upon the teachings of Jesus Christ but upon pure, unadulterated materialistic greed, racism, and domination. Aside from representing the corrupt intentions of the Vatican, the Papal Bulls had been decreed by the very religious institution that had publicly and universally condemned the young Queen Elizabeth threefold as a heretic, a bastard, and a whore. Even so, palace courtiers continued to hound Elizabeth making demands upon her to marry and to produce a (male) heir --- which she refused to do. In 1603, Queen Elizabeth I died, ending the Tudor reign in England to become forever immortalized as the "Virgin Queen".

Despite the rivalries among royal siblings, the political antagonism aroused by the coronation of Elizabeth I as the second queen (after her sister, Mary), and the vitriol brought about by the fierce competition to gain influence over her; the religious fanaticism and vengeance between and among her extended royal family members, Queen Elizabeth's rule resulted in producing many of the world's greatest literary giants in European history with William Shakespeare topping the list. His works flourished under her reign and is one of the most well-known playwrights in the world. Sir Walter Raleigh, accused by the Spanish for being a sea pirate, explored and founded the first English colony in America (Virginia), and Francis Drake, a British explorer matched Magellan's exploits by circumnavigating the entire world. Both explorations contributed to the forging-out of unknown lands and the staking claims upon a world where indigenous peoples lived unaware of the competition between Spanish and British imperial aspirations as they staked out their turfs, setting the stage for the world's complete and total colonization.

Shakespeare, Christianity – Othello, Islam

Artistic, political, and religious symbolisms are found in every civilization on the planet, and the symbolism of Shakespeare's classic 'Othello, the Moor' is no exception. The character of Othello, the Moor, is an accurate illustration of the position held by the Moors in Europe, which depicts him as a general in the Venetian Army. The origin of the Othello character is traced to the tale "Un Capitano Moro" in Gli Hecatommithi by Giovanni Battista Giraldi Cinthio. In that original tale, Othello is simply referred to as the Moor.

Here we will evaluate what determines civilization and being civilized for either the character of Shakespeare's play 'Othello' was crafted based upon his personal relationships and observations, travels and research, or this classic Shakespearean play is pure fiction. All artists reserve the right to embellish their characters with attributes that they deem befitting. But as the old adage confirms, 'you can't have your cake and eat it too'. This is important to state right at the onset because the very premise of racial supremacy is that all Africans and their descendants have always been uncivilized pagan savages, a people with no history, no education, no religion, and no civilized social skills whatsoever. This notion must have been circulating around the palace and is the same idea that young Elizabeth would have heard either as an official pronouncement or mutterings of sheer gossip.

With her royal status, and all her intellectual and language skills, the basic question regarding her views on race is --- was she a white supremacist? In a misogynistic medieval culture such as England, if there was ever an argumentative shrew to be tamed it was Elizabeth! Evidently, she must have had views on this matter considering the manner in which she embraced the establishment of British colonies in an unknown land she had never visited. She had no direct experience with either the indigenous people of Africa or the Americas. It is reasonable to assume that the descriptions of these peoples whom she had never personally encountered included disparaging terms like "savages" and "pagans", and who, in comparison to her own conquered subjects, had not colonized foreign lands, had lived in relative peace with other tribes, had never sought to colonize her own land, and for over the millennia had erected kingdoms and empires even older than her own. Or did she even know that?

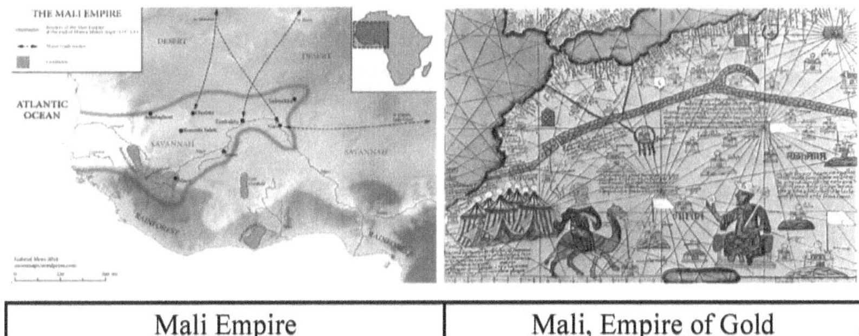

Mali Empire	Mali, Empire of Gold

Mansa Musa on pilgrimage to Mecca

Apart from ancient Kemet (renamed Egypt by the Greeks), African kingdoms were known entities throughout Asia, the Levant and Europe. In the 15th century, Mali was well-known among European royals and were well aware that Mansa Musa, King of Mali, was the richest monarch on the planet (as depicted above). The Mali Empire was a trading empire that flourished from the 13th to the 16th century in West Africa, and was founded by its first king, Sundiata Keita. His Royal Highness, Mansa Musa was the Muslim ruler of Mali, and in 1324, he made pilgrimage to Mecca in Saudi Arabia. The pilgrimage to Mecca numbered an entourage of over one thousand people and 100 camels, each camel loaded with 300 pounds of gold. And as they crossed the desert sands of the Sahara to North Africa, as he went, huge sums of gold coins were paid in every city along the way. And when he arrived in Cairo, Egypt, he spent so much in gold coins there that it had such a negative effect on the economy that it made his pilgrimage to Mecca one of the most publicized events throughout the medieval world.

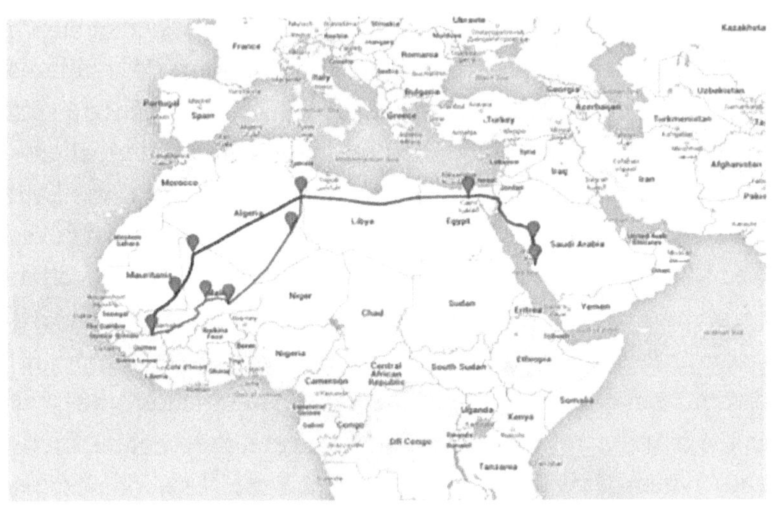

Timbuktu
Cairo

Mali was not the only African kingdom in possession of huge gold deposits, neither was gold its only natural resource. Traditionally, Africans in the 15th century did not live in crowded urban centers the way Europeans lived, and their religious views and practices was their worldview. The way of life in African kingdoms was lived in harmony with nature which has always been the paramount covenant between man and God. The transatlantic slave trade changed all of that. In spite of the assertions against these kingdoms, assertions that countries like Portugal, Spain, Italy, and other regions of the Mediterranean that traded with West African kingdoms knew to be false, the branding of these kingdoms was that they were uncivilized savages which served the aims by which the 'Law of Discovery' was put into full force. Unfortunately, these assertions continue to be the principle of white supremacist ideology and has led to the minimalization of the many contributions African kingdoms have made to world civilization. Finally, race supremacy asserts further that Black African peoples themselves had no history of their own, and that their existence began not with God's creation of the universe and humanity but with the European transatlantic slave trade. This crude absurdity is the crux of white supremacy and racism.

The transatlantic slave trade was initiated by Portugal but was quickly appropriated by the Spanish. In time, the British, the Dutch, the German and other European nations soon jumped on board as the competition for world dominance and wealth mounted. However, the civilizing influence of Islam in Europe grew ever more indisputable. Clearly, the Moors were inspired by something greater than wealth for Europe had no gold, oil, gems, salt, or any other natural resource to speak of. It was nothing more than the sacred teachings of Islam that inspired the advances made on the Iberian Peninsula. This fact remains indisputable to this day. It was this inspiration that brought light to the medieval minds of 15th century Europe which, in turn, inaugurated the era known as 'the Enlightenment' which, until that time, Europe had never experienced the tremendous advances in science, in medicine, in mathematics, in *metallurgy*, in architecture, in astronomy, in engineering, indoor plumbing and irrigation. For the first time in European history the Arabic concept of 'zero' --- a numerical innovation that replaced the clumsy Roman numeral system and revolutionized mathematical computation with digits instead of letters --- all gifts of the spiritual teachings of Muhammad brought by the Moors over their 800-years presence in Spain.

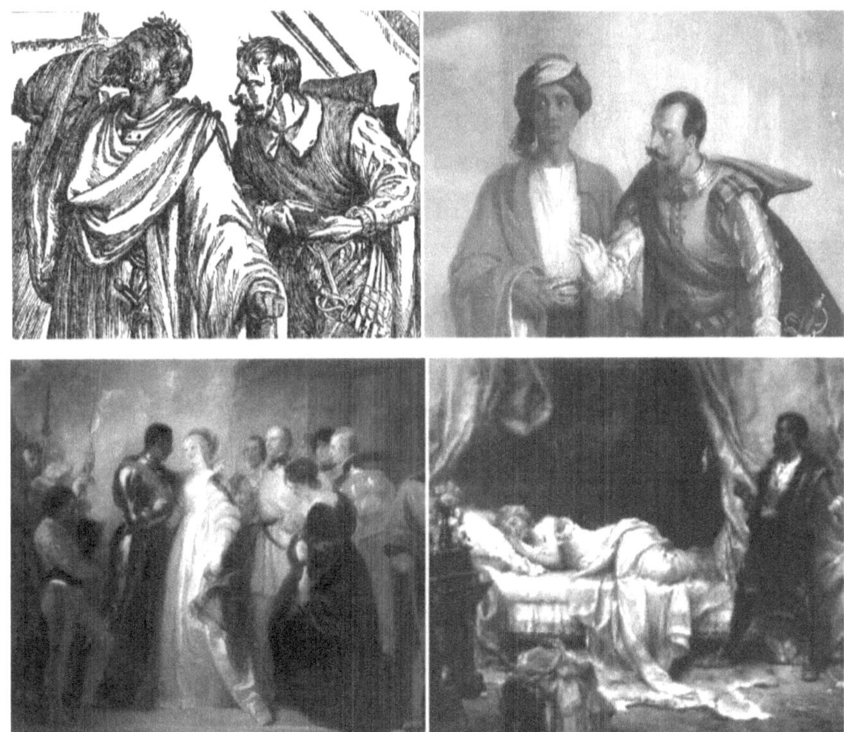

The name, Othello is of Hebrew origin and has two meanings: "he has the sound of God" and "wealth". The motivation for William Shakespeare to write Othello should be understood in context with the growing anti-Moor sentiments in England at the time. William Shakespeare wrote 'The Tragedy of Othello, the Moor of Venice' in 1603, which coincided with the final year of Elizabeth's reign. The first public performance of Othello was held at the king's royal residence at Whitehall Palace in London on November 1, 1604; seven years before the Geneva Bible was retranslated and replaced by the King James Version.

Shakespeare's theater company was often commanded to perform at Queen Elizabeth's court, and certainly, she knew his work very well. It was common practice for monarchs to make requests to see playwrights' plays before they were staged, and, more likely than not, she would have requested to see the 'Tragedy of Othello before its first public performance given that it was among the most requested of Shakespeare's play by British monarchs. Elizabeth would have been extremely sensitive to Othello's plight given the sexual abuse she had suffered in childhood and the constant reminders of her unworthiness being the child of a woman accused of royal infidelity against her father, King Henry VIII. Elizabeth was just two years old when her mother was beheaded by command of her father for adultery, and this must have surely left an indelible scar upon her consciousness. I would think that she would have empathized with Othello's predicament for like Othello, she too had not a single soul upon whom she could place her full trust. Iago must have been a symbol that she would have immediately recognized, symbolizing all the men who surrounded her to embody all the political intrigues and unfaithfulness directed squarely at her. By the time she was coronated at age twenty-five, the first British colony had been established and her reign as 'the Virgin Queen' (despite evidence to the contrary) was memorialized when Sir Walter Raleigh suggested naming the first American colony, 'Virginia'.

CHAPTER EIGHT

Rethinking Ancient African Civilizations

Basil Davidson, British journalist, world renowned historian and author of <u>African Civilization Revisited</u>, published in August 1991 writes: "When our grandchildren reflect on the years of the 20th century, especially on the years from 1950 to 1960, and think about the unbiased contemporary writers of African history --- the history of black peoples, I think that they will see European's emergence from a time of ignorance and cultural misunderstandings. For these were the liberating years when accounts began to be squared with the malice and mystification of racism."

That *mystification of racism* should never imply that there was any kind of spiritual or religious absolution to be gained for the brutal effects of colonialism upon the people of Africa was devastating. Two of the greatest fields of human study are anthropology and archaeology. Combined, these two sciences have enabled the generality of people around the globe to view humanity in its most holistic splendor for it is the study of real people -- their ancient origins, adaptations and ecology, population distribution, customs and languages, their social, political, economic structures, as well as their spiritual and religious beliefs --- all aspects of African civilization that were completely unknown to Europeans under the Law of Discovery. What neither of these sciences will ever be able to excavate out from the bowels of the earth are their dreams, for dreams dwell not in matter and forms but in the souls of black folks; and the soul is a sign of God. Both of these scientific pursuits range from studies of human genetics to personality and society, from the prehistoric past to an ever-expanding future, from preliterate tribes to modern industrial urbanites, exploring in new depths the customs of ancient civilizations such as Ancient Kemet (aka Egypt) to the beliefs of today's everyday people. Both archaeologists and anthropologists explore human evolution, reconstruct societies and civilizations of the past, and analyze the cultures and languages of a diverse range of ethnicities from Iran to Papua New Guinea, Kemet, India to the Americas, the Innuits, Polynesian and Indonesian, and just about every people who live upon this single interdependent, interactive ecosystem that we all call home --- planet earth.

Both archaeology and anthropology emerged as serious professional and scientific disciplines by the early 1920s. It is the study of all aspects of humanity at all times. Science in the 18th and 19th centuries had yet to include these disciplines as sciences; and carbon dating was yet to be invented (1946). Today, more than ever, we can uncover the ancient civilizations of the past as if they were still alive today.

Clearly, when unbiased and unprejudiced scientific facts about African kingdoms and its peoples is known, and when anthropology, archaeology and linguistics are used as the objective tools for establishing fact from fiction, we discover that there are many abject omissions and power-driven agendas in the Papal Bulls of the 14th and 15th centuries that were decreed to discredit African peoples and the civilizations they created long before the transatlantic slave trade began. These omissions point to the overall obsolescence of the

Catholic Papacy having fulfilled its 1,000-years cycle long before 1452. This obsolescence becomes obvious when considering what happens to any institution when the spirit of its purpose has been spent --- desperation soon sets-in, religious fanaticism replaces that spirit, and bigotry, intolerance, prejudice, and small-mindedness replace spiritual principle.

Unfailing Rubric for Determining Fact from Fiction

Essentially a 'rubric' is "an authoritative established rule, tradition, and custom." It is generally used as a guide listing specific criteria for grading or scoring academic papers, projects, or examinations in the pursuit of truth. That said, the rubric I have chosen to use are the Sacred Writings of the Baha'i Faith, one of the fastest growing religions in the world. The reason I've chosen this rubric can be understood by the following statement contained in its message to the people of the world entitled The Promise of World Peace: "No serious attempt to set human affairs aright, to achieve world peace, can ignore religion. Man's perception and practice of it are largely the stuff of history. An eminent historian described religion as a "faculty of human nature". That the perversion of this faculty has contributed to much of the confusion in society and the conflicts in and between individuals can hardly be denied. But neither can any fair-minded observer discount the preponderating influence exerted by religion on the vital expressions of civilization. Furthermore, its indispensability to social order has repeatedly been demonstrated by its direct effect on laws and morality." The Baha'i teachings further explain that we humans all need an educator; that without education, we would never acquire *the means of comfort, civilization, and human virtues,* and that education is of three kinds: material, human and spiritual. Material education aims at the growth and development of the body and consists in securing its sustenance and obtaining the means of its ease and comfort. This education is common to both man and animal. *Human education,* however, *consists in civilization and progress, that is, sound governance, social order, human welfare, commerce and industry, arts and sciences, momentous discoveries, and great undertakings, which are the central features distinguishing man from the animal."*

So, let us evaluate ancient African civilizations and kingdoms by using a rubric that authoritatively evaluates human education as the means to acquire comfort, human virtues, civilization, sound governance, social order, human welfare, commerce and industry, arts and sciences, momentous discoveries, and great undertakings as noted above.

Cheikh Anta Diop Casts a Floodlight on Ancient African Civilizations

Cheikh Anta Diop was a made a member of the UNESCO International Scientific Committee and is recognized for the Drafting of a General History of Africa in 1971. In addition, he wrote the opening chapter about the origins of the ancient Egyptians in the UNESCO General History of Africa, a work that continues to strongly influence continual developments in the research that is still being carried out to this day. Dr. Diop was born into a Muslim Wolof family in Senegal and is a noted historian, chemist, politician, anthropologist, and physicist. His fluency in many languages include Wolof, Pulaar, Mandinka, Balanta-Ganja, Mandjak, Arabic, Noon, French, Serer, Soninke, and English. He began his studies at the Sorbonne in Paris in 1946 and was awarded a doctorate in physics. In response to scientific racism's fixation on cranial studies in its efforts to prove and justify white supremacy among humans, he wrote and performed exhaustive cranial and DNA tests in his hands-on research as part of his research into the human race's origins and pre-colonial African cultures. The questions he posed about cultural bias in scientific race research contributed greatly to the post-colonial shift away from racial bias in the study of contemporary and ancient African civilizations, kingdoms, and peoples.

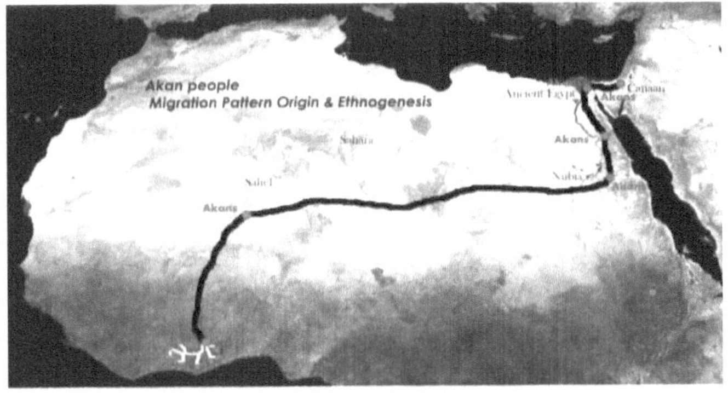

The map above shows the pre-colonial migration of the Akan people from west Africa to Ancient Kemet (Egypt).

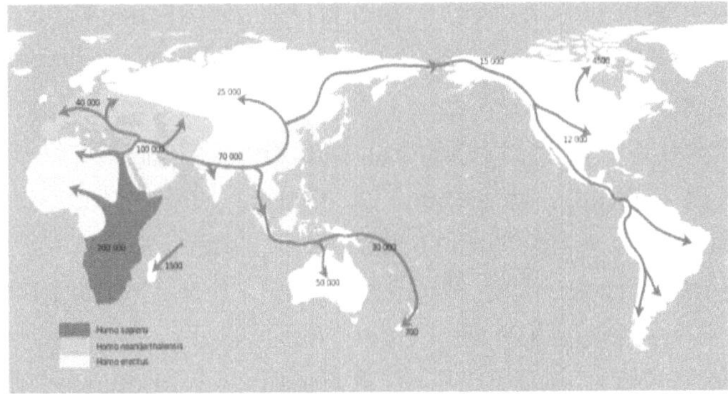

The map above shows the global human migration from the Cradle of Mankind in East Africa.

Traditionally, accounts in world history school textbooks rely upon the *recorded* historical accounts of ancient civilizations. The majority of African civilizations practiced the oral tradition where an entire familial line of *griots* is relied upon by tribal kings as the sole repositories of knowledge about his peoples' ancient history, their religious teachings, and the ancient accounts of laws and traditions. This formal system is called the *oral tradition*. Griots are often viewed as leaders because of their position as advisors to members of a royal family. Early European practitioners of archaeology and anthropology ignored, discounted, and even mocked these prehistory oral accounts because they could not immediately confirm their veracity. However, references to the activities of these ancient kingdoms when considered in the cosmological and geological records, that is, what astrophysics and astronomy now reveal about our origins and our ancient past, the oral tradition has resurged as a viable source of knowledge and information. The oral tradition has been vindicated as remarkably reliable.

Akan Religion and Social Organization

The Ancient Akan people worshipped *Onyame*, the one Supreme God, A*sase Yaa* (the goddess of the earth), and their ancestors by offering sacrifices. The Akan were a traditional matrilineal culture where royal lineage is dependent on women. The Akan are a religious group of people. Through their contact with Europeans Christianity was adopted as a primary religion, but others identified as Muslims.

One of the most prominent individuals known today from the Akan community is Kofi Annan. As a Ghanaian diplomat, Kofi Annan served as Secretary-General of the United Nations from 1997 to 2006. Both Annan and the United Nations were co-recipients of the Nobel Peace Prize in 2001. Kofi Annan was founder and chairman of the Kofi Annan Foundation, as well as chairman of The Elders, an international organization founded by Nelson Mandela. Other prominent Akan figures are Kwame Nkrumah who started the pan-African movement, which 2009 to 2012.

CHAPTER NINE

Napoleon Bonaparte I

World history is replete with both prehistorical (oral) as well as the recorded (written) ancient historical accounts of neighboring tribes fighting over territory and natural resources. These conflicts were universal throughout the world and were often motivated by family squabbles among royals, sibling rivalries among the elite, environmental changes, as well as to exact revenge for previous incursions exacted against a sovereign people. Our greatest example of this is Alexander of Macedonia against King Darius of Persia. It has always been about greed, power, and retribution. Again, this has been the defining characteristic of many, many, many kingdoms all around the world. Napoleon's curiosity was no different and was motivated by vanity and supremacy. That is what gave birth to Egyptology.

After the first millennia A.D., the rulers inhabiting the regions known today as England, France, Germany, Italy, and the Turkey emerged as the fiercest and most bitter rivals for the conquest of all of Europe and the Levant. Their ferocity towards one another led to both WWI and WWII and their feelings of resentment toward one another continue to this day.

In 1798, Napoleon I invaded Egypt., and along with his troops he brought an "army of scholars" whose studies of this ancient culture was the catalyst for the birth and establishment of two new sciences: archaeology and Egyptology. Initially, these two "sciences" gave respectability to what otherwise would be called the looting of ancient holy burial sites. By any other name the confiscation of the gold, silver, ebony, and onyx statuary from their birthplace --- Africa; the taking of dazzling gems, as well as the mummified remains of pharaohs and funerary artifacts, now imprisoned in famed museums of Paris, London, Berlin and other European capital cities cannot be minimized by the crating, shipping and hoarding of precious artifacts.

Jean-Léon Gérôme's painting (pictured above left), titled "Bonaparte Before the Sphinx", captures Napoleon's imperial ambition to harness the glory of ancient Egypt, and to exalt French power worldwide. The painting also depicts the Sphinx's most recognizable physiological appendage gone from its face (its nose), and this still Remains controversial to this day. Some European scholars claim that Napoleon commanded his soldiers to shoot it off it being one of the single-most recognizable features of Egypt's Black Pharoah

Khafre – *his nose.* "Others" attribute the missing nose to erosion. But then, in 1920, British archaeologists unearthed remarkable and unexpected finds that shook the sensibilities of European aristocracies and adherents of scientific racism to their very core …

Clearly, there would be plenty of changes that lay far beyond the horizon of the 19th and 20th centuries' view of the world, advancements of which neither Napoleon I nor his grandnephew Napoleon III could have ever conceived; changes that would pry open minds prone to resist change, flouting their own limited grasp of history and all who had preceded them, reducing civilization to their own putative imagination. Napoleon had much to learn about the peoples on the African continent. I am left to wonder had he been able to see into the future or had witnessed the horrors of the two greatest wars in human history that were yet to come, and the tremendous surges in scientific and technological advancements, how, as he sat upon his horse marveling at the Sphinx and the pyramid of Giza, that might have forced him to contemplate the very nature of the rise and fall of civilizations; even his own. But the future is proscribed --- it is the forbidden. Any urgency to know what lies ahead only ends in frustration. The *now is reserved for the living!* The only thing that can be known for a certain is change. Change alone has the power to release mankind from centuries of ignorance, forcing reason upon consciousness to ever-expand. What mankind can now be certain of is that the firmament that was brewing inside Napoleon's own mind could never be realized by him. It could only redound to an unprejudiced people equipped not only with unfettered curiosity but the ability to realize it in *real time.* Napoleon's dream was to be Emperor of the world, and that the prerequisite for that to happen is an agreed upon principle. That, the 21st century now has the capacity to do! Once sequestered in isolated tribal groups, contending kingdoms and warring nations, mankind has exploded beyond its tribal nurseries and traditional ways of thinking because knowledge, too, has exploded. Yes, World I and II, Vietnam, 9/11, the Iraq war, the Ukranian-Russian war, the Israeli-Palestinian war, the rise of authoritarianism and threats to overthrow well-established democracies, including its very heart and legislative chamber, the citadel of democracy itself --- the Capitol building of the United States of America.

Pharaoh Tutankhamen

When we consider the name "Africa" we would do well to consider what the indigenous people themselves called it. It is the ancient name --- Alkebulan. It means "mother of mankind" or "garden of Eden" and is the oldest and the only word of indigenous origin that identifies this vast land. This designation continued to be used by the Moors, Nubians, Numidians, Khart-Haddans (aka Carthagenians) and the Ethiopians long before and after the Persians conquered Egypt in 525 B.C, and after the Arabs had ravaged the remains of ancient Kemet in 639 AD.

That said, the respite that for hundreds of centuries has enabled racism to persist is nearing its end. The hour has struck. The revelation of God's unerring divine plan for humanity has been unveiled and its impact continues to reverberate throughout the entire planet. This unveiling is as much a blessing to mankind as it is its greatest challenge, for, like the invincible Emperor Napoleon I seated high upon his steed, gazing out into the abyss, mystified, awestruck and perhaps even confused; staring in disbelief at the weathered limestone face of Khafre, the ancient Pharaoh of Kemet --- the Sphinx --- humanity now stares out into that same abyss dumbfounded, recalcitrant, hesitant and torn by the efficacy of this unifying principle as it takes shape in the hearts of millions. This unveiling of the spiritual principle of the 'Oneness of Humanity' was launched in the 19th century. It is a key component of the fulfillment of the Age of Promise, bringing to the fore the pivotal axis round which all impermanent social, political and material coordinates revolve. It is the divine recognition that humankind has attained a new station that extends far beyond the limits of geography, tribe, skin color, and diverse religious systems, thus firmly establishing mankind's perceptions and place in the universe one again. This station stands in stark relief against the self-inflicted isolation, ignorance and prejudices of the past which have stymied its realization for millennia. It has rendered all forms of racial classifications, classes and other man-made hierarchical concepts of supremacy obsolete. It is we, the ordinary people of the world who, compelled or not, unlike Napoleon, have the capacity to recognize our impotence and yet move forward. However bewildered we may feel, however bowed by its implications, we can now conceptualize the need for the divine outpourings of a divine grace in ways Napoleon could not. Yet, racism continues to rear its head, signaling over and over again that contentiousness is not dead. Such was the state of the Hebrews at the foot of Mount Sinai, terrified of the unknown, left to their own devices, impatient for their Lord to return. An impasse has been reached. Its aim: to prevent the acknowledgment that humanity is *"one people"*, that "the earth is *one country"*, and that "all mankind its citizens". For, despite the overwhelming scientific and archaeological evidence, the descendants of the founders and creators of the "mother of all civilizations", Kemet (Egypt), have been denied their rightful place as the progenitors of world civilization. The thousands of Nubian and hundreds of Egyptian pyramids built long before Napoleon had ever set foot on African soil are just the tip of African history. Born of the soul of one of Africa's greatest minds, *Imhotep*, Kemetic polymath, high priest, physician, astrologer, scribe, vizier and chief architect during Pharoah Djoser's reign; a man worshipped as a *god* of medicine and healing (not only in Kemet but by the Greeks) established Kemet as the greatest ancient civilization in the ancient world. It was Imhotep who designed and built both the Step Pyramid at Saqqara and the first stone pyramid in Kemet. It was *Imhotep* who presided over the construction of the first pharaonic temples and burial sites. Priceless artifacts that adorned these sites alone attest to the genius of the trustees of Kemetic civilization, confirming over 4,000 years of civilization, proving beyond doubt that the migration of numerous Black African tribes from throughout the continent to the Nile Valley was the catalyst to the creation of the greatest civilization known to man. Finally, *Imhotep* was in himself sufficient evidence of Kemet's profound historical contributions to the very notion of empire itself, including the empire over which Napoleon ruled.

Unfortunately, Napoleon Bonaparte was born too late to either know or be truly interested in Kemet's ancient achievements; nor would his vanity allow it. In his efforts to undermine Pharaoh Khafre's obvious "negroid" facial features, he ordered his soldiers to blow off the signature feature of Khafre's ethnicity --- his *nose*. Soon thereafter, Napoleon then commissioned his scientists, artists, philosophers and scholars to propagate his own racial bias that black Africans had no history. However, most disturbing to him was that face; the face that adorned the Sphinx. And with the subsequent discovery and translation of the Rosetta Stone more nagging questions arose: who, They wondered, constructed the pyramids? How did they do it? What did the linguistic symbols mean? Who was the 'Aten" referred to in the text? And what was the origin of the Kemetic religion that referred to Him? Later, with the discovery of the Rosetta Stone written in the ancient Egyptian and Greek languages, and three writing systems --- hieroglyphics, the cursive Demotic script form of Egyptian hieroglyphics, and the Greek alphabet, all indelibly etched into the black granite stella and was taken out of the land of its birth to France where it was deciphered. What shocked them all was that the stella contained the ancient historical record of Kemet (now called Egypt), with the names of its Black African Pharoahs and Queens, who had founded the greatest civilization on earth. Frantic excavations ensued and the desecration of royal tombs began. The preserved secret remains of ancient pharaohs dating back to Kemet's earliest beginnings were removed and displayed museums throughout Europe. Precious artifacts of gold and ebony; funerary masks encrusted with diamonds, sapphire and rubies, jade, ivory, and turquoise and were hurriedly and secretly absconded to avoid detection as the unlawful sacking of holy temples, monumental pyramids, and sacred sarcophagi grew ever intense, looting every nook and cranny, and most frantically, the Valley of the Kings. But, that too, wasn't enough.

When viewed through the disbelieving eyes of the 18th century emperor of France, his goal was nothing short of fulfilling the edict known as the people ball where domination and perpetual slavery of indigenous African peoples, the confiscation of their lands and sacred pharaonic remains, their properties, their art and statuary; and the desecration of their ancient religions deafened him to what was screaming out all about him and what is now apparent for all the world to finally acknowledge. And with all its antiquity still screaming out the names of its founders, the battles fought and won, the architects and engineers, the mathematicians and astronomers, the administrators, the builders, and the Black African pharoahs, their queens and their peoples; people who lived and created this eternal and magnificent gift to humanity, yet still, there was even more to discover. There were over thirty engineering monolithic wonders taken from the land of Kemet, each reaching up to the heavens, known to this day as obelisks. The only obelisk that was neither built nor taken from Egypt was built and erected by the Baha'is on Mt. Carmel in 1971. A.D. This Obelisk marks the position of the Baha'i Faith's future MASHRIQU'L-ADHKÁR (Temple) on Mt. Carmel, in Haifa]. The first Egyptian monoliths were constructed between 2465-2323

BCE by pharaohs of the 5th dynasty and were all constructed by ancient Eygptians to revere what Europeans misrepresented as being paganistic, proof of their own narrow understanding of polytheistic beliefs. For these Europeans, Ra, the "Sun God," was nothing more than polytheistic hog-wash; proof that the European Christianity (and thus, them) were superior to all who dwelled on earth. But what exactly is paganism? The answer to that question is both intriguing and surprising and will be thoroughly examined in chapter seventeen. Hold on to your seat belts!

As colonialism spread throughout the continent, these same obelisks were eventually raised from their foundations and shipped as far away from Kemet as possible --- to Rome, to Paris, to Washington, D.C, and to New York City, suggesting that wealthy patrons in these cities either personally financed or used their influence in the halls of city government; or both to finance 'The Scramble for Africa' in the 19th century. These ancient obelisks, which, in Kemet, had divine and kingly inferences, were the spiritual symbols of the relationship between the pharaoh's spirit (ka) and the one eternal God (symbolized by the "sun"). Yet, this short-sighted religious provincialism was once the vehement "protest" against the Papacy for its materialism and corruption in the Vatican (aka the German and British Protestant Reformation) were now disemboweling the very soul of Alkebulan (Africa's ancient name). It was the Romans who invented the term 'Africa'. Initially, it was applied for regions of North Africa (Alkebulan). All historians agree with this fact. And now, some 2000 years later, Africa is the name that is still in use today. Innumerable artifacts were taken from royal tombs which included regal golden masks lifted off the faces of royal mummified bodies of pharaohs along with an array of precious gems and metals. The Book of the Dead, a sacred religious document and other sacred texts which had been carefully inscribed in hieroglyphics on multiple scrolls of papyri, demonstrated Kemet's ancient belief in a single Creator the bulk of which were all confiscated, packed, crated and shipped to Europe under the guise of "scientific inquiry", birthing never-ending and coordinated undertakings all shrouded in corporate and governmental secrecy designed to obscure and hide their overarching intentions to extract ancient Egypt out of Africa, and resorting to pseudo scientific methods to justify the subjugation of African peoples. These were the descendants of those who had not only cultivated the land for millennia but given birth to multiple kingdoms and to civilization itself. Its indigenous name was Alkebulan, Mother Africa.

This exploitation was a total disregard for the sacredness of African life and revealed the urgency of European exploits to hasten the establishment of a colonial system. But for the Canaanites, though on a much smaller scale in the annals of world history, this bold disregard and usurpation on such a massive scale against a peoples' God-given sovereignty had never before been undertaken. This racist frenzy, perpetrated under the watchful eye of Christian monarchs included the dehumanizing racial categorization of African peoples and the dismantling of the origins of these self-same people; an act, once again, that had never been inflicted upon any other population on earth. Their hastily erected new science (archaeology) became known to the world as a benign examination of the land of Egypt, and was dubbed Egyptology, the study of Egypt, its artifacts, its stela's, its monuments, and the entombed ancient pharaohs whose remains were exhumed, crated, dated and stamped, sealed and delivered to far away foreign lands where groping hands impatiently awaited.

Though intensely denied as theft, all of the above frenzy to extract these treasures from Egypt (Africa) goes to the heart of intent. It was done to eradicate and obfuscate the history of black peoples in Africa. Yet, the opposite has taken place. Todays unbiased archaeologists have revealed what (before the 16th century colonial powers concept of race was invented) was then, and is now, clearly apparent: that Ancient Kemetians (Egyptians) were an ethnically diverse peoples composed of Libyans, Nubians, West and East Africans, desert nomadic tribes of the Sahara and sub-Saharan regions, and among these nomadic tribes were the Garamantes.

The Garamantes

Deep in the desert mountains of Southwest Libya in the Sahara desert, contemporary researchers have uncovered the mummified remains of a three year old child. The remains have been carbon dated to be between 5400 to 5600 years old, predating the founding of Egypt by some 3200 years. Take a moment and let that sink in. According to archaeologist, Dr. Savino di Lernia of the University of Rome, the Garamantes had invented and perfected the practice of mummification over a period of 12,000 years long before Egyptian mummification, which by any standard is a significant indication that the practice was not only continued but was embellished and later incorporated into ancient Kemetic burial practices. This demonstrates that Kemet was not only founded upon a religious concept involving an after life but a reverence for a power beyond the grasp of finite beings. What that power is continues to boggle the mind of even the best religious and scientific minds of our own day. There were other such mixed African nomadic tribal ethnic groups and cultures who lived within and around the Saharan desert, forever confounding European efforts in their attempts to arrive at a unified consensus. This failure can clearly be seen in the light of scientific and spiritual reality --- that there is but one human race --- a scientific principle that exposes the ideology of white supremacy as an archaic tribal form of wishful thinking. And it is because of this self-praising belief that racial categorizations have been written into laws, legislative policies, racial housing covenants, employment policies, social engineering, economic policies and all social institutions despite numerous constitutional amendments and political platforms, unity continues to elude the generality of humanity.

This need to categorize the race of the tribal inhabitants of Mesoamerica (after Spanish conquistadors decimated the Maya, the Olmecs, the Tzotzil of Chiapas, and the Aztecs in 1519) was equally catastrophic. This aching for supremacy over indigenous peoples as decreed by the Vatican Papal Bulls continues to show up nearly 400 years later when archaeologist, Leopoldo Batred, "discovered" the Pyramid of the Sun in Teotihuacan (Mexico). He too seemed unwilling to attribute what he saw (with his own eyes) to the people who were still living in its shadows, ignoring what would inevitably become known to all the world that these "Egyptian-like" pyramids, these indigenous civilizations too were built by the ancestors of the same indigenous peoples who are still living within eye-shot of their all-embracing protection to this day.

Pharaoh Akhenaten

The bust of Queen Tiye,
Queen of Ancient Kemet (Egypt)

Queen Tiye, Queen of Kemet

Queen Tiye, mother of Pharoah Akhenaten and grandmother of Pharoah Tutankhamen was one of the most powerful and illustrious queens of ancient Kemet (Egyptian) history. Queen Tiye was born in 1400 BCE. She reigned Egypt from 1390 BC to 1353 BC. To put that timeline in perspective, consider that the account of Moses' year of birth according to the Hebrew calendar is recorded as the 7th of Adar of the year 2368 from creation. This date corresponds to 1393 B.C. The authenticity of the bust remains irrefutable and unchallenged to this day. This ancient bust of Queen Tiye was taken out of Africa by British archaeologists during Howard Carter's defiling of the sacred temples of King Tutankhamen and other Pharaonic tombs seemingly for no other reasons than material gain, personal notoriety, and, of course, to suppress the knowledge of the ethnicity of the faces that were carved into these ancient stone and ebony artifacts. In 1920, Carter's pillaging included the mummified remains and statuary of both predynastic and dynastic Kemet (Egypt) with a total of over

1,150,342 ancient Kemetic and Egyptian artifacts that were shipped to museums throughout Europe, the Americas, Australia, Israel and many, many other western countries.

The bulk of these precious sacred artifacts are still housed in the museums of London, Berlin, New York City, Boston, Massachusetts --- all in the name of the 'Law of Discovery'.

<u>Lest We Forget</u>

Here, we must pause to ask the question – what was in the heart and minds of those who would enter upon the sacred grounds of a people to pillage sacred burial sites? What moral purpose was there to steal all their possessions and properties, and then dismiss the descendants of these pharaohs --- those royal 'symbols of the presence of God' --- the very station of all Egyptians pharaohs, kings and ancient Rulers --- and use demeaning language; conflating terms like pagan, uncivilized, and savages to describe these same people in an effort to dispossess them of all they held sacred and to undermine the spiritual influence with which these Pharaonic rulers had been invested? Who were *these* people? In order to get a clearer picture of those who would go against their own spiritual principles, their own values and religious standards, let us review the wording of the 1452 Papal Bull that was mandated to all of Christendom by Pope Nicholas V. It was a directive of unprecedented gravity in the affairs of men. Its initial proponent was with King Alfonso of Portugal. It established the 'Law of Discovery' which decreed the confiscation of indigenous lands and all their possessions for the Papacy and the Vatican in Rome. Again, let us review… him to go and conquer West Africa:

> "… go to the Western coast of Africa to invade, capture, vanquish and subdue all Saracens (Muslims), pagans and other enemies of Christ; to reduce their persons to perpetual slavery and to take away all their possessions and properties."

The above directive was re-issued six more times in 1455, 1456, 1481, 1493, 1506 and 1514. In that same misguided spirit, the Papal Bull of 1493, issued by Pope Alexander VI, states: "That it is pleasing to the divine majesty that barbarous nations be subjugated." The term used in the document is *deprimatur* which means to deprive, to subdue, to cast down … to hold down. The document further states: "We trust in Him from whom empires and dominations and all good things proceed."

King Alphonso of Portugal

At this point, I would like to submit the Papal restrictions placed upon royal marriages as existed in the Holy Roman Empire from its inception until its demise. It is important for modern readers to understand that these marital restrictions upon the royal houses of Europe were essentially incestuous in nature. In general, royal marriages were not a matter between a man and a woman who were in love, but of a matter State; a system devised to maintain papal control over monarchs and their kingdoms, to secure and maintain power, wealth, and influence, and were not a matter between individuals. More often than not, the parties to these arranged marriages were brother and sister, cousins, and other extended family members whom they had never personally met. Many knew nothing of this precarious arrangement until days before the marriage was to take place. This system was modeled after marriage arrangements among the royal classes of ancient Rome. Such marriages were considered to be fundamental to the stability of the monarchy and to society. Among the Roman elites, it was primarily used as a tool for *interfamilial alliances.* This means that during the 1500 years that it took Christianity to be established on the continent, the Holy Roman Empire (aka Christendom), in its efforts to unify warring European kingdoms, had the power to enforce and prevent marriages between royal parties. Therefore, a royal marriage was primarily used to inter-monarchal alliances rather than interfamilial and is the reason that the royal houses of Europe are blood-related to this day, which has been a major cause of hemophilia, and figures prominently in the history of European royalty particularly in the 19th and 20th centuries. These realities of European royal life begs the question --- is it possible that family members of the royal houses of Europe were all aware of the significance of the Vatican Papal Bulls? I will leave the answer to that question for readers to determine on their own. However, considering the razor-toothed, piranha-like ravaging of Egypt's ancient tombs and artifacts --- the mummified remains of Pharoah Ramses II, Seti I, Thutmose III, and King Tutankhamun, it would stand to reason that King Alphonso of Portugal was not the only monarch who was privy to the significance of the Papal Bulls. These documents were essentially State documents and not intended for Alphonso alone. It was Christendom itself that Pope Nicholas V, Pope Alexander VI, and all subsequent popes to this day were aiming to preserve. Personal enrichment and power over these indigenous regions were not directly stated but implied in the Papal

Bull. Regardless, 'the Law of Discovery' was not intended for a single monarch and kingdom. It was meant for any faithful Christian willing to fulfill the papal mandate.

We now know that the 'Law of Discovery' was not limited to West Africa and Egypt; it was applied liberally throughout the entire African continent, especially north African states, the Sudan and Ethiopia, and was applied to the lands of all indigenous peoples throughout the world. Today, one can visit the museums of numerous countries and can see with their own eyes the exhaustive pilfered collections of ancient African artifacts from Egypt, Benin, Mali, Kenya, Zimbabwe, and many other African kingdoms. They are all on full display throughout the museums of Europe, the United States, Canada, and other countries. And with exorbitant entry prices ranging from $210 to $425 for adults, and $170 to $350 for children, any middle-class family can view these stolen objects and human remains with their very own eyes. The excitement and attraction they arouse in those who come to view these dead bodies is nothing less than the consummate realization of all the Papacy's 15th century Papal Bull and its decree for the "perpetual enslavement" of African peoples. More than that, it is, in my opinion, the *necrophilic obsession to purloin* --- to take without right and detection --- these ancient African human remains and artifacts to be displayed as perpetual tribute to the supremacy of whiteness. This perpetual enslavement, which implies enslavement long after one has become deceased, is not only a show of arrogance in an attempt to usurp the final judgment of individual persons and an entire ethnic group (which is God's alone), but is the unforgivable and dehumanizing consequence of the Vatican Papal Bulls that Pope Nicholas V envisioned in his 'Law of Discovery'.

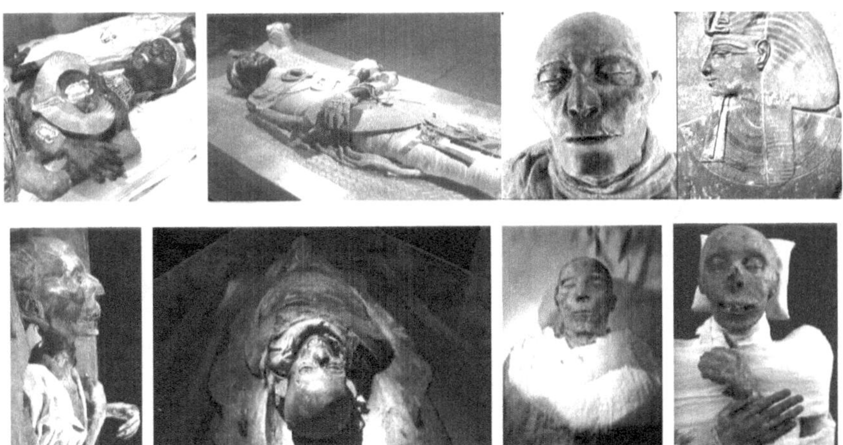

Many may remain firm and unmoved by this commercial ravaging of African spirituality, their societies, and cultures, let them consider then putting the recent entombed remains of England's Queen Elizabeth II transferred to a transparent acrylic display in some distant land where all the world can shelve out an entry fee, take selfies, and gawk at her regal corpse. I am certain that the remains of Alexander of Macedonia and Cyrus of Persia would fetch a handsome entry fee; and let us not leave out Isabela of Spain. Perhaps the remains of U.S. President George Washington, Thomas Jefferson, Benjamin Franklin could be put on display at basement bargain prices since, after all, they are not royals. And then, there are those successive popes who endorsed the Papal Bulls who are now entombed in St. Peter's Basilica in Rome. Would that satisfy this necrophilic obsession?

White supremacy is not simply a matter of racial hatred towards black people as exists today in modern society. It is more than hate. It is pure, unadulterated materialism; the epitome of greed, dishonor, dehumanization, ignorance, self-delusion, vanity, and arrogance; and breaks down all restraints against the degeneration of its perpetrators; and could signal the desecration of God's most noble creation on earth --- the human family. For when honors are bestowed upon the deceased, the act itself transforms the human heart from mere flesh and matter to become the throne of God. Bahá'u'lláh writes: *"O Son of Being! Thy heart is My home; sanctify it for My descent. Thy spirit is My place of revelation; cleanse it for My manifestation."* (24)

This honor that we show is not the pomp and circumstance of royal processions but is the inherent nobility of one's own human life, enabling all mankind to affirm that death is not the end but is the beginning; that each human life is a trust which is to be treated with great dignity and care whatever their station in life. Above all, it demonstrates the victory of the eternal soul of man over the changes and chances of this nether world, for the soul does not die when the body ceases to be; and, like the earth, the body is its temporary home and not its eternal abode. The soul does not die when the body ceases to be, for the body is its temple. Thus, to embalm or cremate this sacred temple goes against that which is seemly in recognizing the awesome sanctity of a loving, All-Knowing, Ever-Forgiving God. Recognition of this reality is why the prophets of God have sacrificed their own sacred lives for ours. This recognition not only shows basic respect but testifies to the faith of the one who has passed "whose body," as Shoghi Effendi attests, "... though now dust, was once exalted by the immortal soul of man!" Effendi, further acknowledges "that donating one's body to science or receiving human organs ... seems a noble thing to do, but again, the remains must be very adhering to the *laws of nature* and not to be embalmed or cremated.

Thus, putting an embalmed body on display in museums seems to be a magnification of the dereliction of the Covenant between man and God which includes honoring the dignity and nobility that is inherent in each human creation. It seems appropriate then that to honor the life of any deceased person we are encouraged to provide a natural burial of such human remains and left undisturbed.

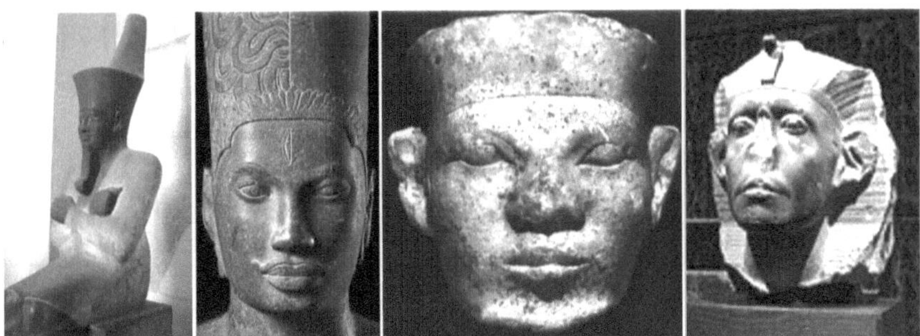

Narmar, the First Pharoah of Egypt

It is imperative for those concerned about the apparently ever-present ideology of white supremacy to realize that vanquishing it is the most challenging issue of our generation. In order to extract it from our midst, individuals and leaders of thought must recognize above all it is not and never has been God's plan for humanity. Again, Bahá'u'lláh addresses the notion of white supremacy as a way of thinking in supremely elegant language saying:

> "O Children of Men! Know ye not why We created you all from the same dust? That no one should exalt himself over the other. Ponder at all times in your hearts how ye were created. Since We have created you all from one same substance it is incumbent on you to be even as one soul, to walk with the same feet, eat with the same mouth and dwell in the same land, that from your inmost being, by your deeds and actions, the signs of oneness and the essence of detachment may be made manifest. Such is My counsel to you, O concourse of light! Heed ye this counsel that ye may obtain the fruit of holiness from the tree of wondrous glory." [25]

Today, the push for the elimination of white supremacy has reached fever pitch among all people of good will. Across the board, African, European, and scholars from around the world know and diligently support the need to establish an authentic description of the true history of ancient Egypt and other African kingdoms and civilizations. The founders of these African kingdoms and civilizations should be the first priority on a list of priorities acknowledging their contributions to the ascendance of humankind, and to learn why early archaeologists of the 19th century summarily dismissed black Africans as the creators of these civilizations, including that of sub-Sahara Africa. We are also called upon to examine the region's three most well-known civilizations --- Kemet (Egypt), Ethiopia and the Sudan to determine whether or not their relationship to one another was symbiotic or antagonistic. In order to achieve this, unbiased archaeological studies must continue to be put into place. For once these relationships are resolved a portrait of reality will surely emerge to identify the imposition of Eurocentric interests upon the African continent in clear historical perspective.

In Michael Eli Dokosi's November 2019 article titled, <u>How Kings from Nubia (Sudan) Became Pharaohs of Ancient Egypt and Ruled both Lands</u>, he points out just how interesting this exchange of power between the two states was. However, Alexander Balogun, of Obafemi Awolowo University makes the case that "Nubians from the south in today's Sudan were the first to forge many of ancient Egypt's cultural and spiritual systems that recent archaeological digs have now come to be noted for." He further notes in the platform known as Quora: "that discoveries of the Archeological Research by Dr. Keith C. Seele from the University of Chicago's Oriental Institute, during the excavation of the Upper Nile of Aswan for the construction of the Aswan dam and inundation of the Upper Nile, led them to the thesis that the earliest Pharaonic monarchy in the Nile Valley was from the region of Lower Nubia, Qustul (Modern day Aswan) as the excavation proved that the White Crown (later used by Upper Egypt) originated from Qustul about

1,000 years before it was used in Egypt. This discovery, he stated, further showed hieroglyphics was earlier used in Qustul before the founding of ancient Egypt while the religious symbol of Horus, the falcon deity, was earlier used in Qustul before the founding of ancient Egypt. During the New Kingdom period (ca. 1550 to 1050 BC), Egypt succeeded in occupying most of Nubia. At the site of Tombos in northern Sudan, Egyptianizing of Nubians is so fused [it makes it difficult] to determine if Egyptian colonists or Nubian leaders ruled." [26]

This is what we do know for certain: geographically, Egypt was divided into two regions: (a) Upper Egypt, the southern part of Egypt in the heart land; (b) Lower Egypt, the northern part of Egypt that is on the Mediterranean Sea. This is all counter-intuitive because Lower Egypt lies north on the Mediterranean Sea, and Upper Egypt is to the south bordering Sudan. Narmer was the first pharaoh, however, he did not conquer all of Lower Egypt during his lifetime. It is estimated today that his forefathers, successive kings of Upper Egypt, gradually annexed much of Lower Egypt piece by piece. However, it was Narmer who is the pharaoh who completed the conquest of Lower Egypt. This conquest was more peaceful than military since the merchants and inhabitants of Lower Egypt appreciated the prosperity and protection that the mighty Upper Egypt brought to them.

Verifying Narmer as Menes, the "Heroic Pharaoh"

It is important to note that Pharaoh Narmer and Pharaoh Menes (sometimes considered Narmer's successor) are more likely to be the same person. Indeed, according to many Egyptian religious writings from 500 BC, the first pharaoh of Egypt was not Narmer but Menes, a pharaoh portrayed as a heroic figure who unified Egypt. Menes is said to have succeeded Horus (the falcon-headed god of royalty"). And, as the personification and manifestation of Horus, the Kemetic Pharaoh-god, the anointed 'Sky god', who represented the sun, kingship, the sky, the weather, storms, health and healing, loyalty, war and protection, anointing Narmar, the first pharaoh of Kemet, empowered by Horus to unify lower and upper Egypt and to protect the land and its people from all would-be invaders. And for a time, this was so.

The prevailing view among both African and European historians today is that Menes is a misrepresentation of the *name* Narmer. This conclusion is quite accepted because at the time when <u>Menes</u> should have existed, there is no record of any mention of the name of such a pharaoh. Unlike the kings of Egypt before him, Narmer is considered to be the first pharaoh because he controlled the entire Egyptian territory in 3125 BC. In this case, the term pharaoh can be likened to the European term emperor, a station above that of a king.

Ancient Egypt, therefore, was founded by Pharaoh Narmar for it was he who established ancient Egypt's very first dynasty. They were a people from the Upper Nile Valley (located to the South) which was known as Kush, Nubia, and the Sudan. The people of the Sudan have always been black people, builders of the first pyramids in Africa, and based on Narmar's name (aka Menes) he came from the Sudan and was the first Pharoah of a "unified Egypt", united by him into a single centralized monarchy. Egyptian settlement and colonization is attested from about 3200 BC onward all over the area of southern Canaan with almost every type of artifact: architecture (fortifications, embankments, and buildings), pottery, vessels, tools, weapons, seals, etc. 20 serekhs attributed to Narmer — the first ruler of the Early Dynastic Period — have been found in Canaan. There is also evidence of Egyptian settlement and occupation in lower Nubia (Sudan) after the Nubian A-Group culture came to an end. By the Early Dynastic Period, the Egyptian state had likely imposed its authority as far north as modern Tel Aviv and as far south as the second cataract in Nubia.

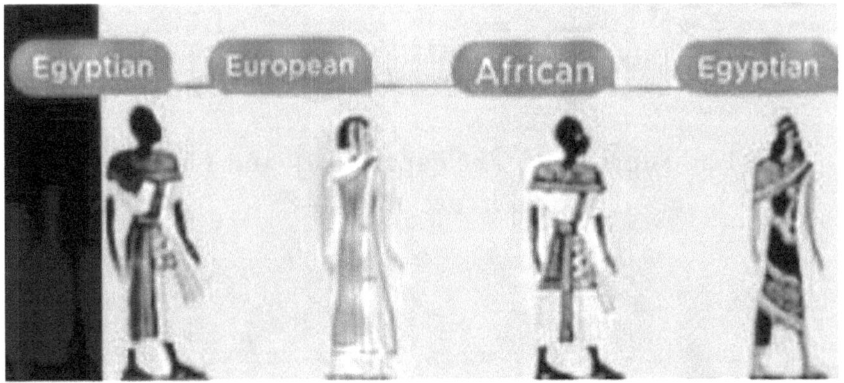

Queen Tiye was the wife of the 18th dynasty King Amenhotep III, the mother of the so-called 'heretic' pharaoh Akhenaten, and the grandmother of King Tutankhame. The bust of Queen Tiye's was hidden from public view and ***kept in a vault*** in Berlin for nearly 100 years. Why, we must now ask, was the bust of Queen Tiye hidden in a vault away from public view and knowledge during the rise of Nazism in Germany? The answer should be both obvious and a wake-up call to any fair-minded student of history and anyone else who is a seeker of truth about Africa and its peoples.

Pharoah Akhenaten ("Servant of the Aten") was the Egyptian pharaoh who ruled during the 18th Dynasty of the New Kingdom period of Ancient Egypt. Akhenaten was the pharaoh who changed the traditional religion of Egypt from the worship of Amun and many gods to the worship of a single God (monotheism) called Aten --the Sun. Pharaoh Akhenaten was born in Egypt approximately 130 years before Moses in 1380 B.C.

CHAPTER TEN

White Supremacy, The Papal Bulls, and The Berlin Conference of 1884-85

The Berlin Conference of 1884-85 was held to divide Africa among European colonial factions who attended the conference. The conference was held during the period deemed as the "new imperialism" and coincided with Germany's sudden emergence as an imperial power. The conference was organized by Otto von Bismarck, the first chancellor of Germany. Its outcome was called 'the General Act of the Berlin Conference'. It targeted the natural resource rich Kingdom of the Kongo, the largest land region in Central West Africa. The conference was the formalization of what became known as the European colonial powers' "Scramble for Africa". [27]

This brings us to some very critical questions. Here are a few: for whom was colonialism implanted in foreign lands? Who would be the beneficiaries of this system of plunder? Who would gain from the enslavement of African peoples? And who would benefit from the goals of the Berlin Conference? To begin to answer those questions, we must consider the Papal Bull that annulled the Magna Carta in 1215 AD. It was Pope Innocent III who issued the Papal Bull that annulled the Magna Carta on August 24, 1215.

The Pope's two principal roles in all of Christendom was as overlord of Christendom which was comprised of numerous European fiefdoms and kingdoms. He was also the *"protector of the monarchs,"* that is, those who had taken a crusader's vow and helped to fund the Crusades against the Muslims to retake Jerusalem. The term Magna Carta means the 'Great Charter'. To this day, it is one of the most famous political documents in Western civilization and was written under the threat of Civil War to force England's reigning King John, to grant it on June 15, 1215. The document declared for the first time in history that *the sovereign was also subject to the same rules of law* that governed all (sound familiar?), and it provided the major foundations for the pursuit of individual rights for landowners and barons in Anglo America.

The charter itself was drafted up by Stephen Langton, the England's Archbishop of Canterbury. However, the clauses of the charter were actually formulated by three parties: the archbishop himself, the rebel barons, and the King. In this way, all the three parties were the original authors of the charter. What is important about the English barons who wrote the Magna Carta is that these men were not members of the royal court but lay people and landowners; and for the most part were members of the hardline baronial opposition to King John for exacting heavy taxes upon them and other abuses of power. For this, the barons continuously plotted rebellion within the kingdom. In addition to this threat, others, namely clergy, stood in hostile opposition to the king and were eager for his overthrow. The committee of landowners (barons) that contributed to the writing of the Magna Carta was seen in clear and unequivocal terms. They were enforcers, a group whose chief responsibilities were of a military nature. In other words, they were ready if necessary to depose King John by civil war to achieve their goals.

Pope Innocent III had already sent a string of letters to England berating the English barons. Now he explained how, 'by such violence and fear as might affect the most courageous of men', they had forced John to accept an agreement 'illegal, unjust, harmful to royal rights and shameful to the English people'. The Pope declared Magna Carta 'null, and void of all validity forever', a judgement which reached England the following month.

> "By 1215, thanks to years of unsuccessful foreign policies and heavy taxation demands, England's King John was facing down a possible rebellion by the country's powerful land barons. Under duress, he agreed to a charter of liberties known as the Magna Carta (or Great Charter) that would place him and all of England's future sovereigns within a rule of law. Though it was not initially successful, the document was reissued (with alterations) in 1216, 1217 and 1225, and eventually served as the foundation for the English system of common law." [28]

For generations, the British aristocracy would continue to celebrate the Magna Carta as a symbol of freedom from oppression. This fight for liberty by the British upper and merchant classes was the quintessential reason for Pope Innocent III's annulment of the Magna Carta in 1215. Its reverberations were felt for hundreds of years down through the centuries to King Henry VIII's *English Reformation* and the formation of the Church of England, whereby its ties with the Vatican were severed forever. However, the Magna Carta continued to have its influence as it did upon the victors of the American Revolution and the writers of the Constitution of the United States of America. In 1776, the Magna Carta was the primary model used to hash out the details of the request for liberty from monarchal oppression.

The Papal Bulls, Leopold II - the King of Belgium, Leopold II, and the Kingdom of Kongo

After the Berlin Conference, the first action taken by King Leopold II of Belgium was to rename the Kingdom of Kongo. He officially renamed the kingdom the 'Congo *Free* State'. This name changes from 'Kingdom of Kongo' to "The Congo *Free* State" was nothing short of euphemism. At best it was a political and economic decoy. For "free" it was not. The choice of name was intentional and was selected to seduce other European and American government leaders to condone, to endorse, and to delude investors. The name change was sanctioned by the United States and Britain; however, the Catholic king's true intent soon became clear and was grounded in the historical Papal Bulls. King Leopold of Belgium officially made the Kongo his own colonial 'private property'. The sanction given to King Leopold gave him sole ownership of the Congo and not to the administrative government of Belgium though this colonial arrangement in the Congo Basin lasted for only 23 years. Yet, within that relatively short period, the King's rule and policies towards the Congolese people resulted in the deaths of 10 million people in pursuit of personal profit for the King. His dominion over the 30 million Congolese people included rampant mutilations, murders, brutal slavery, and disease, and is still considered to be among the worst atrocities of European colonialism. The many narratives that have been recorded recount the litany of brutal crimes committed, and repeatedly underscore the Belgian king's intentions for renaming the Kingdom of Kongo to what he surreptitiously dubbed "the *philanthropic* Congo Free State" --- in an effort to reap unimaginable wealth for *himself.*

Pre-colonial History of the Kingdom of Kongo

Human habitation of the region that came to be known as the Congo basin, known today as the Democratic Republic of Congo, began circa 100,000 to 40,000 BCE. In the southern regions of the Congo, the Bantu people migrated and imported agriculture and iron-working techniques from West Africa into the area (circa 3,000 B.C.), establishing the Bantu language as the primary language for the Congolese people. After the 1885 Conference in Berlin, the

Legacy of the Vatican Papal Bulls "The Law of Discovery" was applied absolutely in the Kingdom of Kongo by King Leopold II of Belgium without him knowing anything of the region's history.

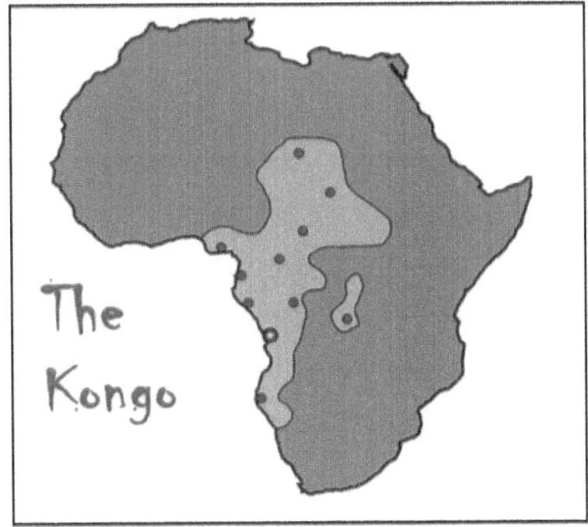

In the 1990s, human remains were discovered in the Democratic Republic of the Congo. The remains have been dated to approximately 90,000 years which extends well beyond the Adamic Cycle which began some 6,000 years ago. The first real states, such as the Kongo, the Lunda, the Luba and Kuba, appeared south of the equatorial forest on the savannah from the 1300s and onwards. The Kingdom of Kong controlled much of western and central Africa including what is now the western portion of the Democratic Republic of the Congo between the 14th and the early 19th centuries. At its peak, the population of the Congo was as many as 500,000 people; it's capital was known as Mbanza-Kongo (south of Matadi) in modern day Angola.

In the late 1400s, Portuguese sailors arrived in the Kingdom of Kongo in late 1440s. With Portugal's economic power being founded on trade in West Africa and the Kongo primarily seeking gold, the small kingdom began to enjoy great prosperity and consolidation. After the Papal Bull of 1452 was issued to King Alfonso, raids in West Africa began in response to neighboring Portuguese districts' requests for slaves. After his death, the Portuguese kingdom underwent a fundamental, deep, and devastating crisis.

CHAPTER ELEVEN

The Birth of British Global Imperialism

Essentially, colonialism was forged from the blood, sweat, and tears of indigenous peoples. A systemic institution was put in place with the sole purpose of depriving these same ancient peoples of their humanity, their languages, their dignity, and their ancient religions. This heinous operation took place in lands that were taken from indigenous peoples throughout the world. The primary beneficiaries of this system were the monarchs and land barons whose exclusive preoccupation was the ownership of everything material that could be monopolized and converted into commodities to reap vast fortune's at any cost for a collective few. The only thing that threatened to stand in the way of their ambitions was their own basic religious teachings found in Matthew 7:12 and Luke 6:31-38 --- "Do unto others as you would have others do unto you, for this sums up the Law and the Prophets." In order to prevent conscience and morality from undermining this goal, minority European religious groups like the Puritans and the Pilgrims had to be marginalized and silenced. And since those who would gain from the enslavement of these people --- the monarchs and barons, the very text of their sacred books had to be modified. The notion of teaching Christianity to people who were considered "heathens" though it was these supposed *heathens* who graciously taught the Puritans and Pilgrims what specific foods (at the time unknown to them) to eat to keep them from starving during their first frigid, bitter and unforgiving winter in the *new world*. Initially, the idea of actually teaching indigenous people anything about the Christian sect that they practiced was an anathema to most of these British men and women who had fled religious persecution in England. The reason for this persecution was that they held that the newly-formed Anglican Church of England, it's ostentation, pomp and rituals were indistinguishable from that of the Roman Catholic

Church which they had refused to accept, protesting against the Church of England and demanding reformation just as Martin Luther had protested against the Roman Catholic Church.

Romans in the 5th century. From the early 17th century onward this religious climate persisted and continued its hostility towards all religious nonconformists especially the Celts in Northern Island, and the Puritans in England. During that same period, in 1620, the first slave ship from West Africa arrived in Virginia. This signature event signaled what 265 years later would become known as 'the Scramble for Africa' --- the carving up of the entire African continent. This "scramble" was the negotiated outcome of the Berlin Conference of 1884-85 where the distribution of indigenous lands throughout Africa were decided among European powers; thus fulfilling the terms outlined in the Papal Bulls of the 15th and 16th centuries' --- a Papal call for the domination and perpetual enslavement of African peoples. The strategy was comprehensive: impose upon indigenous peoples everywhere their ideas, their traditional religious beliefs, their class systems, their world views, and to transplant all of these with the agenda given to them by goals of the Papal Bull. The first step taken was the creation of a global system that would be both profitable and morally justifiable. The system that was to be put in place would have to adhere to the specifications that had been laid out in the Vatican Papal Bull to King Alphonso of Portugal in 1452 and the decrees written later by other popes. However, the domination and enslavement of the people, the confiscation of indigenous lands and its natural resources under the premise of the 'Law of Discovery' whereby they would redound to the Papacy in Rome were now to be taken in the name of the British monarchy and the Church of England into perpetuity. To achieve this goal, the East Indian Company, the Virginia Company of London, and The Royal African Company were all established by the British monarchy and powerful land barons to administer the occupation of "discovered" lands and the enslavement of human beings. The one caveat that threatened to stand in their way was the moral consequences of their actions. Typically, for a civilized people to take over foreign lands by force was seen as part and parcel of the "spoils of war"; however, the forced capture of unsuspecting people and the subsequent trading in the enslavement of these same human beings where neither were signatories to a *declared war* was considered uncivilized and un-Christian. In order to legitimize the transatlantic slave trade European monarchs and their aristocracies turned to a system that had been used for centuries to suppress their own people --- *the system of indentured servitude.*

The East India Company, was a private company chartered by Queen Elizabeth I in 1600 AD. It's mission: to trade spices at islands in present-day Indonesia and eventually all of Asia.

The London Company (also called the Virginia Company of London) was an English joint-stock company established six years after the East India Company was established, in 1606. It was endorsed by King James I in his royal charter with the intended mission of establishing colonial settlements throughout North America which included Canada, the United States, Mexico and throughout the Caribbean.

Founded at Jamestown in 1607, the Virginia Colony was home to about 700 British colonists. By 1619, the total population of the Virginia colony was about 1000 British colonists. Up to **75 percent** of all the British individuals who came off the transatlantic ships in the 17th century were indentured servants. During Jamestown's first 20 years, the majority of the women who arrived, and they were few, were indentured servants. The first 20 enslaved Ndongo captives from Africa to arrive in Virginia disembarked at Point Comfort, in what is today known as Fort Monroe.

The Royal African Company (RAC) was an English mercantile trading company set up in 1660 by the royal Stuart family and City of London merchants to trade along the west coast of Africa, fifty-four years after the Virginia Company of London was established.

Its business plan was the enslavement of black tribal Africans (with no regard to religion (be it Christian, Muslim or indigenous), whether isolated tribal villages or kingdoms; social status, level or age of civilization or any other consideration) to work as unpaid labor in numerous sugar, coffee, and cotton plantations throughout the British colonies which by then was increasingly spreading around the globe.

It was led by the Duke of York, the brother of King Charles II, and in 1685, York took the throne as James II. It was chartered just five years before the publication of King James' new "version" of the Geneva and Catholic Bibles known to this day as the 'King James *Version*'. This London-based venture allowed the Crown to reap the benefits of colonization: natural resources, new markets for English goods, and leverage against the Crown Heads of France, Portugal, and Spain — *without bearing any costs.*

Step 1 - Indentured Servitude

The ruling class term "commoner" has been used in England for centuries. It is a term used to objectify human beings and to keep them in check by class (a form equivalent to India's 'caste system'). This class stratification is always subtextual given the rules of "proper British social etiquette", and is used to emphasize upper class 'superiority' over the downtrodden whose conditions they, by divine right, are obliged to accentuate in speech and manners as one of the prerogatives of royalty "in serving the people," and was exacted by the aristocracy to exploit the 'common people', that is, serfs, peons, vassals, etc. But what exactly does the term "commoner" in a 21st century-instantaneous-social media-gotta-tweet-it-tik-toking-multi-lingual-communication world that strives to disregard British traditions and etiquette world even mean? Who were these 16th century British "commoners"?

One of the best illustrations of what it was like to be a "commoner in 16th century Europe is found in the 1964 film 'My Fair Lady'. It demonstrates how speech, accent & dialect marked the differences between London's upper-class aristocrats and the lower-class Cockneys, that is the "commoners." It was these people who served as indentured servants in the Virginia colony. It also hints at the reception that the Ndongo tribespeople of Africa received in 1619 when they were shipped to the Virginia Colony as slaves to English society unable to speak the language.

As in most European monarchal class societies, the term "commoner" has always been used to maintain a strict distance between upper and lower classes. Throughout the world, class and social demarcation has either been strict or implied. Royal and class apartheid is not the same as racial apartheid though they may appear to be indistinguishable when viewed dispassionately as part of any social organization. However, it is the hallmark of monarchy and influences every aspect of such societies. As long as wealth and power are on equal par skin color is not an issue.

What it Meant to be an Indentured Servant

To achieve the goals of colonialism, the <u>East India Company</u>, the <u>London Company of Virginia</u> (the British colony in North America), and the <u>Royal African Company</u> (ideally, the whole of Africa per the Papal Bulls) needed bodies; people who were loyal and subservient to the British Crown. The companies were set up to ensure that England won the fierce and often frantic competition between other European powers, mainly France, Holland, Portugal, and Spain. Each of them was endorsed, financed, commissioned, and promoted <u>not</u> by public consensus or the approval of the underclass or "common people" of 15th century England, but by aristocratic landowners and the autocratic British elite. It was not a democracy. The "common people" did not matter. The acquisition of knowledge was the privilege of none but the ruling classes. Knowledge for peasants and serfs was usually homespun 'wives' tales,' day-to-day health and pastoral concerns, deaths, gossip, and recaps of sermons that distinguished heaven from hell by invoking simplistic images such as 'milk and honey' (food) to describe heaven; and 'fire and brimstone' to describe hell. These invented notions were fully embraced by often horrified and illiterate serfs believing them to be the Word of God. Such dramatic sermons as these were crafted to appeal to the existing superstitions of the time and were presented in sermons by priests standing high above the flock below behind elaborately sculpted stone and wood pulpits.

Knowing anything more than the basics, that there is a God, selective teachings of Jesus Christ, the holy "sacraments," the existence of man's soul, obeying land barons, and reciting church prayers was secondary to the constant reminders of *their low station.* In effect, this was their religious life. From the moment a peasant was born --- from dawn to dusk --- subservience was the fiber of their life and had been deeply woven into the fabric of their lives for generations.

To illustrate how "funky" the lives of indentured servants was, the pool of people from whence they came were those living in the slums of London. Nearly three hundred years after the first indentured servants were brought to Virginia, the most notorious serial killings took place in what was considered to be the most impoverished slum of London's East End. The serial killings were attributed to a man dubbed "Jack the Ripper." Though this man was never identified, all his murders took place in and around the same Whitechapel district of London where all of his victims were women who lived and worked as prostitutes in that same slum of London's East End.

The slums and orphanages of London's East End were full illiterate and desperate people. A peasant's primary concern was the daily struggle to avoid death and to eke out a meager living. And with a lifespan of about 35 years, avoiding eternal damnation when certain death did arrive, generally kept them all in check. The rule was simple: obey the rules, know your place, and milk and honey would be the reward they'd receive in heaven. It was a miserable life! It remained the same multi-generational 'nose to the grindstone' existence that afflicted the disenfranchised in most medieval societies be it France, Belgium, Russia, Rome, or Spain; a material and spiritual affliction that, indeed, had been embedded into the very soul of medieval life itself. This atrocious system was called serfdom, sharecropping and peasantry; and by any other name it was slavery with benefits –– a meagre portion of the crops they had sown and reaped, beer and ale to bloat the body and stay drunk, and rehearsed blessings from the pulpit. From this class of people 'indentured servitude' was legally instituted, binding the people to a withering life as unworthy peons in a society that itself was considered the wart on the hip of Europe. With no higher aim other than to survive and to avoid eternal damnation and hellfire, any other aspiration was deemed a 'pipe dream' – itself a phrase which originated in 19th century Britain when peasants would smoke opiates through a pipe. When they were high from the drugs, they would talk about impossible dreams and ambitions which they never truly believed they would reach, therefore coining the term 'pipe dream'. With opportunity not even a part of the peasant lexicon, the "common people" remained in a state of perpetual subservience and ignorance of the broader world that lay just outside their forested hamlets --- oblivious of the more than likely exploitive machinations of their masters bent on keeping it that way. How could they then know the global aims of their "sires" who would become the sole beneficiaries of a new political and capitalist economic system that would soon emerge as British colonialism.

Clearly, this state of affairs would easily predispose the ruling class to operate with legal and moral impunity. The persecution of religious minorities (namely the Puritans and Pilgrims) had begun to stir up popular defiance against the Crown with numerous, though powerless, factions of serfs and peasants beginning to at least question their own conditions. Then, as now, such worldly matters were deemed "heretical" and against biblical teachings though few even could have read the bible due to their illiteracy. It was all better left in the hands of land barons and members of the social hierarchy who, according to them, had by 'divine right' been handed the power of governance. And wield the power they did and were able to maintain a relatively undramatic pastoral system in which subservience was its own reward. Plainly speaking, the masses of Europeans were considered to be so far beneath the royal economic stratosphere that wealthy Anglican Protestant aristocrats and landowners who remained loyal to the new Church of England could busy themselves with that which preoccupied them most: *building a global colonial empire on the backs and graves of indigenous peoples around the world.* This system of 'indentured servitude', already a social stable of governance in English society is the same unimaginative system that English monarchs and land barons transplanted in the New World; North America --- the Virginia colony.

Step II - Key Differences & Similarities Between Indentured Servitude & Chattel Enslavement:

Indentured servants were members of England's lowest economic and social class. Servitude as unpaid laborers in the Virginia colony was set for a predetermined number of years based upon the amount paid to ship these servants to the American colony. Indentured servitude was not an inherited state; it was contractual. In other words, children were not bound to indentured servitude for life. Indentured servitude was a form of debt bondage in exchange for unpaid labor, as well as an alternative form of criminal punishment in England of the 1600s. The contract was a one-way agreement. It could be bought or sold like currency which meant that owners could buy or sell servants as punishment or retribution for unsatisfactory service. Indentured servants were bound to a contract and had certain laws and rights such as "freedom dues" which at the end of the term of the contract allowed indentured servants to gain freedom and citizenship in society. It was an agreed or forced term of unpaid labor (determining upon whether the servitude was criminally induced or not). The term was based upon the costs for the servant's room and board, and immigration to America. Indentured servitude was the single-most profitable labor system of the Virginia Company of London during the 1600s because many farmworkers were needed to work the flourishing tobacco plantations of the Commonwealth. before slavery was introduced. In the beginning, indentured servitude was an extremely profitable venture for the Virginia Company of London but disputes with ex-indentured servants with its increasingly high costs of providing food and housing gave cause to find an alternative system --- permanent enslavement. The contract of an indentured servant could be bought by the indentured servant as well as sold by its owner.

Step III - Enslavement Under the System of Chattel Slavery:

Chattel slavery meant a human being was an *item* of property other than real estate and was considered to be legal personal possession. Enslavement of members of different African tribal societies by both African and European slave traders were captured and sold into slavery with no respect to class, language, religion, culture, or tribal status. Chattel slavery was not a social class; it was an economic system whereby adult human beings and their offspring were enslaved for life. An enslaved person was bound by the will of his/her owner. Chattel slavery was forced labor without terms or conditions. Chattel slavery was instituted to be an inherited state in perpetuity without any rights or possibility of citizenship. It eventually replaced indentured servitude as the single-most profitable labor system of the Virginia Company of London and subsequently served as the model in the original thirteen colonies that did permit enslavement. In the southern regions of the United States, chattel slavery was the preferred and exclusive form of unpaid labor. Enslaved persons were considered property however, the enslaved individual could neither buy nor sell his or her own freedom. They were not and never could be a free agent.

Step IV - Practice Makes Perfect: Indentured Servitude, Slavery - the Roadmap to World Empire

In 1619, a British General Assembly convened, bringing limited self-government to selected American colonies, starting with the Virginia colony. In that same year (1619), the Virginia Company brought the first captive Congolese to Virginia. For most of the 1600s, white indentured servants worked the colony's tobacco fields, but by 1705 the Virginia colony had become a slave society of enslaved African labor. Nearly all power was in the hands of white male _landowners_, who ran the government and, by law, belonged to the Church of England (the Anglican Church).

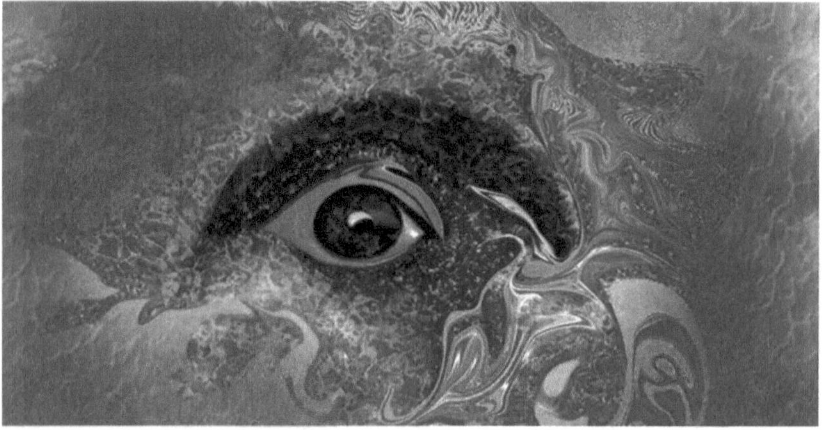

Pupil of the Eye: The Spiritual Insight and Soul of Africa Comes to the Americas

In 1898, Robert Turner became the first African American to embrace the Baha'i Faith. Turner was honored as the recipient of a tablet addressed to him by Abdu'l-Baha, the eldest son of Bahá'u'lláh, which introduced his father's now famous metaphor "pupil of the eye". In this tablet, the metaphor was applied generously to all people of African descent.

> "Thou art like unto the pupil of the eye which is dark in colour, yet it is the fount of light and the revealer of the contingent world. The pupil of the eye is a portal which

admits and regulates the flow of light to the retina. There is no perception without this passage, and no image can be perceived without it." ---'Abdu'l-Bahá [29]

Clearly, the 'Pupil of the Eye' as a metaphor is neither a glib, nor casual patronizing pronouncement as it came from the Mouth of the Supreme Manifestation of God. Naturally, I was intrigued. When understood in the brilliant light of Bahá'u'lláh's Revelation, its power to infuse spiritual insight into human consciousness as well the *transformative effect* to permeate all trials and tribulations with immeasurable spiritual grace, confers upon the soul an inner strength to enable it to overcome overwhelming earthly adversities. This inner strength is a requisite not just in this world, but throughout all the worlds of God. In particular, for most people of African descent, the many unimaginable trials and tribulations that Bahá'u'lláh Himself endured in Persia as a prisoner in the "Siyah Chal", and later, in the Ottoman Empire's "Most Great Prison", struck a deep chord that deeply resonates within the hearts of all African peoples throughout the diaspora. His sublime endurance is proof enough of His divine station.

Dr. May Khadem Czerniejewski, M.D. ophthalmologist, and Dr. Richard Czerniejewski, M.D have written extensively on the bodily function of the pupil and how it relates to the metaphor 'pupil of the eye':

"At the retina, our consciousness is intimately in contact with physical reality, for the brain's cells themselves flow out to the retina to receive information through the illumination modulated by the pupil. The pupil has the dual function of light gathering and modulation. Light, which unites all colors and is composed of all colors, illumines physical reality, but at the same time its intensity can destroy the delicate structures of the eye. When light levels are high, it constricts to protect the retina from intense and even damaging exposure. Since sight is often described as our most precious sensory ability, we can say that the pupil helps to protect this most precious gift. On the other hand, when there is very little light the pupil admits more light through dilating, thus permitting sight even in very dark places. The black appearance of the pupil is deceptive. The pupil appears black only until the inside of the eye is illumined. Then it becomes radiant, filled with a warm, reddish-orange glow. With this reflection from the inside of the eye, the pupil itself becomes a source of illumination. The most remarkable quality of the pupil is that despite its vital service, it is the embodiment of "the hollow reed from which the pith of self hath been blown," for it is the absence of physical structure that permits it to facilitate the harmonious functioning of all the other components of the eye that make sight possible." [30]

Additionally, Christopher Buck, in his Part 40 of a series of 'The Universal Emancipation Proclamation' punctuates the above citation in the following remarks:

"Although a narrow [understanding] of this metaphor might otherwise limit its interpretation to 'light that travels *into* the pupil of the eye and onto the retina', a broader reading of this "pupil of the eye" metaphor has another meaning—it recognizes what African-Americans and people of African descent have witnessed and experienced historically as one collective body, and thus collectively endowing them with a heightened sensitivity to suffering and oppression and deepening their capacity for empathy, social justice, and interracial harmony." [31]

Observe here Buck's clear association of the physical "pupil of the eye" *both* as the "source of light" <u>to the physical retina</u>, and the "source of spiritual light which is "the Love of God" <u>to the all-receptive spiritual retina which is essential to human consciousness and the transmitter of the knowledge of God to man's indivisible eternal soul</u>. The profundity of this should not be underestimated. For it is this association alone that transforms the intensely palpable and lasting memory of the trauma that has been endured by African Americans for generations into radiant acquiescence; not to be confused with either passivity or resignation but rather spiritual awareness. 'Abdu'l-Bahá calls radiant acquiescence the most practical way to handle the disturbing aspects of life. It allows the individual to drop resistance to things that cannot be immediately changed and enables self to recognize that it is life's unpredictable circumstances combined with ignorance and fear that lead people to be unjust, unkind, impolite, or disagreeable.

In another sense, it is the trials of a brutal slavery, the cultural and emotional isolation, the corporal violence that was inflicted, the random brutality of rape --- meted out as if it was a form of parental discipline rather than the crime against humanity *which it was*. More than this, these heinous acts were perpetrated not just against the dignity of a people but against God's divine *sovereignty over the entire creation as humanity's Creator*. It is this *sovereignty* that throughout the African diaspora black people have continuously risen up to defend. The Spirit of Christ did the same in destroying the money changers' tables and overturning them in the temple; the Spirit of Moses atop Mount Sinai did the same by casting down the stone tablets upon which the commandments of God to the Hebrews were inscribed, destroying those who had returned to idol worship. Black people act not out of anger towards their aggressors but from their own inherent spiritual imperative --- indignation. It is this indignation, this recognition of the injustice against them that is the core principle of life itself. It has no skin color! His Holiness Bahá'u'lláh writes:

"O Son of Spirit! The best beloved of all things in My sight is *Justice*; turn not away therefrom if thou desirest Me and neglect it not that I may confide in thee. <u>*By its aid thou shalt see with thine own eyes and not through the eyes of others, and shalt know of thine own knowledge and not through the knowledge of thy neighbor*</u>. Ponder this in thy heart; how it behooveth thee to be. Verily justice is My gift to thee and the sign of My loving-kindness. Set it then before thine eyes." [32]

Since the beginning of the transatlantic slave trade and throughout the past 400 years, white people have continuously characterized the defiance of black people as "anger." However, anger is not the cause of their defiance. What black people did and continue to express, however, is, in fact, indignation. Indignation is a vibrant disdain at what is experienced as *unjust treatment raised to the level of spiritual principle*. Unlike indignation, anger is an attachment to acts of hostility, deprivation, and displeasure and seeks revenge. The difference between the two is that anger results from a desire to exact revenge for material deprivation while indignation results from deprivation of spiritual values. Spiritual values are instilled within the soul and, unlike anger, is not purely psychological. Values are an inherent noble sense created to resist injustice. It is this that compels human beings to seek justice. And of all mother earth's inhabitants, black people have had to confront injustice more that any attachment to material things. Therefore, they tend to be the most adaptable, resilient, spiritually self-reliant people on the planet. This capacity has deepened our ability to internalize Bahá'u'lláh's vision of the oneness of humanity despite the historical oppression, the economic and social disenfranchisements, the generational psychological and physical trauma, the denial of access to education, and even death. For in spite of these, the generations of our own age possess the capacity to communicate in multiple languages --- African, European, as well as Semitic languages and dialects --- should be considered a positive by-product of that oppression. When viewed as a by-product of these it has the potential to serve as a function of transforming a consciousness of injustice into one of justice, war into peace, hate into love, and rancor into diplomacy with all the peoples of the earth. For, for a newborn babe, it is the soul of man that records everything it encounters into its consciousness during this state of incubation where consciousness has neither speech nor understanding of words to express itself. It is during this phase of existence that the soul comprehends what the mind cannot. What other peoples, by virtue of that oppression, are better prepared to awaken the spiritual reality within all who seek true freedom? From the very beginning, Black people have continuously striven to free themselves from the bonds of slavery and to establish justice wherever it is. Seen in this light, this is the gift that keeps on giving; a quality of spirit that neither colonialism, lack of formal education nor enslavement has the power to diminish. And with this gift, black people are seen as inherently capable of fully recognizing, believing, and living according to the principle of the 'oneness of humanity' in all its glory. This is the in-born fount of insight that the metaphor 'pupil of the eye' enshrines, enabling people of African descent to intuit our spiritual bond with the rest of humanity --- the very power that **Bahá'u'lláh** attributes to the 'pupil of the eye', it being the very soul of black people:

> "O Son of the Throne! Thy hearing is My hearing, hear thou therewith. *Thy sight is My sight, do thou see therewith,* that in thine inmost soul thou mayest testify unto My exalted sanctity, and I within Myself may bear witness unto an exalted station for thee." [33]

Here, it seems appropriate to apply Albert Einstein's observation that "time is an illusion" a hypothesis that speaks to human affairs and to the nature of being human. It is due to the common experiences with freedom and oppression that human beings are intimately aware that freedom is to be preferred; it is not a mere political convenience but rather the very essence --- not of man's will, but of God's. Ancient

African histories, religions, cultures, and traditions --- rather than being eclipsed by colonialism and white supremacy have become enshrined not in brick and mortar but within the very souls of African peoples, shining forth as beacons of light for all the world to witness. It has been through the crucible of slavery and its oppressive weight that black people in particular yet have retained our spiritual ties to God and to one another despite the cruelty, the abject efforts to dehumanize --- and the crucible of injustice that has steeled our insight and determination. The potential of what this holds for the future New World Order of **Bahá'u'lláh** is nothing less than the miracle of divine justice and a gift to all humankind. Our common unity (comm*unity*) is our experienced life stories, our art, our music, our vision all combined to enshrine a very rich history that must be shared with one another to make whole the whole human family. We are one people and must never forget that. Despite our past tribulations and separations here are a just a few of the gifts by which the soul can express itself through multiple languages that enshrine God's ageless covenant with humanity: Amharic (Ethiopian), Coptic (the ancient Kemetic [aka Egyptian] language), Hausa, Igbo, Kriol (the Australian Aboriginal language - spoken for over 60,000 years), Oromo, Shona, Somali, Swahili, Yoruba (and many other ancient indigenous African languages). As well as Arabic, Farsi, Hebrew; Dutch, English, French, German, Italian, Portuguese, Russian, Spanish, Swedish; Japanese.

These are the spiritual capacities with which the pupil of the eye is endowed. Binding the body in chains, imprisoning it, or enslaving the body can never prevent these capacities from becoming realized. Unbeknownst to the British Virginia colonists, this is the imperishable gift the Ndonga people had in their possession. When they placed their feet upon the sacred soil, the indigenous lands of America in 1619, this spiritual endowment was already scanning the new horizons. May this knowledge bring all who love God a deepened faith, certitude, and a more profound understanding of the ways of God in protecting His lovers, the Supreme Manifestation of His Own Self.

The Ndonga People: First Enslaved African People in the Virginia Colony

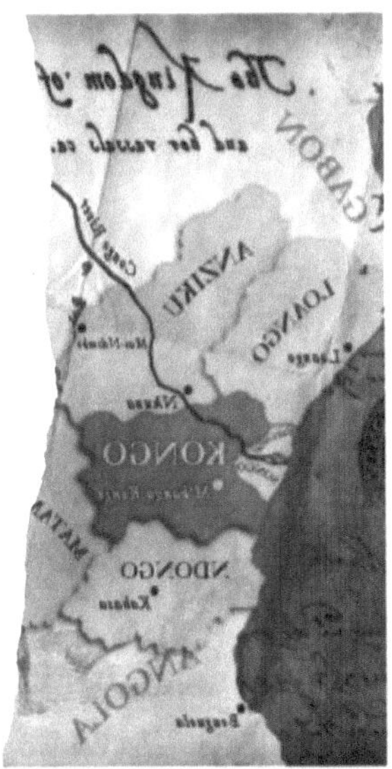

Freedom of religion is said to have been the primary reason for Puritans and Pilgrims to flee England. Freedom of being is religion for African peoples. However, neither of these two fundamental freedoms animated the *raison d'être* for members of the British aristocracy. It wasn't until after the land had been cleared, dwellings erected, and the rules of the settlement had been firmly established that it was even permissible for them to set sail across a vast and tumultuous ocean. Their primary role was as appointed overseers of the Virginia colony. These individuals and families had not fled England. They were heirs of the British aristocracy. Teaching the Christian religion to indigenous African peoples receded and became a tertiary concern to their primary vision and material interests which, whether directly mandated by the Papal Bull or not, was calculated to carry out the spirit of the Papal decrees in the form of British colonialism.

We are talking about human beings. In doing so, we must avoid the tendency to reduce people to just bodies, to their social rank and titles. Rather, principle must prevail over superficial and impermanent designations for it is by seeing human beings as having been 'created in the *spiritual image* of God' that justice either shines or diminishes that image. Human thoughts then either reflect that reality or denies it. As proverbs 23:7 states "For as a man thinketh in his heart, so is he." The apostle Peter believed yet denied Christ three times. Beliefs are neither proofs nor convictions. Some say beliefs are neurospasms of the brain struggling to make sense of things, desperate to keep up with an ever-advancing world while navigating deep chasms that harbor the unexpected. Beliefs are mental representations of the ways our brains expect things to workout. Beliefs are nothing without proofs and convictions. Much of what we believe is handed down generation to generation and therefore are not always sustainable as reality changes, yet people still hold on to ideas that no longer serve them. And here is where such periods in history such as the 'Enlightenment' should be evaluated in terms of its long-term effect upon human consciousness. The Enlightenment not only encouraged the study of science and the investigation of natural phenomena but applied science and reason to just about every problem that humanity faced, ultimately replacing the inherent impulse to supplicate before acting with pure reason alone when both are needed.

English philosopher John Locke *believed* (there's that term again) and argued that *"each person is naturally free and equal under the law of nature.* His doctrine of natural rights was to become profoundly influential in politics. Yet, Locke owned stock in slave trading and was the secretary of the Lords Proprietors of the Carolinas where slavery was constitutionally permitted.

Locke believed two things about slavery: one, that there was what he called "legitimate slavery" where it was described as "captivity with forced labor" *and was imposed by the victor who won the war;* and the other was what he dubbed "illegitimate slavery" *which he described as "authoritarian deprivation of natural rights." (34)*

The lemon on this unsavory expression of belief was that Locke avoided trying to justify either the enslavement of African people or the genocide and oppression of indigenous people who he dubbed "Amerindians" most likely because there had been no formal declaration of war! For him to attempt to justify either "legitimate slavery" or "illegitimate slavery," terms that came out of <u>his</u> own mouth as justification for *capturing and forcing African people to labor with compensation;* or to justify *authoritarian deprivation of indigenous peoples' natural, God-given rights in their own land* (which is what he *believed* to be true), there necessarily would have to have been a <u>*declared war fought*</u> to make it legitimate in order for his deluded reasoning to make it a moral or legal argument. For, as according to the standards of the time, a war would have to be declared by *both sides.* However, this was not the case; and, apart from skirmishes and battles between American Indians and European settlers, however violent, *were never formally declared wars by either side which would have been consistent with British standards as practiced between Spain and England at the time and throughout Europe.* But between 1622 and the late 19th century, a series of skirmishes that were called the *Indian Wars* took place. From the Powhatan perspective, these so-called wars were viewed as British incursions and were fought over land that the Powhatans had thrived on for thousands of years. These so-called Indian Wars had begun almost immediately when, in 1607, the English colonists arrived in Jamestown, Virginia. And when the British settlers' intention to own and control the land became clear an uneasy relationship with the Powhatan tribe (incorrectly dubbed 'Indians') began. They were not Indians. Long before their arrival, millions of indigenous peoples became spread out and had settled across North America in organized and structured tribal nations with their own religious beliefs and practices. The point here is that there never was any *declared war* ever fought against any tribe in the New World or any of the African kingdoms. The United States as a nation had yet to be established, so again, it would have been localized skirmishes rather than wars. Locke's mental-mealy-mouthed-and-racist-beliefs-rationale overlooks this fact, and it illustrates the ease at which impromptu justifications were used to disassociate himself from his own supposedly deeply held religious teachings enshrined in words in Leviticus 19:18 where Christ answers the lawyer's question --- "who is my neighbor?" Christ's answer was simple enough for anyone to understand and that is why Christ gave the lesson in a parable: The Good Samaritan --- "to love thy neighbor as oneself." But this command was preceded by a much deeper love than love of one's neighbor; and is the essence of why human beings were created in the first place. It is referred to as the Greatest Commandment of all: "'Love the Lord your God with all your heart and with all your soul and with all your mind and with all your strength.'" The second is this: 'Love thy neighbor as yourself.' No other commandment is greater than these." And the lawyer, unable to dispute with Christ any further said, "Right, Teacher, you have stated correctly that God is One and there is no other but Him." And, since then, biblical commentators have been obliged to repeat this parable from scripture, teaching that we must "love everyone we come into contact with, regardless of their ethnicity, beliefs, or actions" a clarification which speaks to us today for it is based upon the parable that Christ taught. These verses were true when Jesus said them, they were true at the time of Locke's conflicted writings, they are true today, true tomorrow, and true forever. However, the spiritual milieu of 1619 Virginia colonists when the nineteen Ndonga captives disembarked from the San Juan Bautista slave ship (a Portuguese name that is equivalent to the name in English, St. John the Baptist) was already 619 years after the initial decline of the Christian 1000 year-cycle had begun, and only nine years after the decline of Islam's 1000 year-cycle had begun. Little did these Africans know that they were taking their first steps upon an already blood-soaked indigenous land, now hailed by the British as the first successful English colony in the new world.

Just Who Were the Ndonga People?

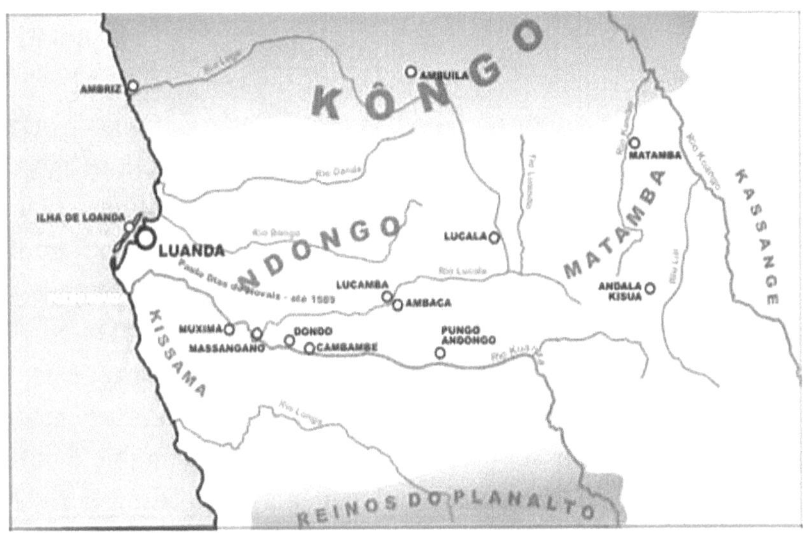

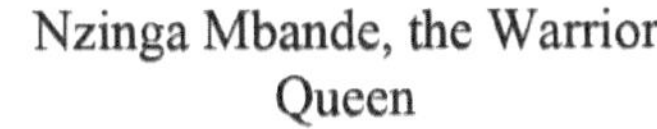

| Nzinga Mbande, the Warrior Queen | King Ngola Kiluanje kia Samba |

The founder and first historical King of Ndonga, Ngola Kiluanje kia Samba, reigned from 1515 to 1556. He became king only a few decades before his daughter, Queen Nzinga Mbande of Ndongo, was born. Ngola Kiluanje kia Samba was a peaceful consensus builder, but it had been a complex mix of political intrigues and tribal battles that had precipitated his rise as ruler. Founded in the highlands of modern Angola near the Atlantic coast, the kingdom of Ndongo's political history was to be inextricably tied to Portuguese colonial interests in west-central Africa. For nearly a century, the armies of Ndongo battled with Portuguese in multiple wars that resulted in the loss of most of Ndongo's territory, until the rise of Queen Njinga ended the deepest colonial expansion into central Africa.

Isaac Samuel, author of 'The Effects of Early Colonial Warfare in Central Africa', describes the warrior queen in the following way: "Queen Njinga of Ndongo is the undoubtedly the best-known Queen in pre-colonial Africa's history. During her remarkable reign, she was involved in dozens of wars with the Portuguese, and forged trans-regional alliances with the Kongo kingdom and the Dutch. She skillfully performed and manipulated several legitimating practices to overcome challenges to her rule that were based on her gender, and the precedent she set produced an equally remarkable dynasty of women with at least six queen regnants succeeding her —an exceptional number in World History."

The Ndonga captives were Kimbundu-speaking people from Kabasa, the capital city, and other urban areas targeted by the Portuguese invasion. The landing of the first Africans in Virginia is one of the most significant events in American history. Although English colonists in Virginia did not invent slavery, *the transition from a handful of bound Ndonga laborers to a legalized system of full-blown chattel slavery took many decades. The year 1619 marks the beginning of a race-based relationship that defined the heart and soul of the American experience for over 400 years.*

However, despite the transformational and civilizing potential of the early 17th century 'Enlightenment' period in Europe, when it came to religion, the general population remained steeped in nightmarish superstitions driven by dramatic visual images that streamed from pulpit sermons filled with graphic depictions of fire and brimstone. This seems to have been the preferred means of religious education and to gain and maintain control of illiterate serf-parishioners during the Middle Ages. The sermons were intended to harangue these uneducated and gullible congregations into obedience and subservience in a culture where the images they did encounter in religious books of the times served to reinforce those same superstitions. John Milton's poem of 1667, *Paradise Lost*, was one such impactful literary mediums for engendering some of the most persistent and disturbing images of life after death.

John Milton's biographer, John Aubrey, writes that Milton began writing the manuscript in about 1658 completing it around 1663, and adds that parts of the poem were written during his "early youth." By 1652, Milton had gone blind and wrote the manuscript entirely through dictation with the aid of friends and secretaries. In addition to his being blind, Milton suffered continuously from acute inflammatory arthritis (known as gout), as well as suffering emotional bouts with depression and guilt after both his second wife and their infant daughter died while he wrote the epic poem.

Paradise Lost is indeed an epic poem. It is divided into ten books filled with terrifying images of hell. Simply put, it is a tale of *good and evil*. Whatever thoughts may emerge when one considers those two fundamental expressions of human nature, there were many superstitions that prevailed among both illiterate commoners and wealthy aristocrats they represented the medieval mindset of a people still emerging out from the dark ages. Many imaginary notions were lifted from the bible as literal truth, and perhaps, that is what kept them from recognizing the common humanity of people who looked and worshipped differently from them in whatever form they may have witnessed. Indentured servants especially, probably would not have had much direct contact with such people although the Moors, known as Blackamoores in medieval England, were indeed an integral part of British society. The "Blackamoores" were Black Muslims, many of whom held high positions in the Royal Court. The English Surname "Moore" is derived from this appellation: "Blacka*moores*".

CHAPTER TWELVE

Draft Proclamation of 1601 To Expel British Blackamoores from England

There were many large aristocratic households (including that of the Queen herself) who also employed black African servants and musicians. As well, parish records show abundant evidence of black people working in London and its surroundings. But at the end of Elizabeth's reign, the Blackamoores were specifically targeted in the 'Draft Proclamation of 1601', a document that was written to expel them from Elizabethan England. she issued several official warrants requesting the removal of 'Blackamoores'.

Draft Proclamation of 1601 on the Expulsion of 'Negroes and Blackamoores'.

This draft proclamation of 1601 is an important document revealing that there must have been a significant proportion of people of different ethnic backgrounds living in Elizabethan England. But the proclamation asks for the deportation of black people, described as 'Negroes (which is the Spanish word for 'black') and 'Blackamoores' from the realm of England. This was justified on the grounds that these people were viewed as Muslim 'infidels' who were draining resources needed by the Queen's 'own white British subjects' at a time of hardship. The full transcript of this manuscript appears on The National Archives website.

In the late 16th century, repeatedly failing harvests had caused an increase in poverty, starvation, and vagrancy. In terms that might sound unnervingly familiar to a modern reader, the expulsion of black people was presented as a *solution*. In fact, the presence of the Blackamoores was so small in number that their absence would have had done little to relieve English suffering. In 1596, a letter was sent to the mayors of London and other cities, arranging for a Lübeck merchant named Caspar van Senden to transport the 'many Blackamoores' (and sell them). This was in exchange for 89 English prisoners whom Van Senden had helped to release from Spanish and Portuguese jails. Yet the masters of these black workers did not consent to the deal, so the demand was repeated in 1596 and again in 1601.

The language of these documents has disturbing implications, suggesting wide-scale racial prejudice [racism]. Importantly, however, some critics like Miranda Kaufmann have challenged the idea that this was a calculated 'piece of racist immigration policy'. Instead, in her book 'Black Tudors', Kaufmann regards it as 'one of many scandalous proposals made by merchants and courtiers in the later part' of Elizabeth's reign, *suggesting* that the 1601 manuscript "may never have gone beyond draft form'. However, the 'Draft Proclamation' remains as a testimony of the *thinking* of the monarchy which led to the establishment of the Royal African Company's business plan – the transatlantic slave trade for it was initiated by 'the Law of Discovery' issued by Pope Nicholas V as a directive to King Alphonso of Portugal was the Papal Bull of 1452. The wording of this document is unequivocal and was directed at Black African Muslim Moors, Arab Muslims, and all indigenous people throughout the world. Again, the Papal Bull were initially directed to the King of Portugal in these clear words: *"to go to the Western coast of Africa and invade, capture, vanquish and subdue all Saracens (Arab Muslims), Moors, pagans and other enemies of Christ and reduce their person to perpetual slavery and to take asway all their possessions and properties."*

This directive was later reissued in 1455, 1456, 1481, 1493, 1506 and 1514, during the reign of King Henry VII from 1485 to 1509. King Henry VII was the immediate predecessor to King Henry VIII who ruled England and who initiated the Protestant Reformation from 1509 to 1547; followed later by Queen Elizabeth I who ruled from 1558 to 1603. Clearly, these directives stood in sharp contrast to the directives given by Jesus Christ Himself when he spoke to His disciples saying: "And he said unto them, Go ye into all the world, and preach the gospel to every creature," --- Mark 16:15, with no mention or suggestion that spreading the gospel meant to 'vanquish, capture, subdue, reduce to perpetual enslavement, and to take away all their possessions and properties' in His Name. In fact, the ignorance, greed and disregard for these peoples and their ancient kingdoms spoke volumes of their lack of humanity. For example, despite the suspicious behavior of the Powhatans when they captured Captain John Smith upon his arrival, he was taken to Powhatan, the chieftain of the village of the empire. This event is reported in <u>Document A & B</u> which were written by Smith himself. In these documents, Smith describes what happened to him which illustrates the civility of the Powhatans: *Pocahontas, the king's dearest daughter, took my head in her arms and laid down her own upon it to save me from death."* [35]

The sweetness and simplicity of Smith's words in Document-C should alert us to the need to take pause and not rush to any judgement. We must take care to put all events of the time into context. To condemn European Christian theologians, men who were responsible for upholding Christian theology in the colonies, would be a form of joining partners with God, for He alone is Judge. However, the demonization of the Powhatans as savages was and remains a strategic weapon which upheld not the teachings of Christ but that of decrees as outlined in the Vatican Papal Bulls of the 15th and 16th centuries. This is deserving of our condemnation.

A hundred years after Spanish conquistador, Hernan Cortes arrived in Mexico in 1519, the Ndongo tribesmen arrived aboard the English privateer ship White Lion in what is today's Fort Monroe in Hampton, Virginia which suggests that England was late getting in on the exploitation of Africa and its millions of black Africans.

In 1491, King Nzinga of the Kongo Kingdom, of which Ndongo was a powerful vassal state, converted to Roman Catholicism, taking the Christian name João, after coming into contact with Portuguese colonial explorers. The conversion facilitated trade with the Portuguese and other European nations. Once arrived in Virginia, these African people were traded in exchange for supplies. Several days later, a second ship (the Treasurer) arrived in Virginia with additional enslaved Africans. Both groups had been captured by English privateers from the Spanish slave ship San Juan Bautista. They are the first recorded Africans to arrive in England's mainland American colonies. Although English colonists in Virginia did not invent slavery, and the transition from a handful of bound African laborers to a legalized system of full-blown chattel slavery took many decades, 1619 marks the beginning of a European ethnocentric-based imposition of bondage that defined the foundation of the African experience in America --- slavery. Hampton's status as the location for the first landing is a double-edged sword. Today, we are uniquely positioned to tell a powerful story, but it is a challenging narrative fraught with myth, controversy, and contradictions that strike at the heart of the intersection between slavery in America and the freedom it espoused.

For any serious discourse on this subject, it must include what took place at Point Comfort in 1619. If for no other reason the weight of this consequential event is important for it changed the course of life on the entire planet and its legacy has and continues to affect every aspect of our lives today. In order to grasp the complexities of how *human thoughts* manifest as history, legacy, and life itself any serious social activist must suspend generational anger, bitterness, confusion, guilt, or denial, and look for opportunities to transform society from division and ambiguity to unity. But first, let us take in three major considerations that demonstrate that capitalism, racism, and slavery did not come into existence as some happen-stance phenomenon. They were and remain the three pillars of an ideological framework which is expressed as *world power by a single race or tribe of people, extremes of wealth and poverty, and consumerism* --- how to get it, how to expand it, and how to maintain it.

In order to achieve all of the above, a system based on the above features can only be put into place if the adherents of this philosophy can convince a majority of people to identify with it. It does not require others to *believe* in materialism in the same way that religion requires a belief in God, and neither does it require any formal education or indoctrination nor an awareness of any possible adverse psychological effect that it may have for both the individual and society as a whole. In the soul of the materialist all that is required is the willingness to sublimate that which is unwanted for that which is desired: poverty for wealth, obscurity for fame, weakness for power, high-minded aspiration for expediency. However, what eventually becomes clear to the materialist is that to persuade a significant amount of people to abandon that which has been considered a spiritual imperative, a substitute philosophy must needs be found to neutralize its influence. Seduction, therefore, must replace these inherent imperative, and involve such trickery as deception, manipulation of religious texts, the marginalization of natural inhibitions., and a wanton disregard of all spiritual principles. Greed, then, necessary must be raised to the level of economic principle whereby the concept of survival of the fittest can take root. It must be enshrined and maintained as the highest achievement anyone can attain.. And, to assuage any possible sense of guilt or injustice, and to reduce tax liability on wealth, a system must be put in place to provide a guiltless off-rank to those who make charitable donations to mitigate the needs of the dispossessed and the poor, thus ensuring an undisturbed and continual accumulation of riches for the wealthy few, further dividing humanity into waring camps. Every civilization, ancient to modern, eventually has its rendezvous with materialism, that is, the tendency to consider material possessions and physical comfort as being of more importance than spiritual values --- love, peace, honesty, non-violence, faithfulness, trustworthiness, etc. Because materialism is as much a philosophical concept as it is a concrete objective, views that contradict it are seen as undermining the very premise of society and a threat to its existence. This view eventually has to deny the existence of spirit and gradually becomes accustomed to a reliance upon the concrete evidence of mankind's singular preoccupation with survival in a material world. Many see this as standing opposed to mystical and spiritual concepts, and seeks to explain all phenomena, including the workings of the human mind, as observable and quantifiable --- how much lava flows from a volcano; how much gold has yet to be mined--- material concerns having nothing to do with spiritual imperatives that, since the emergence of human life on the planet, transcend human consciousness to safeguard human survival in a material world

In its 1985 'The Promise of World Peace: A Statement to the Peoples of the World', the Universal House of Justice addresses this phenomenon in the following manner: "Most particularly, it is in the glorification of material pursuits, at once the progenitor and common feature of all such ideologies, that we find the roots which nourish the falsehood that human beings are incorrigibly selfish and aggressive. It is here that the ground must be cleared for the building of a new world fit for our descendants."

CHAPTER THIRTEEN

The Papal Bulls -- Europe's Revised Version of the
Teachings of Christ:
'The Law of Discovery' and 'The Age of Exploration'

In 1852, economic theorist, Herbert Spencer published "A Theory of Population." Spencer described his concept as being similar to Charles Darwin's "survival of the fittest" after reading his 1864 publication of 'On the Origin of Species.' In Spencer's book, he draws the parallels between his own economic theories and Darwin's biological, evolutionary theories. He writes: "This survival of the fittest, which I have here sought to express in mechanical terms, is that which Mr. Darwin has called 'natural selection' ... the preservation of favored races in the struggle for life."

At this juncture, it's a good idea to note the humble beginnings of the Papacy. In the Church's first three hundred years, many of those who succeeded Peter were obscure figures none of whom were actual apostles of Christ. When we reflect upon the death of the apostle Peter, his death bring to mind the essential quality of spirit that characterized his papacy --- absolute humility in the face of death.

He was executed by crucifixion, which was ordered by the Roman Emperor Nero. Nero had blamed the city's Christians for the terrible fire that had ravaged Rome and rather than being crucified head up, Peter requested to be crucified upside down because he felt unworthy to die in the same manner as Christ.

Many of the early popes also suffered martyrdom right alongside the early faithful of the Church especially during periods of persecution. This relationship with the lay people of the Church was intimate, nurturing, and based on the kind of ministry that Christ Himself had practiced in Israel which, by the 15th century was a far cry from the papacy as the Church evolved, while attracting new adherents throughout the centuries. By 1452, when the Papal Bulls were decreed, all that had changed. Few believers had ever traveled to Rome, and certainly even fewer had ever even seen or knew who the pope was by name. To this day, the papacy is the office held by the pope as the head of the Catholic Church. The term, 'catholic', means 'universal'. With this term, the ministry of Christ was made clear. It was intended to spread far beyond the narrow confines of Judaism and Israel and embrace the far reaches of the planet regardless of tribe, ethnicity, color, previous religious affiliation, gender, nationality, etc. As a religious institution, the Papacy spans from the time of the disciple Peter to the present day. The Vatican had become the administrative center of all Christendom. To describe it as an administrative center alone in 1452 is misleading. The Vatican had become the Seat of Christianity and had issued a number of Papal Bulls ranging from canonical law, granting royal marriages, and excommunicating the same for disobedience to the pope. By the 15th century the function of the pope was no longer as *co-religionist* but as the Vicar of Christ, that is, Christ's representative on earth. The first recorded use of the term "Vicar of Christ" is found in the epistles of Tertullian, written in the late 2nd and early 3rd centuries. At the time, the term referred to the Holy Spirit since Christ was no longer physically present to perform miracles. It was therefore considered to be the Holy Spirit who intervened on His behalf as his Vicar, performing miracles and protecting the Church by granting the pope infallibility. There were other more mundane roles that Tertullian attributed to the Holy Spirit as Vicar such as "the direction of discipline, the revelation of the Scriptures, the reformation of the intellect, and the advancement toward the better things." As a result, by the 15th century in Europe, the pope's decrees held both a powerful spiritual and political leverage even above that of emperors and kings, elevating the Papal Bulls and the 'Law of Discovery' on par with 'the Word of God'.

The impact of the Papal Bull decrees upon young Catholic European adventurers cannot be underestimated. Just as space exploration today has radically broadened our sense of who we are in the universe, completely transforming our way of thinking and being, "global exploration by sea" had the same life-changing effect upon the young minds and imaginations of 16th century lads throughout Christendom. To be able to "see the world," travel long distances aboard massive expeditionary sea vessels was enough to spur on many a young lad, adventurous peasants to trade in their plain., heavy wool and linen handmade clothing and straw hats for seaman's life on the wide open seas. It was just too hard to resist. On New Years Day, 1726, a publication was released to the British public. The name of this publication was titled, 'Gulliver's Travels.' Once again poor British lads were suddenly caught up in a frenzy of excitement as they heard or listened to readings of tales about exotic peoples in far away lands that they never heard of, while learning at the same time that what they had always believed to be a flat earth was a round rocky mass of dirt and seas floating in space, circling round the sun rather than the sun circling around *it*. The story was written by author and Anglican clergyman, Jonathan Swift. Those must've been very exciting times. Some, I'm sure, only wanted to heed the call to spread the Faith of Jesus Christ in foreign lands; however, others wanted only a chance --- a shot at whatever paltry slice of the colonial pie that were rumored to be had in orphanages, in the streets and country sides, in the taverns, and in the pubs of London. Simultaneously, they would be hailed as patriots, beneficiaries, and investors .... seamlessly replacing whatever religious beliefs that they may have had with the new materialist concept of Darwin's 'preservation of favored races in the struggle for life' also known as *the survival of the fittest*. This whole new world had opened up not just for the Portuguese and the Spanish but redounded to the French and British too. Right before their eyes, with new visions pummeled their imaginations as new possibilities ... new ideas swirled throughout these European capitals, the butcher shops, and unlettered peasant country sides of the entire continent, captivating the imaginations of every young wanna-be explorer, with inventions like the printing press having already put the Bible within easy reach and understanding of everyone. Spreading the gospel was now made far easier for it was written in plain language that even the least literate sharecropper could understand. However, that was not necessarily sufficient reason to risk life and limb upon those newly chartered, perilous, pirate infested waters to unknown lands no matter what we've been led to believe. However, gold, power, and unimaginable wealth, now these were the stuff of dreams --- big dreams, big enough to spur on even the most-timid of adventurers among them. Then as today, major British and Spanish commercial enterprises were moving preemptively to lay claims to lands in both Africa and the new world. The Papal Bulls had laid out to them what can only be considered by them to be a religious mandate: the 'Law of Discovery, and were feverishly developing campaigns to exploit this new craze for global domination. Young explorers, eager young men --- dreamers --- were even being signed up as they boarded ships ready to sail. These well-connected wealthy enterprises would see to it that these young, illiterate boys and men got plenty of action on the high seas, unwittingly impregnating their hearts and minds with visions of conquering unsuspecting indigenous tribes across the globe, giving birth to even greater and newer ideas that would later come to fruition: individual liberty and independent wealth.

It may be reasonable to conclude that the anglicized interpretation of that which Christ instructed His disciples, that is, "to spread the gospel throughout the world" resonated with the belief that they were entitled to the "keys of heaven". In hindsight, if this new idea was a chimera --- intended to obscure and deflect attention from some future form of earthly kingdom whereby the promises of Christ upon His return would redound to them _alone_, it would be right to say, perhaps, that Christ's words were pure speculation and open to interpretation; or, perhaps it was thought that "commoners" of whatever color were excluded from entry because their lives were considered to be the very antithesis of the spiritual virtues inherent in the teachings of Moses and Jesus Christ. This would have inclined them to rely upon their lower nature and to look down upon subservience in the same way the elite of India did, believing it was their right to do so. For certainly, spreading the gospel on a global scale would require strategy, material funds, shrewd business skills and a belief that what they were doing was consistent with the teachings of Christ. For how else could wealth and power possibly shut them out from attaining entry into the very "Kingdom of God" that the gospel had instructed them to strive for?

Thus, the acquisition and application of such a virtue as *justice* could be considered a prerogative and not a moral imperative.

Charles Dickens' Ebenezer Scrooge

However, it was Jesus Christ Himself who warned His disciples that "it is easier for a camel to go through the eye of a needle, than for a rich man to enter into the kingdom of God. Therefore, speak I to them in parables: because seeing they see not; and hearing they hear not, neither do they understand. And in them is fulfilled the prophecy of Isaias, which saith, 'By hearing ye shall hear, and shall not understand; and seeing ye shall see and shall not perceive: For this people's heart is waxed gross, and *their* ears are dull of hearing, and their eyes they have closed; lest at any time they should see with *their* eyes, and hear with *their* ears, and should understand with *their* heart, and should be converted, and I should heal them. When any one heareth the word of the kingdom, and understandeth *it* not, then cometh the wicked *one*, and catcheth away that which was sown in his heart. This is he which received seed by the wayside." -- Matthew 13:16

According to the Hindu Tantra tradition spiritual reality is "a single, infinite, indivisible whole whose nature is consciousness (aka pure knowing). By this definition of reality, it is means *everything there is*; that which is outside of oneself and that which is inside of oneself." Thus, one can conclude that this conundrum that Matthew recounts in 13:16 has always been the same inner battle or jihad, as Muhammad called it, for every individual in every generation. This inner battle with reality, or truth, will either result in an individual's sense of peace and tranquility or a very disruptive sense of cognitive self-disassociation. Any form of disassociation from self is accompanied by willful denial! The closing of the eyes and ears is what rebellious Hebrews did in Egypt under Moses, and what the pharisees did in Jerusalem under Jesus Christ, ultimately twisting the Sacred Words of these prophets in pursuit of their own moribund agendas, unmindful of the inner meanings of Their Words. This is the crucible of all who wield power and religious influence over the "common man". Those who choose to interpret scripture to fit their own imaginings to maintain control and influence for their own personal gain. The Divine Reality may have been in place to protect them, but greed, covetousness, murder, and theft can never outwit the Will of God. After all, not coveting one's neighbor's house, or wife, or his manservant or maidservant, or his ox, or his ass, or anything that belongs to his is neighbor, including his wife, have always been temptations too great to resist. And so it is that a good offense beats a good defense and sets into perpetual motion the need to justify the immense land grabs, the enslavement, and the genocide of a people --- by any means necessary. Blind faith has never been a spiritual path in any religion. Corruption, greed, and hypocrisy, however, have always been the mainstays of kings and rulers, leaders of religion and industry, and those who just shut their eyes and ears to attain their worldly dominance.

Ancient Indigenous Civilizations in the "New World"

What none of the European 'spreaders of the gospel' could ever have anticipated was the ancient Mayan religious prophecy that had thousands of years earlier prophesied this Old World – New World encounter:

"Whether by sheer luck or by providence, the time of Cortés' arrival in the Yucatan (Mexico) coincided with the prophesied return of the Aztec Prophet, Quetzalcoatl. During the 16th century, Quetzalcoatl – whose name in the Nahuatl language means "precious serpent" or "plumed serpent", was one of the principal Aztec deities in the region. According to the Maya, Quetzalcoatl, who was among the "deities of creation", was forced into exile by Tezcatlipoca, another principal Aztec prophet. According to the narrative, Quetzalcoatl sailed away east into the Atlantic on a raft with a promise to return on a specific date and year, the First Year of the Reed (aka New Fire Ceremony) which occurred once every 52 years." [36]

On November 7, 1519, Spanish explorers Hernan Cortés, Bernal Diaz and a shipload of a military force numbering 1,000 men arrived on the shores of the Yucatan, exactly one hundred years before the African Ndongo captives arrived in the Virginia colony. Their arrival occurred exactly on the date that Quetzacoatl had prophesied He would return, so reminiscent of Jesus Christ's exhortations to His apostles. Bernal Diaz del Castillo, one of Cortés' men, writes in his journal in 1519 and gives a description of the land known as Tenochtitlán:

> "Warriors, seated in serried rows on the beach, facing east, waiting peacefully as our ship sailed to the shore. I saw palaces and temples, towers … women dressed in white robes. We saw all those cities and villages built on water; and the other great towns on dry land, and that straight and level causeway leading to Mexico, we were astounded." In closing he writes, "To convert them to Christianity, we had to destroy that city." [37]

CHAPTER FOURTEEN

Entropy, White Supremacy and Systemic Racism

Author, James Clear's 'Entropy: Why Life Always Seems to Get More Complicated (Mental Models)' takes on a familiar adage that's been around for decades. It is called 'Murphy's Law' which states that "anything that can go wrong, will go wrong." He writes further that "this concise statement refers to the annoying tendency of life to cause trouble and make things difficult. Problems seem to arise naturally on their own, while solutions always require our attention, energy, and effort. Life never seems to just work itself out for us. If anything, our lives have become more complicated with life itself gradually declining into disorder rather than becoming a peaceful social and political structure where coexistence can thrive. But why is that?

As a common adage, Murphy's Law is tossed around in conversation without much thought given to it in an era when nanoseconds are the measure of time. This shift is not just related to technological advances but is one of the great forces of our universe. This force is so fundamental to the way our world works that it permeates nearly every endeavor we pursue. It drives many of the problems we face and leads to disarray. It is the one force that governs everybody's life --- entropy."

According to theoretical physicist, Professor Sean Carroll, "entropy is the measurement of disorder. A chaotic and disorderly state can be said to have high entropy, whereas an efficient, harmonious state is a state of stability, order, and balance and is considered a *low entropy state.*"

This interconnectedness of these two forces, the yin yang of existence is the history of the world. At its most superficial level, the written accounts of world history is born of accounts of wars of the past --- its heroes, its victories, and perhaps with forced humility its losses. At its most sublime, however, it is humanity's intimate and personal often unspoken collective accounts and memories of what was, what is, and what can be with none of the guardrails that time and scholarly interpretations later impose. This kind of history is the essence of low entropy for it is a seamless stream of shared consciousness that continually evolves taking humanity to higher and higher states of consciousness even after we have passed. For it is *His* story, not ours. And when inevitably high entropy resurges, low entropy, like a dancer waiting in the wings, remains hidden from view so that to whatever level consciousness has evolved that it stands poised for a new and stronger resurgence despite the chaos. No matter which state we find ourselves living in both high entropy (chaos) and low entropy (harmony) are necessary in order for humans to recognize the need to abandon outworn and obsolete concepts of reality. Thus, low entropy exists as a consolidation of the gems of wisdom that creates civilization itself. It is the foundation of peace, justice, love, and all the virtues that humankind has continued to strive for millennia; and high entropy exists in order to shift human consciousness away from corruption, disorder, and injustice; and towards higher and higher states of low entropy.

High and Low Entropy Plays Out as the Christian Religious Cycle Comes to an End

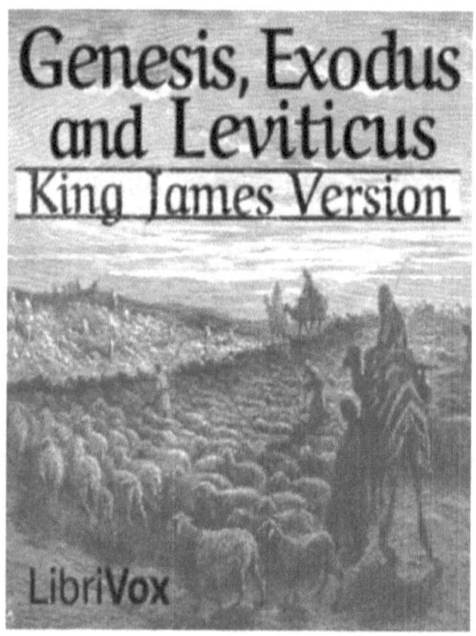

The first complete Bible in Spanish was printed in Basel in 1569, translated and authored by Casiodoro de la Reina. The first complete Bible in English was published by the Protestant 'Church of England'. The name 'Protestant' perfectly described the aims of the English Reformation which was to protest against the Pope's authority. To this day, this act is considered by the Roman Catholic Church to be heretical. The King James Version was commissioned by King James I and printed in 1611 AD.

Europe's complete conversion to Christianity took about 1,500. Over time, the King James Version **slowly replaced** the much older original texts of the Geneva, the Catholic Codex, the Coptic and other Bibles circulating around medieval Europe up to that time. Before then, the Eastern Roman Empire had officially adopted Christianity in AD 380. The First Council of Nicaea had been convened in AD 325 and was attended by Christian bishops from all around the empire as mandated by then Roman Emperor, Constantine I, who himself had been a "pagan" (a person holding religious beliefs other than those of the main or recognized religions) before converting to Christianity. The Council was held in what is known today as İznik, Turkey. As regards Constantine's conversion to Christianity, the narrative is that he converted after having had a 'vision of Christ upon the cross' suspended in mid-air. This ecumenical council was the first effort to attain consensus on beliefs and practices, and to select from the many narratives circulating throughout the empire, effectively unifying the content of the Bible. Intense debates ensued among its diverse racial, cultural, and political factions --- often bitter enemies --- who all participated as church bishops in the assembly representing all of Christendom from Northern Europe to Egypt and Ethiopia.

Among the many bishops in attendance at the Council of Nicaea was Saint Moses, the Black, so-called because of the dark color of his skin. Although an Ethiopian, Saint Moses lived in 4th century Egypt. In his youth he had been conscripted into slavery to an Egyptian government official, but after he committed a murder, he was banished and joined a band of robbers. Years later, Saint Moses repented and became an ascetic monk, and then became a priest and a notable Desert priest. Tested and proven by his efforts and sincerity, he was later instated as Bishop of Coptic Egypt.

The 'Curse of Ham'

> "And Noah said, 'Cursed be Canaan; a servant of servants shall he be unto his brethren'" --- Genesis 9:25, the Geneva Bible.

This **"curse of Ham"** is described in the Book of Genesis, Chapter 9, Verse 25, as having been imposed by the patriarch Noah upon Ham's son Canaan, Noah's grandson. It occurs in the context of Noah's drunkenness after "the Flood" and is provoked when Ham sees "the nakedness of his father" and he and his brothers cover him. According to biblical scholars, the exact nature of Ham's transgression and the reason Noah cursed Canaan when it was Ham's son who had "sinned" have been debated for over 2,000 years. And, according to these same biblical scholars, the original purpose of the story had to do with justifying the subjection of the Canaanites to the Israelites who, after some 430 years of enslavement in Egypt, were newly arrived in the "Promised Land". But, centuries later, from the 16th to the 19th centuries, new "interpretations" commissioned by the royal houses of Christendom (Europe), that is, France, British and Germany were published and circulated as an explanation for the existence of black-skinned Africans and to justify their enslavement in what would be (for them) one of the most lucrative commercial world enterprises launched on a scale that had never occurred in human history – the transatlantic slave trade."

Europe had been steeped in multiple superstitious beliefs for millennia. By the Dark Ages, which lasted from the 5th to the 14th centuries was a period of 900 years following the fall of the Roman Empire to the Renaissance and was still undergoing Christianization.

During this period the growing sectarian religious rivalries among Christian European monarchs and religious clerics often clashed violently over different Christian tenets, principles, and beliefs of the faithful. The diverse, rival kingdoms that comprised what we refer to today as Europe were constantly at each other's throats for power and territory were held firmly in the grip of the Holy Roman Empire under the head of the Roman Catholic Church, the Italian Popes. These popes themselves came from competing rival tribal factions and were at constant war with one another. For instance, the Guelphs and the Ghibellines were rival families with one faction supporting the Pope (Pope John XXII) and the other supporting the Holy Roman Emperor (Charles V) who lived in the city-states of Central and Northern Italy. Throughout this volatile political situation in Europe over the next few centuries, the popes managed to maintain control over the Papal States. When the Carolingian Empire broke up in the 9th century, the papacy fell under the control of the Roman nobility.

European history is the history of powerful monarchs' failure to recognize the station of any divine Prophet as Messengers of God other than Jesus Christ in spite of the biblical record of progressive revelation which named forty-eight such Holy Personages in the Old Testament --- *Abraham, Isaac, Jacob, Moses, Joshua, Phinhas, Eli, Elkanah, Samuel, Gad, Natan, David, Ahijah the Shilonite,* Solomon, all the way up to Micah. Any espousal of a "foreign prophet" was seen as apostasy and heretical and was met with swift, vehement, and violent consequences that precipitated the fall of any monarch and expulsion from the Catholic Church. Any monarch who disobeyed the Pope was publicly declared a heretic and marginalized by order of Papal Decree. Apostasy among the common people was always met with accusations of witchcraft, public beheadings or being publicly burned at the stake. Yet, the gleaming gem of "progressive revelation" – the progressive and eternal Plan of God through His Prophets -- lay hidden within those ancient pages of historical revelations which are filled with spiritual intersessions as described in literary metaphors and parables that preserved the essence of God's relationship with humanity --- His covenant which is explicitly stated in Deuteronomy 31:6:

> "Be strong and courageous. Do not fear or be in dread of
> them, for it is the LORD your God who goes with you.
> He will not leave you or forsake you."

And in Hebrews 13:5 we are reminded of His presence in our lives:

> "Keep your life free from love of money, and be content
> with what you have, for he has said, "I will never leave
> you nor forsake you."

God's Covenant *is* the relationship that humanity has with God. But only the *pure in heart*, those infused with the power of the Holy Spirit, can recognize it: "Blessed are the pure in heart, for they will *see* God" is what Matthew 5:8 unequivocally states. Therefore, human interpretations of the Torah and the multitude of disputed canonical texts of the New Testament throughout the centuries have clouded that which was and is as apparent as the noonday sun --- Progressive Revelation, the eternal Divine Covenant between God and man extended necessarily over time in evolutionary stages.

The sacred texts were again re-translated in 1604 by commission of King James I in an attempt to unify *his* kingdom under the newly established Church of England (aka the Anglican Church); and, as noted earlier, was published, and widely distributed throughout the American colonies.

From the very beginning of the Age of Enlightenment and the Age of Exploration, that which galvanized the colonial goals of European powers to invest and to commission explorers to circumnavigate the earth was in direct response to the six 'Papal Bulls' decreeing "the Law of Discovery." That "law" was intentionally ordained by Pope Nicholas as an obligation for the explorers to confiscate indigenous lands, its gold and abundant natural resources, to enslave its peoples and to decimate indigenous cultures, religions, and languages all in the name of Christ. It was then essential to this mission to win over reluctant adherents to its colonial cause. Enter the translations of the original Geneva Bible into English, an act which drove even deeper the wedge that had been created when King Henry VIII divorced and banished Catherine of Aragon and married Anne Boleyn. By now the English Reformation was beginning to take shape as other more pressing needs were yet unfulfilled, namely a moral justification for the brutal usurpation, exploitation, and colonization of ancient peoples and their lands. The establishment of the transatlantic slave trade stood in sharp contradiction to the teachings of Christ. In order to enlist public support of uneducated and illiterate, marginally Christian serfs and peasants, a remedy had to be found to relieve this underclass of any guilt and fear of divine retribution. And, considering the fact that this same underclass was undergoing deep confusion by the discovery that the earth was not flat but a sphere, a program of "re-education" had to be put in place.

Throughout the Middle Ages, the most common modes of persuasion to influence public opinion be they rebels, illiterate serfs, sharecroppers, or peasants was the use of sermons, superstitions, imprisonment, public burnings at the stake, public floggings, and decapitation (the guillotine in France). However, in 1611, in order to gain control over the aristocracy and to unite his kingdom under a single biblical narrative (just as Constantine had done in convening the 'Council of Nicaea), a new translation was commissioned to replace both the Geneva Bible (one of the oldest Christian Bibles in all of Christendom) and the *Vaticanus Codex* which was the Roman Catholic Church's Version of the Bible. Again, this re-translation was intended to support the king's own royal aims and was considered 'heresy' by the Catholic Church of Rome.

Today, that Bible is the "sacred" text of the Church of England. It is exactly what it states, a version, the King James Version of the Bible. King James I not only had the Bible re-translated, but he also changed it. Until 1611, there was only one common version of the bible in England, namely the Roman Catholic Codex. The Roman Catholic Codex is made up of seventy-three books. King James published the KJV with sixty-six books, seven less than the Roman Catholic Bible. So, what does this all have to do with white supremacy, racism, colonialism, and the Papal Bulls? Fasten your seat belts.

CHAPTER FIFTEEN

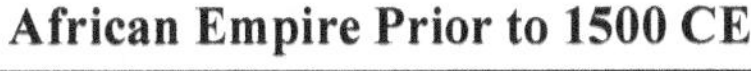

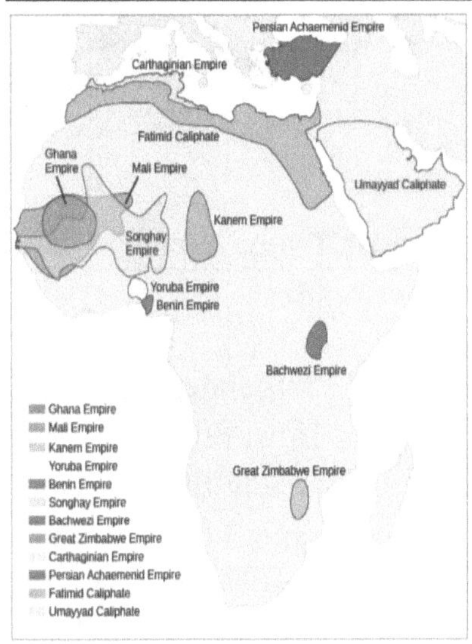

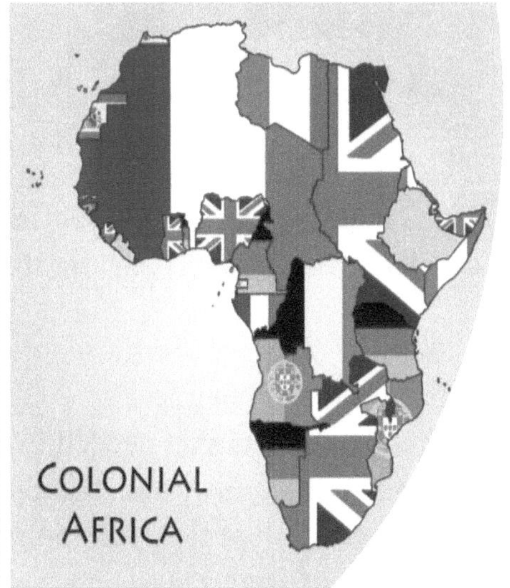

Before 1500 C.E., little was known about Africa and its Ancient pre-colonial Black African Empires. By the end of 1800 CE European Colonialism on the African continent was hailed as a thing that had already taken place and decided before affected African countries and peoples even heard anything about it, leaving them with no option but to accept it --- the very definition of a *fait accompli.* But this had not just happened on the African continent. On a distant continent, The United States of America as well as the United States of Mexico were busy with their own usurpation of land and decimation of peoples, cultures, histories, languages, and religions all under the guise of spreading the *Word of God.*

The Groundwork for Extracting Egypt from Africa – The Establishment of the Transatlantic Slave trade

And so, after the Berlin Conference of 1885 ended, the work of slicing up the continent of Africa began. However, there were numerous problems that needed to be _fixed_, namely the thousands of Kemetic sculptures and the Sphinx of Kemet at Giza which unequivocally identified the founder and pharaohs of Kemet as Black Nubians from the Sudan. So fanatical were the monarchs of Europe to project their own racial and cultural superiority (even amongst themselves) that religious clerics, scientists, philosophers, and scholars were commissioned to extract Egypt entirely from the African continent.

Artists too were among those who were enlisted to Europeanize existing Egyptian monuments in an attempt to erase the origin and history of Ancient Kemet and (especially) its Nubian (Sudanese) connections. And the most profound and efficient way to justify the rewriting of that history and the sacking of priceless Egyptian artifacts --- was the Holy Bible by rewriting, re-translating, and by distorting its original text, and making it the crux of its self-proclaimed mandate for global colonialism.

The Crafting of the Constitution of the United States

The anti-black racial interpretation of the 'Curse of Ham' found in Genesis was deliberate, and it was embedded in the American consciousness for over 400 years. Its near narcissistic theology is directly connected to the racial philosophies of John Locke and Montesquieu which greatly influenced the crafting of the Constitution of the United States in 1787. Today, these two men's thoughts conflate to obscure the West's underlying worldview of reality, history and the civilizations and peoples of what is today called "third world" lands and cultures. The American system is a hybrid form of government. The "democratic system" we now have is not based solely upon Greek and Roman models though that is how it has been presented throughout American history in school textbooks, the media, etc. Indeed, the American system of government was essentially embarked upon as an "experiment" which, at its foundation, is antithetical namely to the European concept of 'the divine right of monarchies'. However shunned, this particular concept as well as Greek and Roman aristocracies, the French monarchy and aristocracy, and the ancient Persian concept of the divine right of monarchy are also shunned. What many American citizens are unaware of is that the Constitution of the United States combines a mixture of political concepts borrowed from the Iroquois Confederacy as well as other indigenous cultures and ancient African civilizations. All of these forms of governments were debated by the Founders and formulated to create the Constitution of the United States of America that we have today.

The colonial period in Virginia began in 1607 with the landing of the first one hundred forty-four English settlers, sailors, and indentured servants at Jamestown on May 13, 1607, and was established by the Virginia Company of London. This corporate entity was called Jamestown, named for King James I, and was the first permanent British colony in North America. The colony ended after the American Revolution ended, and, in 1776, with the signing of the Declaration of Independence, established the Commonwealth of Virginia. Although a thriving Indian society had existed for thousands of years before the English arrived, war with the European settlers and the introduction of new diseases for which the Indians had no resistance spelled disaster for them. Meanwhile, the English colonists just barely survived, suffering through summer droughts and near winter starvation. Salvation came to the colony in the form of smoking tobacco, when John Rolfe cultivated a variety of tobacco that sold well in England. In 1619, a General Assembly convened, bringing limited self-government to the Virginia colony. That same year Virginia brought the first Africans to Virginia. For most of the 1600s British indentured servants worked the colony's tobacco fields, but by 1705 the Virginia colony had become a slave society. Nearly all power was in the hands of white male landowners, who ran the government and, by law, belonged to the Church of England. Women who were married and worked at home were considered "good wives". Those who refused such "proper" roles were considered troublesome and even accused of witchcraft. And while Virginia's ruling men did not encourage women to be independent, they nevertheless fought for their own independence, taking full part in the American Revolution (1775–1783).

President John Adams

Chief Tecumseh

When the American Revolutionary War came to an end, the delegates to the Constitutional Convention met in 1787 to debate what form of government the United States should have. There were no contemporary democracies in Europe from which they could draw inspiration. The most democratic forms of government that any of the convention members had personally encountered were those of Native American nations. Of particular interest was the Iroquois Confederacy, which historians have argued wielded a significant influence on the U.S. Constitution. The evidence that exists that the delegates studied Native governments appear in the three-volume handbook John Adams wrote for the convention surveying different types of governments and ideas about government. It included European philosophers John Locke and Montesquieu, whom U.S. history textbooks have long identified as constitutional influences; but it also included the Iroquois Confederacy and other Indigenous governments, which many of the delegates knew through personal experience: "You had the Cherokee chiefs having dinner with Thomas Jefferson's father in Williamsburg, Virginia, and then in the northern area of course you had this Philadelphia interaction with the Delaware and the Iroquois tribesmen." [38]

Sadly, to this day, this vital information regarding the contributions made by Cherokee and Iroquois Chiefs to the Crafting of the Constitution of the United States has been completely marginalized with no historical attribution to the Cherokee and Iroquois in American history.

Haiti: Smoke and Mirrors – Now You See It, Now You Don't

The Haitian Revolution of 1803 and the United States' Purchase of the Louisiana Territory

The Battle of Waterloo marked the defeat of Napoleon Bonaparte I in a final two-pronged war, the last of several wars known as the Napoleonic Wars. On June 22, 1815, four days after losing the conflict, Napoleon abdicated as emperor of France for the second and last time and was exiled to the island of St. Helena off the coast of Africa after his defeat. To this day, this reality, like the crusty memories of a defeated old soldier, continues to torment the French people, reducing them to a cantankerous bunch who do not want to be reminded of this life-changing episode of history. For as French novelist, Victor Hugo poetically lamented, "Waterloo was not a battle; it was the changing face of the universe." The facts remain that the Napoleonic Wars took the lives of five million people, and Waterloo, especially, laid the groundwork for the later establishment of both the European Union, NATO and the United Nations. However, in 1806, there was another significant historical shift which *changed the face of the universe.* It was a shift that most historians have completely dismissed as a simple *slave rebellion.* In the midst of France's rendezvous with destiny, by 1806, the Holy Roman Empire headed by the Kaiser of Germany was dissolved. This dissolution created a spiritual vacuum that inevitably demanded to be filled.

Napoleon Exhumes an Embalmed Ancient Kemet (Egyptian) Body

At the end of the 18th century, in 1798, Emperor Napoleon Bonaparte I stepped foot on the desert sands of Egypt for the very first time and faced the Great Sphinx and the Pyramid of Giza and wondered what great people had built such magnificent ancient monuments along the banks of the Nile at the edge of the most inhospitable desert in the world … the Sahara. And thus, was kick-started the very first archaeological study of ancient Kemet, known today as Egyptology. Napoleon was a general with multiple titles: General of the French Revolution and ruler of France, First Consul of the French Republic, Emperor of the French, King of Italy (all under the name Napoleon I) from May 18, 1804 thru April 6, 1814, and was briefly restored as Emperor of France from March 20 to June 22, 1815.

On the other hand, the enslaved African prince from Dohemy (Benin), Toussaint L'Overture was fluent in Fon, French, Spanish, and Yoruba, was elevated to general in the French army, and was a Doctor of Medicine. In 1791, he led the Haitian people in a bloody revolution initially against France, and later against Spain and England, and, in 1803, defeated them all. The failure of these three colonial powers to put down the Haitian revolution made Haiti a commercial, political, and trade pariah but established Haiti as the only 'free' nation in the New World headed by African people. L'Overture was invited to France to negotiate post-war settlements but instead was jailed at the Fort de Joux. Although Louverture died in prison before the final and most violent stage of the Haitian Revolution in 1803, his achievements set the grounds for the Haitian army's final victory.

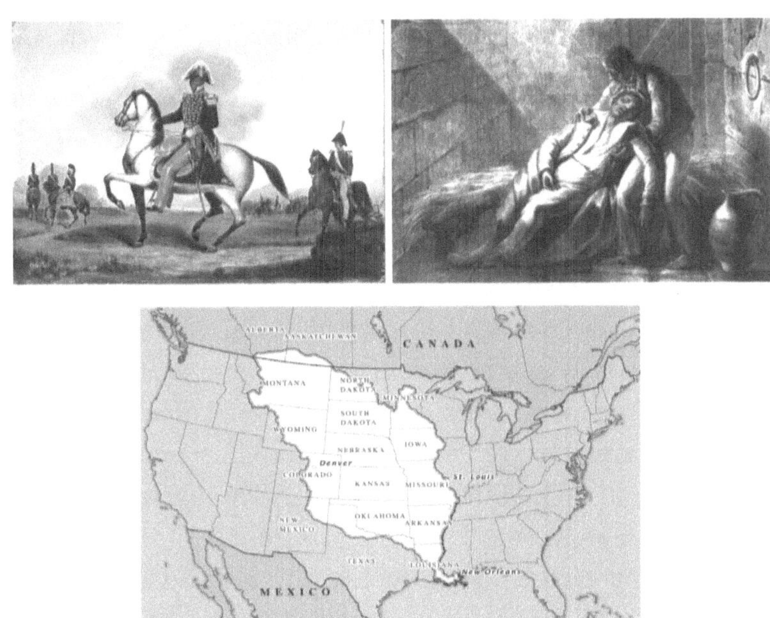

Consequently, the impending war between France and Great Britain and the probable British naval blockade of France, combined with French economic difficulties and loss of prestige and power, prompted Napoleon Bonaparte to sell-off the Louisiana Territory to the United States. President Thomas Jefferson seized the opportunity to double the size of the newly founded United States of America giving it a seemingly inexhaustible supply of new farmland in the mid-Western region while instilling terror within him fearing that the successful Haitian Revolution would spur enslaved peoples in the United States to revolt and undermine the expansionist aims of the young, fledgling nation. The fact that the Louisiana Purchase was made possible by Prince General Toussaint L'Ouverture's defeat of French, Spanish and British forces by the enslaved African Dahomey tribe of Benin remains one the most recognizable characteristics of European thought of the period.

Why, you may ask, is this important to know? Because immediately after the revolution, the United States, under the presidency of Thomas Jefferson severed its diplomatic relationship to Haiti which, as a French-ruled colony, had provided nearly all the American and European imports of sugar and coffee imports. These trade arrangements suddenly came to a screeching halt.

Not only had the United States benefited from the success of Toussaint L'Overture revolution which had forced Napoleon to sell the Louisiana Territory to the United States, Jefferson recognized that the African Haitian's success in freeing themselves from oppression had the potential to spur upheavals against slavery in his own country. White abolitionists, too, were a major concern, and plantation owners' fears of a similar revolution spreading to the South became the government's major consideration. Against this backdrop, in spite of the declared *primary* goal of maintaining social order in Haiti, the United States refused to acknowledge Haitian independence. This refusal to acknowledge Haitian independence was driven by the fact that Haiti was now the *only* African-ruled Caribbean state. The United States immediately imposed trade embargoes on the now liberated island colony despite its substantial trade agreements with French-Haitian plantation owners. The severance of these trade ties was exacted under the guise of *not wanting to upset either the evicted French, or its own U.S. constituents --- the Southern plantation owner --- to abandon Haiti, the only liberated African nation in the Western Hemisphere to fend for itself.*

The Fierce Dohemy Female Warriors of Benin

The Amazons of Dohemy were female warriors who led African Empires and armies against European colonialism and enslavement. From ancient times through the 19th century, women battled colonialists to maintain their power and to prevent enslavement. The Portuguese called these fierce women warriors of Benin "Amazonas". The name is derived from an ancient Greek "myth" about this tribe of mighty women warriors. The Dahomey

Amazons, also known as Mino (meaning 'our mothers' in the Fon language), were an all-female military army of the Republic of Benin which was known at the time as the Kingdom of Dahomey. The kingdom was largely made up of the Fon people, who were situated towards the south of the country sandwiched by Togo to the left and Nigeria to the right. The term 'Amazons' was derived from the Western observers due to their similarities in build to the Amazons in Greek mythology. The region of known today as the Amazon in Brazil, is named after them.

CHAPTER SIXTEEN

<u>**Universal Cycles, Intermediate Cycles & the Rise and Fall of Civilizations**</u>

Typically, when we think of history, we find ourselves thinking of it as a kind of time capsule where world events are organized, precisely dated, explicitly recounted, and where quotations are carefully attributed and filed for ease of recovery to be used as inspirational fodder for political campaigns to remind the masses of just who they are. Typically, the average high school student completes hours of history lessons without ever reading any history account outside what they are obliged to read to pass the class. And, perhaps, none of these young minds are aware that the textbook they've been assigned to read has been selected by members of a State Board of Education outside of their own state. These individuals are tasked with the responsibility of evaluating the quality of writing, the data it contains, its age-appropriateness, and whether or not it agrees with the acceptable narrative from how wars were fought, won or lost; to how people migrated to populate the earth; and, in some regions, a Genesis account of the differences between "the races." Such is the focus of many institutions of learning. Just as typical is the litany of all too familiar names of war heroes as well as indications of how history supports and maintains whatever sense of national pride, self-esteem, and honor that any *proud* nation wishes to have reinforced. Don't misunderstand. I do get it.

However, *real history* is not so neat. In fact, it is very, very messy, and even scary. Authenticity is not a thing; it is an existential virtue. It is a quality of spirit that when given attention and applied can be wrought out like any precious metal or gem. Authentic history is dug out, not hammered; chiseled, not blasted. It requires an enormous amount of mental and spiritual energy, muscle aches and many nights of desperation expended. The eyes tire, the thirst goes unquenched, and the blood may even boil. History is both objective and subjective with many moment-to-moment overlapping and conflicting oral accounts before they are ever written down and later authenticated. Without these, history feels more like a list of self-flattering ruminations mixed with dare we facts and omitted souls who could reveal all the shameful and humiliating very human stuff that tells us what really happened that night. *Authentic history doesn't ask the reader to read between the line; to get at the truth authenticity tells the truth.* Authenticity is Muhammad Ali refusing to be drafted in an unholy war! Authenticity is Queen Elizabeth I refusing to compromise her womanly integrity to uphold Dark Age marital demands from dishonorable chivalrous men and her refusal to compromise her authentic faith even with the threat of excommunication from a powerful and corrupt Christian hierarchy! Authenticity is reality; it is what it is! Moreover, what seems to be missing in our history textbooks is the soul not of one group in opposition to another but rather the soul of all peoples without embellishments or ornamentations, just the actual character of a people, true accounts that speak to the very purpose and meaning of life and the lessons that all humanity must learn to fulfill their God-given purpose. The words that we would encounter in such a history textbook would necessarily speak louder than the words on a page for they would be true. This, I believe, requires what I have come to call seeing *history through the eyes of God.* That is, what life itself means --- when we view it *through His eyes* --- to see it not as man's story but *His Story.*

Universal Cycles & the Duration of Civilizations

Abdu'l-Baha, the son of the Founder of the Baha'i Faith (His Holiness Bahá'u'lláh) shares with us an explanation of Universal Cycles and why they are central to the unfoldment of God's eternal Plan for humanity. Hopefully we will come to understand 'how' and 'why' that during the past 6,000 years many of the world's ancient civilizations rose to such great heights and then fell so completely to be erased from memory particularly, ancient indigenous kingdoms around the globe. With consideration of the theme of this presentation, we will focus first upon African kingdoms. Without the knowledge of Universal Cycles, we have been solely reliant upon archaeological and scientific discoveries that were made during the late-19th century and the scientists whose material and racial biases continue to obscure any spiritual insight that might have been obvious but ignored as expressed by European scientists in the creation of "scientific racism."

Abdu'l-Baha's poignant explanation offers new and deeper insights into how civilizations emerge. According to Him, this emergence becomes the *central perfecting agent for human progress.* In other words, civilizations are the outcomes of the Divine Teachings brought by numerous Prophetic (Teachers) throughout the Ages Who are the Founders of great religions named after Them. Their Holy Teachings have always been the animator of humans to strive to live increasingly improved lives, to organize societies and improve conditions via social and economic measures, through new discoveries in the sciences and the arts, and is the cause of new inventions and new thoughts that have led to the rise of each of those civilizations throughout the Adamic Cycle. Each civilization, therefore, is the manifest "fruit" and the definitive proof of Their Divinity which Christ spoke of when asked by His disciples … "How shall we know Them (the Prophets)?"

Religious scholars generally acknowledge that during the past 6,000 years there have existed six cradles of civilization; four are believed to be the earliest in the Old World --- Mesopotamia, Ancient Egypt, Ancient India, and Ancient China, and two are believed to be the earliest in the New World --- the Caral-Supe civilization of coastal Peru and the Olmec civilization of Vera Cruz, Mexico. While keeping this is in mind, we will explore what scholars refer to as the "Cradle of Mankind" which distinguishes it from all previously mentioned "cradles of civilization." This area is known as the Olduvai Gorge in northern Tanzania, Africa, and is the starting point from which all African and non-African civilizations emerged. The decline of African kingdoms and civilizations such as Egypt, Nubia, Ethiopia, Mali, Zimbabwe, and others is what 19th century Europeans saw but refused to credit the remnants that remained to the Black African peoples they encountered. Without knowledge of universal cycles, any conclusion arrived at by these *raiders of ancient civilizations* reveals more about their myopic sense of exceptionalism be it religious, secular, or even atheistic. The end of a cycle precipitates decline. Yet, the tenacity of defiance, steeped in medieval concepts of divinity based in tribal isolationism, still continues to obscure reality to this day, rendering the geocentric, flat-earth concepts of the creation of the universe both scientifically, logically and spiritually unstable as even new religious cycles (Islam, the Bābī and the Baha'i Faiths) dawned upon the horizon of renewal (or redemption) to re-enliven this infinite and incomprehensible creation once again:

> "When a cycle [e.g., the Adamic Cycle] ends, a new one is inaugurated, and the previous cycle, on account of the momentous events which transpire, vanishes so entirely from memory as to leave behind no record or trace. Thus, as you are aware, we have no record of twenty thousand years ago, even though ... life on this earth is very ancient—not one or two hundred thousand, or even one or two million years old: It is ancient indeed, and the records and traces of ancient times have been entirely obliterated. Each of the Prophets of God has likewise a cycle wherein His religion and His law are in full force and effect. This cycle generally ranges anywhere from 500 to 1000 years and is called an intermediate cycle. When His cycle is ended through the advent of a new prophet of God, a new cycle begins. Thus, cycles are inaugurated, concluded, and renewed, until a Universal Cycle is completed in the world of existence and is followed by a series of momentous events which over time effaces any record and trace of the past ..." [39]

Most people would agree that among the categories of human socio-cultural systems, that is, science, politics and religion, that religion is the oldest system known to man for the perfecting of human thought and behavior and that civilization is its noblest fruit.

A careful study of ancient civilizations reveals that their laws and cultures are the outcomes of Divine Teachings brought overtime by numerous Prophetic Teachers, Founders of great religions from Whom civilizations and religious practices have taken their names. This cyclic procession of Prophets has existed throughout the Ages and will continue to do so, for it is the embodiment of the saying, "God will never leave man alone." Their Holy Teachings have always been the animator of the strivings of human beings aimed at increasingly improving their lives, to organize societies, and to improve conditions via social, material, and economic measures, through new discoveries in the sciences and the arts, and is the cause of new inventions and new thoughts that broaden human consciousness to emerge as a new and advanced civilization. This is apparent throughout the Adamic Cycle. Each civilization, therefore, is the manifest "fruit" and the definitive proof of a Prophet's divinity. This is but one of the meanings of the term 'fruits' which Christ spoke of when asked by His disciples "how shall we know them?" His reply: "every tree that bringeth not forth good fruit is hewn down and cast into the fire" and can be applied to a civilization itself. And when applied to the recognition of a new revelation, His second reply speaks volumes: "a good tree cannot bring forth evil fruit, neither can a corrupt tree bring forth good fruit." In other words, it is the quality of the character of His followers who claim belief in the new revelation that becomes the test for they are either the *good or evil fruits* tested by the new revelation. This is borne out by the following verse from Matthew: *"Many will say to me in that day, Lord, Lord, have we not prophesied in thy name? and in thy name have cast out devils? And in thy name done many wonderful works? And then will I profess unto them, I never knew you: depart from me, ye that work iniquity."* And lastly, "Son of man, thou dwellest in the midst of a rebellious house, which have eyes to see, and see not; they have ears to hear, and hear not: for they *are* a rebellious house."

Africa Before Napoleon's Invasion and Sacking of Egypt

If one should dare take the blinders off, these biblical sayings become abundantly clear; that by these sayings of Christ, *the prophet known to the world as the prophet of love and self-sacrifice*, both the rise and fall of civilizations are determined not upon wealth, power, and weapons but by the fruit it produces, and that fruit today is the transformation from homo sapiens --- the ones who appear to be wise --- to the emergence of *Homo Espiritus* --- the awakened ones who have bridged the transformational leap from physical bipedalism to a being who is capable of spiritual flight.

Humanity has experienced this process of transformation since the foundation of Hinduism (the oldest existing monotheistic religion of the Adamic Cycle with the 'Bhagavad Gita' as its religious Scripture), to the ancient Egyptians with 'The Narmar Palette' and 'The Book of the Dead'; to the Hebrews and the Torah; to the 'Avesta', the Book of Zoroaster; to Judaism and the 'Five Books of Moses'; to Buddhism and its sacred Book, the 'Buddhavacana'; to Christianity and its 'New Testament' proclaiming for the first time in religious history "the Kingdom of God"; to the Hopi, the Choctaw, the Azteca, Inca and the Maya spiritual Teachings of Quetzalcoatl, also known as 'The Feathered Serpent'; to Islam and the 'Holy Quran'; and in our own time, the Bab'i Faith with its Holy Mother Book, the 'Bayan'; followed closely by the 'Kitab-i-Aqdas' (the Most Holy Book) of the Baha'i Faith whose consummate promise is a hierarchal World Commonwealth founded upon the pivotal spiritual principle of the 'Oneness of Humankind'.

The Adamic Cycle

> *"... we have no record of twenty thousand years ago, even though life on this earth is very ancient — not one or two hundred thousand, or even one or two million years old: It is ancient indeed, and the records and traces of ancient times have been entirely obliterated." --- Some Answered Questions, Abdu'l-Baha* [40]

What we do know today is that the Adamic Cycle began 6,000 years ago. Throughout modern history, the Mesopotamians have been typically considered the very first urban civilization in the world. However, several earlier peoples developed complex societies and cultures that are now classified as civilizations. Such were the Sans people, and they are still very much alive today. The Sans created the civilizations known today as Angola, Botswana, Lesotho, Namibia, South Africa, and Zimbabwe. "The Sans trace their history directly to ancient peoples who lived around 140,000 to 100,000 years ago and are the direct descendants of one of the original ancestral human groups called the haplogroup. Simply put, it is the DNA and RNA both of which are essential biomolecules found within all life-forms on Earth. They are obtained in the diet and are also synthesized from common nutrients by the liver. A haplotype is a group of alleles in an organism that are inherited together from a single parent, making the Sans people the most ancient people and civilization in the world. In their earliest stage, the Sans were a semi-nomadic hunter-gatherer people. Today, many are farmers while others serve as caretakers of the many nature reserves within their own countries." [41]

Finally, yet most importantly, recent archaeological finds have uncovered ancient spearheads once used in sacrificial rituals inside a cave in the Tsodilo Hills of Botswana. Modern-day archaeologists, freed from racial biases of the 19th century, consider these hills as containing the largest and most exquisite concentration of rock paintings in the world --- all created by the ancient San people of southern Africa 70,000 years ago.

It is important for people in the 21st century to pause and take this all in and to not underestimate the significance of what this all means. When placed within the context of human evolution, current religious wars and territorial disputes, colonialism, white supremacy, xenophobia, racism, the speed at which unrelenting technological advancements are emerging, space exploration, artificial intelligence, consumerism, materialism, spirituality, atheism, and all the *things* and ideas that pummel the mind, the above words present a stark contrast to all that generations of people have conceived as the measure of *civilization, and thus being civilized.*

> "All great works of art and science are witnesses to this power of the Spirit. The same Spirit gives Eternal Life Man --- the true man --- is soul, not body; though physically man belongs to the animal kingdom, yet his soul lifts him above the rest of creation. Behold how the light of the sun illuminates the world of matter: even so doth the Divine Light shed its rays in the kingdom of the soul. The soul it is which makes the human creature a celestial entity! By the power of the Holy Spirit, working through his soul, man is able to perceive the Divine reality of things." [41]

CHAPTER SEVENTEEN

Kemet - The Crown of African Civilizations

'Kemet' is the original name given to both the land and to the civilization that was built upon the rich, black Nile Valley soil. The ancient term, "Kemet", means 'land of the blacks', which was used to refer to themselves as the Founders of Ancient Kemet, the land of the Pharaohs. The indigenous wisdom teachings date the civilization known as ancient 'Kemet' to around 65,000 years old give or take a few thousand years. Of course, 19th and 20th century Christian Egyptologists were clearly unaware of just how ancient Kemet was and based their assessments upon biblical texts rather than scientific evidence and dated the origin of civilizations from around 6,000 years ago to fit their theoretical model of the origin and development of civilizations in general.

'Kemet' still remains the most mysterious and misrepresented ancient civilization ever recorded in the annals of world history. The modern era has yet to produce anything comparable to its magnificence. Both its mystery and its misrepresentation revolve around two concepts that in modern times have both become conflated and derogatory: *paganism and polytheism.*

In Western cultures particularly, paganism and polytheism are more often than not conflated to insinuate that a given indigenous religion is unfit and that its followers are savage, barbaric, and uncivilized, at least, that is how it has come to be used. However, language itself is very malleable. This capacity for language to be altered or controlled by outside forces and influences give language the vital adaptive quality necessary when unexpected scientific discoveries, new challenges, societal and other changes occur. Often this adaptation is forced upon us in order to redefine a reality that was previously unknown. Moreover, because of this adaptability, religious terms are redefined according to the specific agenda of any of the fragmented and multitudinous *religious sects that abound.* However, defining terms is how unity of thought is achieved. One non-condemnatory definition of paganism is *"a religion other than one of the main world religions."* Traditionally, in Western cultures, it is the Abrahamic religions --- Judaism, Christianity, and Islam --- that are understood to be *main world religions.* But really, what establishes a religion as being "main?" We may want to ask whether or not it is to be determined according to the number of adherents alone, or are there other factors we should consider? This tendency to present human conditions as mathematical data in terms of its superiority or inferiority is key to understanding why white supremacy is even a thing for it underscores the idea that majority and dominance are the same thing which is the key message of all Vatican Papal Bulls. It's like the question: Which sport is better? Football or soccer? These two sports are similar games in that that they both require *opposing* teams, each seeking to dominate the other by scoring points. In football, this is achieved by making touchdowns; in soccer it is achieved by kicking the ball between two goal posts. Both have rules that govern sportsmanship; however, they are two very different sports all requiring high levels of endurance, stamina, teamwork, and motor skills. We all understand that these sports demand a competitive spirit in order to achieve the overall goal of *winning*. However, what is often not considered is the rate of serious injuries on the field. This rate of serious injury is decidedly different, often come with collateral injuries that may not even be diagnosed though they can last an entire lifetime long after players are forced to retire. Here are the injury stats for soccer and football: 1.15% less injuries for soccer (144.895 injuries) and 4.25% for football (222,086 injuries).

The obvious major injuries in soccer are (1) ankle sprains, (2) Achilles tendonitis, (3) Achilles tendon rupture, (4) calf strain, (5) foot fracture. (6) kneecap bursitis, (7) knee sprain, (8) hamstring strains.

The obvious major injuries in football are (1) knee injuries, (2) shoulder injuries, (3) foot injuries, (4) ankle injuries, (5) bone fractures, (6) head injuries, (7) neck injuries, (8) shoulder, (9) head concussion, (10) hand injuries, (11) wrist sprains, (12) leg injuries, (13) anterior ligament injuries, (14) posterior cruciate ligament (ACL/PCL) injuries, and (15) back injuries.

When we consider the long-term effects of these physical and mental injuries, hospitalization, health insurance, medications, surgeries, the effect upon family members, etc., which more often than not are not considered to be injuries; however, the accumulated effects can be devastating not only upon the individual player's body in the present but extend throughout a lifetime upon all who are affected.

Unfortunately, the World Religion Database (WRD) applies the same principle of competition to the religions of the world. WRD reports that in 2020 Christianity can boast of a population of 2.4 billion Christians around the world; approximately 1.9 billion Muslims; and approximately 15.2 million Jews. Those are the three so-called mainstream religions. The WRD also reports that in 2010, there were approximately 1.16 billion Hindus. Lastly, the same report shows that there are 7.3 million Baha'ís in the world and that it is one of the fastest growing religions in virtually every country, in many island nations, as well as dependent territories and overseas departments. What the database does not acknowledge and cannot show is the plight of the *true seeker* who is the leaven of this world, the ones who seek divine truth, who strive to know and love God but doesn't know where to find Him or from Whom to seek His divine knowledge This is the crucible, and is the plight of all past, present and future generations, for as it is written:

> "The true seeker hunteth naught but the object of his quest, and the lover hath no desire save union with his beloved. Nor shall the seeker reach his goal unless he sacrifices all things. That is, whatever he hath seen, and heard, and understood, all must he set at naught, that he may enter the realm of the spirit, which is the City of God. Labor is needed, if we are to seek Him; ardor is needed, if we are to drink of the honey of reunion with Him; and if we taste of this cup, we shall cast away the world." [(42)]

In the Old Testament, the name "Mizraim" is the Hebrew name for the land we call Egypt. The ancient Greeks called this same land (Αἴγυπτος) which by English transliteration became Aegyptos (A-**egypt**-os), and with the passage of generational morphing of this name, a transliterated metamorphosis occurred which became the English name 'Egypt'. This occurrence was based solely upon the English transliteration and pronunciation and not upon any further research beyond the Greek references. However, the ancient Kemetic name for the region prior to the Greek's renaming of the region was all around them in plain sight. In addition, the transliteration that was provided was the English alphabet lettering, itself an Anglo-Norman-Saxon derivation or 'corruption' of Latin. By definition, this makes the evolution of the English language wholly dependent upon what was borrowed from other languages. For example, when the name of the African country 'Niger' is transliterated from the African indigenous language 'Hausa', Germanic and Anglo-Saxon languages, employing their own guttural, harsh 'guh' pronounces the name 'Nigger', a clear distortion of the softer French pronunciation which uses the sound 'zh' (je). Given the centuries of vitriol and bitterness between the Germans and the British towards the French, it is plausible that the guttural mispronunciation by Germans and British was intended to dismiss the French pronunciation giving them license to denigrate the name Niger. Over time, this mispronunciation became the standard Anglo-Saxon pronunciation of the name, eventually becoming the widely used derogatory term *nigger* throughout the long period of German colonialism in Africa, and British colonialism in Africa and India. Of course, white supremacists promoted its use and applied the term to all African kingdoms and its peoples as a tool of disenfranchisement, disrespect and the dismissal of African peoples' ancient languages and religions. But why was this necessary? What benefits did 18th – 20th centuries European archaeologists derive by such an assault on the dignity of these ancient human beings? Why was it important to extract ancient Egypt from the continent of Africa? How could they just shut their eyes to the obvious testaments to Black excellence in Egypt? Nubia? Ethiopia, and South Africa? What virtue lies in confiscating Africa's ancient artifacts? These questions have been haunting humanity for centuries and is now motivating a new generation of scholars, scientists, anthropologists and archaeologists to rethink African history with new eyes. Today, as contemporary archaeologists excavate the very bowels of Africa, literally digging into the earth to get at the truth, examining oral traditions without prejudice, researching ancient African religious texts, studying ancient religious practices, primordial rock art and histories, they are finally beginning to acknowledge the accuracy of African oral histories, and the reality of the "oneness of humankind" is finally coming into view.

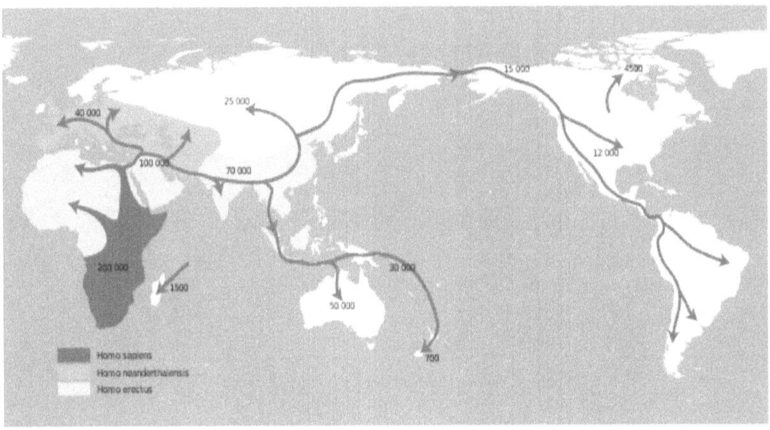

Human Migration is Not a New Global Phenomenon

In our own times, human beings continue or are forced to migrate from one region of the planet to another despite the dangers and difficulties they are sure to encounter. We must, therefore, ask the question: what *inner* motivation beyond physical survival drove the human spirit to risk everything in order to endure and to reach beyond any limitations to understand, grasp, and explore the unknown? Whatever the motivations, it is clear in hindsight that some All-Pervasive Spirit was the animator of the inner power that sustained them.

With no intent to oversimplify, the most widely accepted theory of the dispersion of Homo sapiens (modern humans) within Africa is that the dispersal began within the African continent around 300,000 years ago. According to this theory, modern humans outside of the continent are descended from a population of Homo sapiens who began their migration out of East Africa (Tanzania). This migration began some 70-50,000 years ago; and spread out along the southern coast of Asia Minor to Oceania. 40,000 years ago, modern humans had spread out across Europe. Theory or not, the biblical narrative cites the migration of humans out of Africa in Genesis 11:4.

CHAPTER EIGHTEEN

Genesis 11:4

"And the whole earth was of one language, and of one speech. And it came to pass, as they journeyed from the east, that they found a plain in the land of Shinar; and they dwelt there. And they said one to another, Go to, let us make brick, and burn them thoroughly. And they had brick for stone, and slime had they for mortar. And they said, go to, let us build us a city and a tower, whose top may reach unto heave; and let us make us a name for ourselves, *lest we be scattered abroad upon the face of the whole earth.* And the LORD came down to see the city and the tower, which the children of men had built. And the LORD said, Behold, the people *is* one, and they have all one language; and this they begin to do: and now nothing will be restrained from them, which they have imagined to do. *Go to, let us go down, and there confound their language, that they may not understand one another's speech."* [43]

Whatever one may think of religion, one thing is very clear: *it has been around for as long as human beings have existed.* Of course, the form has changed, but the essence and purpose of religion has remained the same throughout the Ages … until now.

The Origin, Purpose and Meaning of Religion

Human beings have been practicing religion in different forms long before pre-historic times. Throughout history, religion has been a critical part of the human experience in its primordial, prehistoric, ancient, medieval and right up to modern times. Human religious experience pre-dates the 5,000 years of our written history. Although, much of what we know of pre-historic religions is based upon indirect sources, including oral traditions which are the traditions that have been handed down throughout the ages, the archaeological records recognize the existence of these pre-historic religions based upon direct excavations of pre-historic burial sites, suppositions, and other scientific methods. So what exactly is religion?

The English term *religion* derives from the Latin term *religio.* The term was coined by Marcus Tullius Cicero in 106 B.C. Being a Roman statesman, Cicero was also a lawyer, a scholar, a philosopher, a writer, and an academic skeptic. During the political crises that ultimately led to the establishment of the Roman Empire, it was he who sought to uphold the principles of the Roman ruling class. Originally, these principles designated the sense of duty, reverence or conscientiousness towards nature, "gods" and *humans,* and was mainly used to express personal virtue rather than any collective moral-belief system. The original term religion comes from the Latin *relegere* which means *to go through or go over again.* The term was used to refer to thinking or reading something as in a repetitive manner. It is a complex word, that is a word that affixes a prefix (re-) to mean "again" to a root word (legere) to mean "to read" to form a new word which means to read over again. Popular etymology (the study of the origin of words), however, and the interpretation of many modern writers, connects it with *religare (notice the difference in spelling)* which means "<u>to bind fast together</u>." In other words, the word religion can have two meanings: to do over again and to firmly unite.

Unlike prophets of the Adamic Cycle, Bahá'u'lláh, the Founder of the Baha'i Faith, revealed His station to be 'the Manifestation of God' and states in no uncertain terms that He *"did not come to establish one more religion but to revolutionize the very conception of what religion is."* He further states that the purpose of religion is: *"... a stimulus of human consciousness that drives the spiritual process forward."* This new conception of religion, and by stating its purpose in the lives of human beings, is nothing short of lifting the full light of knowledge above both past, present, and future divine revelations higher than what was previously taught in previous revelations. In this way, our concept of the divine is raised whereby religious practice itself becomes an elevated and more transcendent testimony acknowledging the following: "I testify that Thou art sanctified above all Names and holy above all attributes." This affirmation is a spiritual requirement for Baha'is and is to be affirmed every day in recognition that God is *above any* attributes that we can imagine. This necessarily poses the question: is prayer in human worship an affirmation of the attributes of God? If so, then we are talking about the Kingdom of Names and not the Kingdom of Divinity which is sanctified above the comprehension of human beings. In other words, no human can ever attain the station of *knowing the Unknowable God* which such knowing in itself is an attribute; that is, God is in His Essence *Unknowable*. In the Seven Valleys, Bahá'u'lláh wrote: "For God, in His Essence, is sanctified above all ascent and descent, egress and regress; He hath through all eternity been exalted beyond the attributes of His creation and will ever remain so. No man hath ever known Him; no soul hath ever fathomed the nature of His Being."

Words then are too feeble to express the Sanctity of God. What we do have available to us is *God made manifest in the Personage of the Prophet.* At most then, it is the Life and Words of His Prophets that alone have the power to raise human beings out from the abyss of ignorance to the predesigned grandeur which at the very beginning of creation existed in order for us to continue to strive to know our own true spiritual selves, while acknowledging our feebleness to comprehend that sanctity and that divinity which singularly enshrines that Omnipotence and, once again, is the incomprehensible essence that we call God.

All Human Civilizations are the By-Products of Divine Revelation

The Baha'i teachings indicate that our ancestors' "departure from Africa, their successful populating of all the livable continents, their domestication of plants, animals, and themselves ... came about as a result of the creative energy and the knowledge imparted to them by one or more Divine Prophets and Messengers. These, the Baha'i writings refer to as *Manifestations of God.* The entire universe, whether with respect to the realm of nature or the realm of man, proceeds through cycles of major events and occurrences. When a cycle comes to a close, a new one is inaugurated, and the previous cycle, on account of the momentous events which transpire, vanishes so entirely from memory as to leave behind no record or trace. Each of the Manifestations of God has likewise a cycle wherein His religion and His law are in full force and effect. When His cycle is ended through the advent of a new Manifestation, a new cycle begins. In such a cycle, the Manifestations of God shine forth in the visible realm until a universal and supreme Manifestation makes the world the focal centre of divine splendours and, through His revelation, brings it to the stage of maturity. We are in the cycle which began with Adam and whose universal Manifestation is Bahá'u'lláh." [44]

Cosmologist, Stephen Phelps, suggests a unifying way to view the history of our knowledge of the universe and the history of our knowledge of religion, and in speaking about religion and its history uses a very poignant illustration to clarify the purpose of religion. He writes, "words and names are the place holders for the spirit ..." Elucidating further, he offers this clear imagery upon which to contemplate: "... just as notes are the place holders for the music." This analogy suggests that musical notations are the physical expression of an intangible, transcendent reality, that is, the transcendent music that we hear and that moves us. The musician uses these musical notations to produce the original intent of the composer ... a desired sound which of itself is not the note but the means by which transcendence can be experienced. Phelps's insight is based upon the Baha'i view expressed by Abdu'l-Baha which conveys the message that the Divine Reality is sanctified above our conception of both *singleness and plurality* ..." In an effort to make his point clearer, Phelps uses the following example of how people say that God is *unknowable*, yet they go on to say that the one thing they are *certai*n of is that there is only <u>one God</u>, seemingly unaware that using the terms unknowable and certainty to describe a single Reality poses both a contradiction and a quandary that cannot be flippantly resolved with logic alone. "Abdu'l-Baha," Phelps says, "addresses this quandary in the following statement which directly addresses this historical religious conundrum which has led many to condemn others for their belief in a God, one God, or in many gods: "The idea of one God or many gods itself is a secondary feature," he states. Phelps seems to relish this statement by Abdu'l-Baha saying, "If in fact it is a secondary feature of religion, (that is, the singularity of God or multiplicity of gods) then we should be more tolerant of people who have different ways of thinking *about the Divine*, different ways of thinking *about spiritual reality*. Rather than presenting a single, crystallized dogma, a single correct way of thinking about everything above the veil [of our awareness] ... everything above that dotted line ...which is our limited conceptions of God ... into which our rational minds can't reach. Isn't it rather opening up realms of discourse within which we can be united below the veil and continue to have different thoughts and conceptions above the veil?"

Can Polytheism Teach Humanity Anything?

In Memories of the Sojourn of Abdu'l-Baha in Paris, Lady Blomfield documented many of the talks that Abdu'l-Baha gave during his stay in Paris in 1911. He spoke to large crowds of people who had traveled long distances to hear his message. One such message was the following: "All religions of the present day have fallen into superstitious practices, out of harmony alike with the principles of the teaching they represent and with the scientific discoveries of the time. Many religious leaders have grown to think that the importance of religion lies mainly in the adherence to a collection of certain dogmas and the practice of rites and ceremonies! Those whose souls they profess to cure are taught to believe likewise, and these [souls] cling tenaciously to the outward forms, confusing them with the inward truth." [45]

Unknowingly, it is this same veil that becomes evident whenever scholars of history and archaeologists write generally about the *polytheistic belief systems* of indigenous peoples, but specifically when writing about the religious beliefs of the ancient Egyptians and other African kingdoms and civilizations. It is these belief systems that the Papal Bull of the 15th and 16th centuries targeted as being the "enemies of Christ," rather than systems that Christ's teachings were predestined to transform. However, if we hold to what has been proposed as the purpose of religion, that is, *to bind fast humanity to its Creator,* what emerges is the continuous and ever-evolving consciousness of humanity's reliable dependence upon each divine revelation to serve not as a superior weapon of dominance but as divine guidance to achieve a sequential and elevating transformation in the whole of civilization. This is the very essence of progressive revelation. Without this progressive nature of revelation, mankind would be stuck in a spiritual malaise which can only produce harmful and regressive thinking and behaviors that would keep both individuals and societies in a state of social, political and spiritual retrogression or, perhaps even worse, spiritual paralysis. Like the saying goes --- "we are either moving forward or backward." We can't escape it. This is as true for religion as it is for both individuals and humanity as a whole. In all aspects of life, there is no such thing as standing still --- spiritually, physically, intellectually, technologically --- be it personal or professional --- continual learning is the key to a healthy, ever-unfolding, happy and fulfilling life.

I Am God

The problem that religion has faced during the 6,000-years-Adamic cycle is one of attachment. For as each 1,000-year cycle began its decline and as a new religious cycle emerged followers of the former were unable to recognize or even accept that the previous cosmological stage of spiritual evolution had ended. Any form of evolution goes beyond the immediate perimeters of locale. It is a universal confluence that takes place throughout God's illimitable creation involving not only man's quest to live in harmony with other human beings but with the Cosmos itself within which nature and all creation and its manifold species of beings have come into existence and are sustained. We may gain appreciation of the immensity of this ongoing and long-term biological and social interaction between two or more different entities which can be characterized as a spiritual revolutionary process especially when we apply it to diverse religious belief systems. One case in point is the Council of Nicaea where the canons of Christian beliefs and dogmas were formulated by men who held different beliefs regarding the divinity of Jesus Christ as well as other theological tenents of the nascent Christian Faith. There were numerous controversial ideas competing for ascendancy during deliberations; too many to note here. The immediate problem that needed to be resolved was the selection of the writings which were to be included in the New Testament. This topic of debate proved to be one of the most heated among all others and rocked the early church's formation of Christian canons of faith. The most contentious arguments were over whether or not Christianity was an independent religion or a sect of Judaism, and choosing from among the many texts circulating around the empire which would be included in the New Testament (such as the Gnostic writings). This was no easy task for these and other mystical writings of the sayings of Jesus Christ challenged the very essence of what had come to be considered Christian belief, and were ultimately rejected from inclusion. By rejecting these writings, multiple schisms occurred when bishops from as far as Ethiopia, and as near as Greece and Rome threatened or abandoned the councils deliberations, causing irreconcilable differences that dashed all hope of any form of Christian unity.

Melissa Petruzzello, one of several editors at Encyclopedia Britannica recently revised and updated an article in which she describes this state of affairs as follows: "Initially, both the requirements of monotheism inherited from the Hebrew Scriptures and the implications of the need to interpret the biblical teaching to Greco-Roman religions seemed to demand that the divine in Christ as the Word, or Logos, be interpreted as subordinate to the Supreme Being. An alternate solution was to interpret Father, Son, and Holy Spirit as three modes of the self-disclosure of the one God but not as distinct within the being of God itself. The first tendency recognized the distinctness among the three, but at the cost of their equality and hence of their unity (subordinationism). The second came to terms with their unity, but at the cost of their distinctness as "persons" (modalism). The high point of these conflicts was the so-called Arian controversy in the early 4th century. In his interpretation of the idea of God, Arius sought to maintain a formal understanding of the oneness of God. In defense of that oneness, he was obliged to dispute the sameness of essence of the Son and the Holy Spirit with God the Father. It was not until later in the 4th century that the distinctness of the three and their unity were brought together in a single orthodox doctrine of one essence and three persons."

Among the many doctrines contained in the Nicene Creed, the Holy Trinity stands out as the signature Christian doctrine of the unity of the Father (God), the Son (Christ), and the Holy Spirit (The Power of God) as three realities in one Godhead.

This doctrine of the Trinity is considered to be one of the central Christian beliefs about the Supreme Being and is based upon the Old Testament scripture on the nature and reality of God as manifested as a threefold divine figure as Creator, Father, and Judge as described in the Old Testament. The New Testament goes further and presents the human figure of Jesus Christ as Lord who is present in the midst of the lives of human beings; and the Holy Spirit as the Power of God in language to describe the permanent relationship between humans and God. In this doctrine, therefore, the second Person (Christ) is viewed as the human representation of God on earth and therefore viewed as God in the flesh. However, neither the word "Trinity" nor the explicit doctrine appear in the New Testament which came into being as a result of a selective process whereby the collective body of work by Matthew, Mark, Luke, and John were chosen as canon to give official testimony to the life, the ministry, and the teachings of Jesus Christ:

> "The Council of Nicaea stated the crucial formula for that doctrine [the Trinity] in its confession that the Son is "of the same substance [*homoousios*] as the Father ..." ever since. It is accepted in all of the historic confessions of Christianity even though the impact of the Enlightenment decreased its importance in some traditions." [46]

The doctrine of the Trinity continued to develop gradually over several centuries and even as it was being debated during the Council of Nicaea in 325 A.D was considered controversial by its participants. What is essential for critical thinkers to keep in mind is that this doctrine is a human formulation and not a divine exposition given in any of the teachings of Jesus Christ Himself. According to Luke 22:70, when Jesus faced the judges of the Sanhedrin He said --- "But from now on the Son of Man will be seated at the right hand of the power of God. So, they asked, 'Are You then the Son of God?' He replied, 'You say that I am.'" Hearing this, the judges declared, "Why do we need any more testimony? We have heard it for ourselves from His own lips." [46]

Throughout the examination by the judges of the Sanhedrin, Jesus generally remained quiet and did not attempt to defend himself. In spite of this, however, He was found guilty of a number of violations: healing on the Sabbath law, practicing witchcraft, threatening to destroy the Jewish Temple, exorcism of demons, and lastly, but what should have been first on their list of violations, making claim to be the Messiah, which claim He did not make.

Idolatry is neither Polytheism nor Paganism

In the 18th and 19th centuries when European archaeologists underwent the arduous and costly task of raiding the tombs of ancient Egyptian pharaohs, the only religious compass they had was based in the teachings of Judaism and Christianity. Other Abrahamic religions, such as Zoroastrianism, Islam, and the Baha'i Faith, also view idolatry as the *worship of objects* and firmly state that they are not to be worshipped. Islam and the Baha'i Faith go even further by prohibiting even the depiction of prophets in any form of artistic expression.

When it comes to primordial religions and the religions of ancient civilizations such as those of Ancient Kemet, Egypt, and Greece, perhaps the greatest obstacles to recognizing these religions as having a divine origin is due to their extreme antiquity, the primordial forms these religions may have taken, their relative antiquity to the appearance of *the then new concept of monotheism*, as well as many other factors. Each subsequent Abrahamic revelation would have promoted a monotheistic theology that would have had its own linguistic terms to express the who, what, where, when, why, and how of the new teachings which inevitably would have been expressed in a distinctive linguistic style and form unfamiliar to polytheistic believers, further distinguishing the new religion from the old, especially those religions which had been practiced in remote places with very little outside contact. It is this clash of Faiths that I wish to address here.

Polytheism, literally, "the belief in many gods", includes the so-called mythical gods of ancient Rome as well as those gods who are believed to embody the forces of nature as in ancient Celtic, Greek, Native American, Pacific Island and other polytheistic religions which for this reason alone makes them easy targets for monotheists to condemn. But to be fair, the Old Testament is full of stories of the prophets of Israel condemning such religious practices among the twelve tribes of Israel. Yet, this condemnation continues to this day to be attributed almost exclusively to pre-Abrahamic (gentile) religions within and outside of the Levant. Paganism, according to the Oxford Dictionary, is defined as "a *religion that is not considered one of the* <u>*mainstream*</u> *religions,"* and has been condemned and applied almost exclusively to ancient African, Native American, and other indigenous religions around the world. This attitude of condemnation, however, is a two-edged sword, primarily because it assumes that one has the right to condemn while the other has no such right. It also creates the irrational notion that one view is superior to another without investigating the origin of such beliefs, the remoteness of their origins and how they are expressed to safeguard social cohesion in prehistorical societies. Today, both polytheism and paganism remain conflated and are identified with idol worship despite the differences between them. And so, many lay people, scholars, and even anthropologists and archaeologists have dismissed these forms of worship completely, once again, never asking why they exist in the first place. The essential difference between the three forms of worship is that idol worship is neither polytheism nor paganism. *Idol worship is the practice of worshiping an inanimate physical and not abstract man-made object as a god. For this reason, Abraham was told by*

God to leave His father, who himself was a fashioner of stone idols, and to go to a land that God would show Him.

When we reflect back upon the sixty-one major and minor Old Testament Prophets of Israel alone --- from Adam to Noah to Ezekiel to Christ --- perhaps we may be able to reconsider our understanding of how these different prophets with different messages and teachings meant specifically for the times in which they were given, and under the many other impositions of the times --- the non-existence of electronic and print communications, tremendous travel distances, the illiteracy and lack of education of their flock, the differences of language, and everything that could limit Them from serving the greater need with the single purpose of guiding all humanity along the ever-evolving trajectory of God's Will --- it should give us pause to think and reflect on how much conditions have changed since ancient times. Perhaps, then, we can acknowledge that God's Will has always been fundamental to human progress from the beginning that has no beginning and will continue in various forms to be so throughout eternity. According to every prophet, God's Will is dispensed according to His Will and according to the spiritual maturity and the needs of an ever-evolving humanity --- this, necessarily, would apply even to primordial man as well. The following statement may help us to broaden our range of what is considered timelessness and what it therefore means when we invoke the name --- *God, the Omnipresence:* "Were any of the All-embracing Manifestations of God to declare: "I am God, He, verily, speaketh the truth, and no doubt attacheth thereto. For through their Revelation, their attributes and names, the Revelation of God, His names, and His attributes, are made manifest in the world. And were any of them to voice the utterance, "I am the Messenger of God," He also, speaketh the truth, the indubitable truth. Viewed in this light, they are all but Messengers of that ideal King, that unchangeable Essence. And were they to say, "We are the Servants of God," this also is a manifest and indisputable fact. For they have been made manifest in the uttermost state of servitude, a servitude the like of which no man can possibly attain." [47]

Paganism, Polytheism and Progressive Revelation

What biblical revisionism, religious xenophobia, fanaticism, scientific racism and materialism, as well as biased, haste-driven incompetency will never be able to suppress is the essence of the transcendent aspirations which drove the ancient peoples of Africa to create their civilizations in the first place. What followed was a continual recreation of over 30 dynasties to sustain a single civilization for nearly 3200 years. Where, I might ask, did that rejuvenating spirit come from? What was the yearning in the hundreds of generations of black human souls on the African continent --- that neither the invention of Sanskrit and hieroglyphics, nor the replacement of clay tablets with papyrus, could remove from their hearts? Clearly, it was that which inspired the invention of sacred geometry, the erection of towering Egyptian obelisks and pyramids in Nubia, in Japan, China, Indonesia, Chichen Itza and Teotihuacan in Mesoamerica --- all standing to this very day. So awe-inspiring were these testimonies to the Glory of God that modern engineers think them impossible to have been created by any ancient civilization. Unthinkable in splendor and grandeur --- the towering Sphinx, the grand pillar pavilions of Egypt, the temple art, the wood-carved ebony and mahogany statues, golden death masks; the numerous sacred texts --- so rich and complete, testifying over and over to God's glory and purpose. And then there are the many massive sarcophagi, forever attesting to their absolute certitude and belief in the life hereafter -- an idea that only an All-Pervasive, Omnipresent God could implant in the soul of a people. Yet, these are but tokens of His Pre-Eminence, all bequeathed to a humanity that to this day still yearns --- from generation to generation --- to take its place beyond the stars. This is *His* eternal legacy, His testimony of His eternal love for mankind. Perhaps we can now see primordial and ancient civilizations as man's sacred spirit's first baby steps into a spiritual reality continually unfolding. With this spirit, man's earliest civilizations emerged to fulfill and to testify to our primordial origins and the consummate acknowledgment that "He is God, and that there is no other God beside Him!"

What was it that the genius of the ancients could envision but was unable to capture in form even by erecting the most majestic civilization of the Adamic Cycle --- Kemet? It must've been something so unbelievably transcendent that even the wisest, the most prolific, the most powerful would not dare attempt to duplicate it; so beyond the perfect embodiment of beauty itself; so esoteric in its essence that not even a mighty Pharoah could put it into words --- artifacts, yes; pyramids, yes; but how does one put into words the awesome grandeur and magnificence of a Supreme, Unknowable Creator? Is that not what all the ancients and their civilizations were really trying to express --- the yearning to know the unknowable, the inaccessible, the Single, the All-Knowing Creator of all Creation? I believe that more than anything about Ancient Kemet. Whatever it was that inspired these ancient peoples to sacrifice all their strength, all their wealth, all their love for life for that which is barred from ever being expressed by mortal man is the same sacred yearning that every human being --- no matter the historical Age, no matter one's social status, level of education, gender, or ethnicity --- it is this we all strive to express. It is what we all *feel* --- our impotence to know from whence the Light of

Divine Reality comes ... to be unable to accurately describe the visions ... the dreams, the hopes, the love that we all cherish within our very being with any precision. Any true believer of whichever religion knows this feeling, a feeling that is nothing short of humbling.

The only Being Who is commissioned by God with that Divine Right ... to express it as it flows from the Mind of a Single Absolute Power and Divinity is the Supreme Talisman ... the Manifestation of God ... be it thought, form or words ... as elusive as they are ... it is consecrated above human imagination ... how much more than human knowledge where the very atoms of being dwell yet are unable to contain it for it dwells in neither form nor words. It is subtle. It does not demand, it commands ... and it is so ... No human will ever know such a Mind! Even a Carl Sagan or an Albert Einstein is rendered utterly confounded and mute to describe it as perfectly and as unambiguously --- without allusions, metaphors, or mathematical equations --- a Reality so unapproachable yet so apparent, radiating in all its splendor beyond that which even a trillion blazing suns flooding the cosmos remain but an insignificant dim ray of light languishing in its divine brilliance. It is clear that for mortal men to achieve even an inkling of this capacity and vision without considering the spiritual nature of all creation is what materialistic science has been attempting to accomplish for centuries. It must be excruciatingly painful to see a mathematical formula as brilliant as it is to be turned into the greatest weapon of mass destruction in the history of the world, a weapon with the capacity to destroy the earth over 9,000 times. It remains the crucible of our lives. It is as much a pain to the soul of mankind as it is a gift to our new Age; and requires maturity. Ultimately, all materialists share the same failings of all mortal men --- pride, prejudice, and a dearth of reverence. Reverence, perhaps, is one of the highest expressions of the soul and should not be mistaken for flattery or as a tool to entice or bargain with God. So, why were ancient Africans so obsessed with deities? Why were the Pharaohs of Kemet worshiped as gods giving mankind over twenty-five supreme and majestic dynasties of reverence and excellence? To what do we attribute this glorification of a civilization; to the entombments of pharaohs; or to the divinity of a Prophet of God? For this expression of reverence to endure for such an immense span of time --- over 5,000 years --- for it to be so pervasive; it necessarily had to have had a divine origin. For the origin of all things has ever been... and is ... and shall ever be the *Word of God,* inextricably embodied within the very essence of the *Perfect Man* ... and can be deduced by all of His servants to be the Will of a Supreme and Single God.

CHAPTER NINETEEN

Progressive Revelation

Progressive revelation is a core teaching of the Bahá'í Faith. It teaches that there is but one religion and that the name of that religion is the _religion of God_. And because religious truth is revealed progressively and cyclically by God over time through a series of divine Prophets and Messengers, this single religion identifies itself in different revelations by taking on the form, character, and attributes of the Prophet-Founder of that religion during its own 1000-year religious cycle. The fact that their teachings are tailored to suit the needs of the religious cycle of its time (which endures approximately 500 to 1000 years) and not just to the place of their appearance (country) has, like gifts from loving parents to their own children, been made into a source of intense conflict between siblings, the recipients of those many gifts. In Joseph Roy Shepherd's series 'The Basic Elements of the Baha'i Faith Part 24', he writes:

"The process of humankind's spiritual evolution continues because God sends messengers to humanity from time to time. That concept, called progressive revelation, underpins the Baha'i teachings. These periodic messengers, known as prophets, manifestations, and the founders of the world's Faiths, provide the means of humanity's development and progress throughout the ages. They are responsible for our elevation from a lesser to a greater degree of understanding regarding the existence and purpose of God." He further explains that: "Throughout recorded history, many of the messengers of God have arisen in that part of the Asian continent which extends from the shores of the Red and Mediterranean Seas in the West to the mouth of the River Ganges in the East. This part of the planet has been the birthplace of most of the world's best-known religions, and the western part of this region has a great religious tradition which has witnessed a long succession of messengers. However, because of the chronology, the followers of each religion only recognize the ones who came before their particular messenger. For example, Judaism acknowledges both Abraham and Moses; Christianity recognizes Abraham, Moses and then Christ; Islam identifies the succession of Abraham, Moses, Christ and then Muhammad. The Bible itself, with its Old and New Testaments, bears witness to the progressive revelation that led from Judaism to Christianity." Yet, in spite of the biblical record, conflicts still persist over this very observable reality.

Ancient Nubian gods	**Lord Krishna**	**Cernunnos**
From 5,000 BCE	Hindu, India	Irish Celtic god

Polytheism: many gods, or many Messengers of God?

Since my earliest readings about the origin of creation, and as a non-academic lover of ancient histories, I began asking questions of my own and have taken the leap of digging deeper than conventional religious scholars, archaeologists, and anthropologists might be willing to permit. The academic community's attention has always been focused exclusively on *things*: gold artifacts, mummies, tombs, pyramids, precious gems like turquoise and rubies --- all very beautiful and exciting, but I wanted to know the spirit behind the actions ... the essence within that animates all that is ... the intangible essence that is the very life of all creation, including human beings. I wanted more than scientific theory and lab work that was focused on lifeless, inanimate, leftovers and embalmed human droppings. I wanted to know their spirit! I wanted to know the inner life, not dead mummies! So, I prayed for insight! Why, I wondered, would the builders of the pyramids create death masks of gold and precious gems and then place them on mummified Pharaohs that the ancients knew (from their own life's experience) would not physically leave their tombs and would remain so on this earth forever. No, I thought, God has never left man alone; He has always sent divine messengers to all humankind and not to just one ethnic group or tribe, Messengers Who have with the passage of time been forgotten, dismissed, misrepresented, obscured, predated before any historical record ... gone and unknown. They too would have been considered to be Holy Beings Whose sacred teachings were nonetheless from a single Unknowable Divine Source We know the names ... Moses ... Buddha ... Christ ... Zoroaster ... Muhammad ... the Báb ... Bahá'u'lláh --- the spiritual teachings the same though the particular social laws were befitting of the needs of the Cycle in which their ministries occurred. Over that immeasurable expanse of time, since man's first emergence upon the earth, it became clear that God's promise had always been fulfilled by others some we know such as Shiva and Kali, and others Whose names have been lost to time. Indeed, as we were promised, mankind has never been left alone.

This kind of questioning drove the Catholic nuns at my middle school crazy. However, the seed of imagination is curiosity, and it comes from meditating 24/7 on just about everything … work, reading, eating, and marveling at the wonders that captivated me. The bedrock, however, is turning to the written Word of God for spiritual guidance which alone has the power to silence the noise of so much dogma and speculation so that I could at least attempt to hear the numerous explanations given by Bahá'u'lláh on the origin of man, the purpose of religion, and the purpose of civilization. Also, I took counsel in the writings of Shoghi Effendi (Bahá'u'lláh's great grandson), to get his personal take and perspective on the influence of Divine revelation on the emergence of civilizations --- both ancient and modern. As I meditated upon these Sacred Writings, I found myself reconsidering the unquestioned European archaeological concept that the ancient civilizations practiced polytheism rather than seeing them as primordial prophets and messengers who were now being referred to as --- *gods.*

Osiris	**Isis**	**Viracocha**
God of Fertility	Goddess of Life	Supreme God
(Kemet/Egypt)	(Kemet/Egypt)	of the Incas

<u>Mikwabo</u> Goddess of the Universal Womb (Benin, Africa)	**<u>Kali</u>** Hindu God of Destruction (India)	**<u>Quetzacoatl</u>** Azteca and Maya God of life, light and wisdom, and Lord of the day and the winds. (Mesoamerica)

The Abrahamic Judeo-Christian religious community's social and political view of the world's non-European peoples can perhaps be better described as being racially and religiously ethnocentric rather than being ethnically xenophobic. For many thousands of years, practitioners of these two religions, in particular, have had as their modus operandi an unusual preoccupation with either the color of a person's skin or their religious affiliation. Unfortunately, the spiritual component was hardly ever factored in for it was not the spirit or character that animates the human reality but the color of the body itself which is the very definition of *racist*. However, white supremacy goes beyond racism and is not xenophobia.

The Oxford dictionary defines xenophobia as "a strong feeling of dislike or fear of people from other countries, a fear of or antipathy towards foreigners and strangers, their cultures … their customs," and though not included in this definition, language and religious beliefs are factors as well. Though related to racism, xenophobia is not the same as racism. Though inaccurate, whiteness as a superficial descriptor of a particular race is harmless. But when fused with the term supremacy it becomes a statement of intent.

It has taken just a little over 400 years for white supremacy to become normalized. Many consider it the very definition of American life because it is so intricately woven into every aspect of society that it feels normal. In comparison, the speed at which ideas and information can go viral, and the ease at which instantaneous communications (that is, the internet) can be launched to propagate these ideas and information has taken less than thirty years, making it possible to spread any ideology to even the most sheltered, remote, and isolated populations on planet earth. When global institutions begin to spread racist ideologies, their policies reflect them, and beliefs of any kind become meaningless for they are no longer essential to sustaining the institution itself. In other words, the process of implementation is no longer a process but rather a *fait accompli that is carried out without consultation* or *discussion*. It is then that intent becomes universally agreed upon as a *common part of everyday life*. It is in this stage of completion that independence from those same racist socio-political, economic, and religious global systems and institutions that once nurtured it can be disposed of and like the mistletoe rooted into the life force of the majestic oak tree, can thrive independently for it is now hard-wired into a population's neurological responses to otherness. Multiplied by eight billion people it becomes clear why the world is in so much more turmoil than any century ever before it. By any other rubric, at this stage an individual's neurological, mental, and psychological life begins to view skin color, nationality, and social status as the three most significant unifying forces in any society. However, what becomes lost, and is no longer considered to be valid, is humanity's inherent capacity to recognize and implement the teachings of any new unifying principle that challenges or disrupts previously held conceptions of unity. This capacity to faithfully implement the teachings of a new spiritual revelation can only occur at the good pleasure of God for humans tend to shirk new ideas and are entrenched in old ways of thinking. In Matthew 9:14-17, Mark 2:18-22 and Luke 5:33-39 the parable of "new wine in old wineskins" is recounted by all three disciples of Christ to illustrate that new ideas and practices cannot be contained by those who cling to old traditions. The parable employs the metaphor of the old wineskins (old religious beliefs) as being too rigid and therefore unable to handle the new wine due to the expansion of the wineskin because the new wine is spilled and wasted, and the old wineskins are destroyed. Let us reflect upon that for a moment before continuing ...

The causative factors that contribute to human limitations becomes apparent when we consider the above-mentioned parable. All one has to do is to trace any religious institution as far back through the ages as today's archaeological and historical records can allow. However, when applied to the elimination of racism and white supremacy, one off-shoot of this process is the *individual awareness and expressions* of racial prejudice and racial discrimination that many may or may not even be aware of. This is where the rubber meets the road. The moment of truth, so to speak. For example, although unlike xenophobia and racism, both racial prejudice and racial discrimination have become conflated because of the feelings that come with them. Feelings are visceral, and therefore, when experienced they are one and the same thing. Prejudice is prejudging, racial prejudice is prejudging based on race; and racial discrimination is the act of discerning the differences between racial groups and making choices based on one's inner and outer awareness rather than experienced facts. And, although none of the prementioned are the same, especially in these times, they do engender similar feelings and, for most people, this is as far as they need to go whether they mean the same thing or not. That aside, let us now consider the concept of supremacy itself.

> "Every human creature is the servant of God. All have been created and reared by the power and favor of God; all have been blessed with the bounties of the same Sun of divine truth; all have quaffed from the fountain of the infinite mercy of God; and all in His estimation and love are equal as servants. He is beneficent and kind to all. Therefore, no one should glorify himself over another; no one should manifest pride or superiority toward another; no one should look upon another with scorn

and contempt; and no one should deprive or oppress a fellow creature. All must be considered as submerged in the ocean of God's mercy." [49]

What Does It Mean To Be 'The Chosen People?'

This question brings to my mind the wisdom of a young mother when answering a similar question of two or more siblings of who she loves best? At first glance, this may seem a bit of a stretch, but actually because it is a common question that many young children (especially in large families) have asked in every generation. Of course, we all know that there is always that one special child who probably does get more attention than the others, the biggest scoop of ice cream, the spiffiest coat or sweater, the most friends at birthday parties. This has been the stuff of sibling rivalries since the beginning of time --- Cain and Abel, Ishmael and Isaac, Joseph and his ten brothers. I know from experience that for parents to give any hint of preference can be a heartbreaking experience. So, when the question 'who are the chosen people?' is asked, I'm pretty certain that all ears go on high alert.

The Baha'i principle of the "oneness of mankind" presupposes any postulation that any single peoples are God's chosen people. This principle pertains to all people regardless of how one practices their religion or whether or not they even choose to have any religion. This is a radical departure from the teachings and beliefs of religions of the Adamic cycle. The bedrock of all Baha'i teachings is that there is only one God, and that all religions worship a single God. It does not matter which religion we profess because they all come from the same God and the entire human race, Baha'is believe, constitutes the holy people of God. Abdu'l-Baha makes this perfectly clear in the following taken from his writings in Selections from the Writings of Abdu'l-Baha:

> "In every dispensation, there hath been the commandment of fellowship and love, but it was a commandment limited to the community of those

in mutual agreement, not to the dissident foe. In this wondrous age, however, praised be God, the commandments of God are not delimited, not restricted to any one group of people, rather have all the friends been commanded to show forth fellowship and love, consideration and generosity and loving-kindness to every community on earth. Now must the lovers of God arise to carry out these instructions of His: let them be kindly fathers to the children of the human race, and compassionate brothers to the youth, and self-denying offspring to those bent with years. The meaning of this is that ye must show forth tenderness and love to every human being, even to your enemies, and welcome them all with unalloyed friendship, good cheer, and loving-kindness. When ye meet with cruelty and persecution at another's hands, keep faith with him; when malevolence is directed your way, respond with a friendly heart." [50]

I would like to bring our attention back to the opening lines of the above statement which says, "In every dispensation, there hath been the commandment of fellowship and love, *but it was a commandment limited to the community of those in mutual agreement, not to the dissident foe.*" This statement reveals the nature of religion itself. The past religious dispensations during the Adamic cycle include all the religions of the past 6,000 years. Clearly, it is understood that there have been tremendous changes not only in the geophysical form of the earth, but in the ability of diverse populations to interact because of the lack of technological developments to do so. Any human interaction would necessarily have been limited. Most, if not all, would have been based upon relatively simple tribal social structures that had been put in place over generations to protect, guide, and nurture such communities. Given the limited knowledge of the world around them, the unawareness of the various uses of natural resources, and the capacity to make use of them, it is reasonable to assume that ancient civilizations took many thousands of years to emerge, and familiarity with other tribal groups would have taken as much time to develop. Today, humankind lives in the most momentous cycle of all time --- the Cycle of fulfillment. The emphasis, then, has been placed upon the equality and unity of *all* the people of God, and in a single sweep of the pen has done away with both xenophobia and *parochialism*. Again, in The Secret of Divine Civilization, it is written: "Rather, the purpose of His consummate wisdom was to free the people from the chains of fanaticism which had bound them hand and foot, and to forestall those very objections which today confuse the mind and trouble the conscience ..." [51]

This brings us to another step upon the ladder of reconciliation --- the nature of religion itself. Shoghi Effendi, the Guardian of the Baha'i Faith explains that according to the teachings of Bahá'u'lláh, "religious truth and the civil laws that proceed from it are relative, not fixed:

> "The fundamental principle enunciated by Bahá'u'lláh, the followers of His Faith firmly believe is that Religious truth is not absolute but relative, that Divine Revelation is a continuous and progressive process, that all the great religions of the world are divine in origin, that their basic principles are in complete harmony, that their aims and purposes are on and the same, that their teachings are but facets of one truth, that their functions are complementary, that they differ only in the non-essential aspects of their doctrines, and that their missions represent successive stages in the spiritual evolution of human society." [52]

In The World Order of Bahá'u'lláh, he further writes: "When religious laws no longer serve humanity's needs, we must discard them: "The call of Bahá'u'lláh is primarily directed against all forms of provincialism, all insularities, and prejudices. If long-cherished ideals and time-honored institutions, if certain social assumptions and religious formulae have ceased to promote the welfare of the generality of mankind, if they no longer minister to the needs of a continually evolving humanity, let them be swept away and relegated to the limbo of obsolescent and forgotten doctrines. Why should these, in a world subject to the immutable law of change and decay, be exempt from the deterioration that must needs overtake every human institution? For legal standards, political and economic theories are solely designed to safeguard the interests of humanity as a whole, and not humanity to be crucified for the preservation of the integrity of any particular law or doctrine."

The Followers of Judaism are Not Monolithic

Followers of Judaism are not and never have been a monolith, and Jews are often the first to admit that this notion is a myth. There are Sephardic, Ashkenazic, Mizrahi and Ethiopian Jews. The fact that the followers of Moses, despite their affiliation with the Faith of Moses, were not a unified body is clearly described in Joshua 13-21 of the Old Testament. This description is given in excruciatingly clear language of how after the Hebrews had arrived in the Promised Land (in the land of Canaan), Joshua distributed the land among the twelve tribes. The twelve sons of Jacob form the distinctive heads of the twelve tribes and are listed in order from oldest to youngest: Reuben, Simeon, Levi, Judah, Dan, Naphtali, Gad, Asher, Issachar, Zebulun, Joseph, and Benjamin. These twelve tribes had become so antagonistic against one another that their antagonism often exploded into war. So, given this tension among Hebrew tribes, Joshua divided up the land, and then commanded each tribe to wipe out the Canaanites who had remained in the territory in order to preserve the Faith of Judaism. Joshua charged Israel with the task of mapping out and possessing the land for the remaining seven tribes, which were Benjamin, Simeon, Zebulun, Issachar, Asher, Naphtali, and Dan. Joshua then drew lots to consult the Lord and assigned each of the remaining tribes of Israel a specific area of land." [53]

What is important to understand is that the brother's antagonism against Joseph did not end with the deaths of the twelve brothers. The antagonism that existed while they were yet alive redounded to their descendants long after their deaths. This well-known antagonism had begun much earlier as all but his youngest brother, Benjamin, became envious of Joseph for being their father's favorite son. This was no mere sibling rivalry. The brothers hated Joseph and began to plot his death. Each day, this growing antagonism grew and grew until it finally reached its peak when Joseph unwittingly told them a dream that he had had just the previous night. And, by telling them the dream, each of his brothers came to hate him even more:

"We were binding sheaves of grain out in the field," he told them, *"When suddenly my sheaf rose and stood upright, while your sheaves gathered around mine and bowed down to it." His brothers said to him, "Do you intend to reign over us?"* [54]

The brothers then gathered together away from Joseph and decided to kill him but after considering the consequences instead decided to sell him into slavery.

Joseph Interprets the Pharaoh's Dream from God?

In Genesis, Joseph was reported to be known for being a dream-interpreter. After he was sold into Egyptian slavery by his brothers, Joseph served the Pharaoh and interpreted his dreams. By this means, the Pharoah learned of a coming famine. He made Joseph the overseer to administrate the storage of grain, and under his guidance was able to save Egypt from starvation and destruction.

The Exodus

Aaron is described in the Book of Exodus of the Hebrew Scriptures (Old Testament) as a son of Amram and Jochebed of the tribe of **Levi.** Aaron was three years older than his brother Moses.

"After wandering for 40 years in the desert under the leadership of Moses, the twelve tribes enter the land of Canaan with Joshua in command. The land of Canaan was situated in the territory of the southern Levant, which today encompasses Israel, the West Bank and Gaza, Jordan, and the southern portions of Syria and Lebanon. Throughout time, many names have been given to this area including Palestine, Eretz-Israel, Bilad es-Shem, the Holy Land and Djahy. The earliest recorded name for this area was "Canaan." After Joshua and his army took control of the whole land and destroyed or captured the key cities therein they did not take every city or slay every Canaanite." [55]

Joshua Distributes the Land of Canaan to the Twelve Tribes of Israel

To be fair, it is difficult to accurately conclude anything from the Old Testament. It is, after all, the Old Covenant between God and those who believe in Him. The writings regarding Joshua's stewardship of the distribution of land to the twelve very different tribes have become conflated to give the impression that they were twelve *unified* tribes of Israel. The impact of this disunity redounds to us today and can help us understand the critical role that class, education and social status played in Jewish society, and why the humble circumstances of Jesus's life were completely unacceptable to Caiaphas, the high priest of the tribe of Levi and a member of the Jewish sect known as the Sadducees. Above all, Caiaphas was the most powerful Jewish authority in Israel and *the* key figure in the trial and execution of the humble Judean from Judah, Jesus Christ.

Here, is a good place to take pause and take a look at Caiaphas' very human perspective on the claim that Jesus was the Messiah. It is important to know *how* he viewed Jesus of Judah as claimant to be the Messiah. We get a clear picture of his view of Him by referring to two different narratives depicted in the New Testament (the new

Covenant): The first is 'The Parable of the Good Samaritan', and the other is found in 'Acts 4'.

The Parable of the Good Samaritan

The parable of the Good Samaritan appears in Luke 10:25-37. While Jesus is preaching to his disciples, a lawyer stands up and asks Jesus what he needs to do to inherit eternal life. Jesus answers by asking the man what the law says. The man replies that it states that he will love God with all of his heart and soul and love his neighbor as he loves himself. Hoping perhaps to ensnare Jesus in some kind of heresy he presses further, asking Jesus "who is my neighbor?" Jesus replied, "A man was going down from Jerusalem to Jericho, when he was attacked by robbers. They stripped him of his clothes, beat him and went away, leaving him half dead. A priest happened to be going down the same road, and when he saw the man, he passed by on the other side. So too, a *Levite*, when he came to the place and saw him, passed by on the other side. But a Samaritan, as he traveled, came where the man was; and when he saw him, he took pity on him. He went to him and bandaged his wounds, pouring on oil and wine. Then he put the man on his own donkey and walked beside the donkey, brought him to an inn and took care of him. The next day he took out two denarii and gave them to the innkeeper. 'Look after him,' he said, 'and when I return, I will reimburse you for any extra expense you may have.' "Which of these three do you think was a neighbor to the man who fell into the hands of robbers?" Jesus asked. The expert in the law replied, "The one who had mercy on him." Jesus told him, "Go and do likewise."

However, the fact that Jesus cited the priest as a Levite and as one of the men who passed the beaten man on the other side without offering help sheds more light on the parable not just as a story about doing good but about class, hypocrisy, and envy. In identifying the priest as a Levite in Christ's parable of the Good Samaritan, Caiaphas, the high priest, is implicated by association as the Levite without compassion unmindful of the Mosaic law, was as direct an accusation of Caiaphas that only he himself would have been able to recognize.

It is helpful to us to know just what status in society the Samaritans held at that time and how they were viewed by the Levites.

According to the Samaritans, after the Exodus from Egypt and 40 years of wandering, Joshua led the people of Israel to Mount Gerizim, while the Jews hold that God chose Mount Zion in Jerusalem. After the Babylonian Exile, the Samaritans built a temple on Mount Gerizim, and the Jews built a temple on Mount Zion. Samaritan tradition claims the group descends from the northern Israelite tribes who were not deported by the New-Assyrian Empire after the destruction of the Kingdom of Israel. They consider Samaritanism to be the *true religion of the ancient Israelites* and regard modern mainstream Judaism as a closely related but altered religion. Equally distinctive is that the Samaritans also regard Mount Gerizim, and not the Temple Mount in Jerusalem, to be the holiest place on Earth. They believe that the schism between them and the Jews originated by the establishment of a *competing shrine* that was built in opposition to Mount Gerizim by the Jews. With this additional information, the Parable of the Good Samaritan illustrates the disdain Caiaphas held in his heart against Jesus of Judah, foster son of Joseph, the Judean.

Acts 4

In Acts 4, when Peter and John go before Caiaphas after they had healed a crippled beggar in Jesus' name, it was when Caiaphas questioned the disciples' authority to perform such a miracle that his view becomes clear. Peter answered him saying that Jesus of Nazareth was the *source of their power.* In hearing this, Caiaphas and the other pharisees realized that neither Peter nor John had any formal education, yet they had spoken eloquently about the man who they called *their Savior.* After sending them away, Caiaphas and the other high priests agreed that the word of the miracle had already become known among the population and that any refutation would be useless. Instead of refuting, the priests later warned the apostles not to spread the name of Jesus. When they commanded Peter and John not to spread His name, both men refused, saying *"Judge for yourselves* *whether it is right in God's sight to obey <u>you</u> rather than God. For we cannot help speaking about what we have seen and heard."*

After the Roman governor, Caiaphas was the most powerful leader in Judea. Given this powerful position, he would have known that the Romans would not perform executions for violations of Jewish Law and not Roman Law, therefore charging Jesus with blasphemy would not have been a concern to Pilate. Caiaphas' position, therefore, was to establish that Jesus was guilty not only of blasphemy, but also of proclaiming himself to be the Messiah, which Jews understood to be *the return of the Davidic Kingship. One may then conclude that the idea of a man from Judah, a place considered to be impoverished, backward and beneath not only the stature of a Jewish king, but more so, equally beneath Caiaphas himself.*

Apart from this claim challenging the expectations of the Jewish people for the appearance of the Messiah, if true, Caiaphas would have at a minimum considered that Christ's claim also implied the end of what has already been introduced *as the end of a religious cycle.* This end necessarily implies that all things --- religious texts, the status of high priests, religious practices, laws and teachings, traditions, rituals, etc., and all that is associated with that religion would no longer express the Will of God and would eventually lose its spiritual influence signaling its end. At this point, another aspect that should not be overlooked is the moral and spiritual predicament in which Caiaphas, the most powerful high priest in Jewish history, was now cast. An easy way to imagine this for ourselves is to consider what it would be like for us to be directly and physically confronted by the Mouthpiece of God, His Holiness, Jesus Christ. In juxtaposition to the Person of Christ, it is recorded that Caiaphas served as the Jewish people's *"representative to God on earth"*, an assumed title which predates and is equivalent to the station that later popes of the Catholic Faith would also assume --- the *"Vicar or Representative of God on earth."* [56]

As head of the high priests, Caiaphas was also in charge of the temple treasury, controlled the temple police and lower-ranking priests and attendants, and ruled over the Sanhedrin. His 19-year tenure implies that the Romans, who appointed the high priests, were pleased with his service. Once a year Caiaphas would enter the <u>Holy of Holies</u> in the temple to offer sacrifices to Yahweh. As the high priest of the temple in Jerusalem, Caiaphas alone was the sole earthly power to choose to embrace or to condemn, and it was Caiaphas who charged Jesus with blasphemy and who sentenced him to corporal punishment and eventually His death by Roman decree.

Traditionally, Jewish tribal membership was based upon a child's paternal line. Joseph, Jesus' foster father by marriage to Mary, was a member of the tribe of Judah, and this is how his birth would have been recorded in the Jewish census with Jesus as a member of the tribe of Judah. This established Jesus as a member of the tribe of Judah, and this is how St. Matthew recounted Jesus' *paternal* genealogy as it is written in Matthew, 1:1-6; 16-18.

Here, it is appropriate to mention Joshua's land distribution to the tribe of Judah. Joshua returned the tribe of Judah to their original land along with what remained from the tribes of Ephraim, Manasseh, Issachar, and Zebulun, tribes that had not been exiled elsewhere, after the Babylonian Exile. Recent archaeological work indicates that Capernaum, a city important in **Jesus'** ministry, was **poor** and small, without even a forum or an agora. According to the economic standards of 1st century Roman Empire, Jesus was born to poor parents and didn't have a home in adulthood. Jesus' teachings promoted caring for those who lacked the basic necessities of life and taught his disciples not to pursue earthly possessions as well. If nothing more, it is reasonable to conclude that Jesus Christ by His very Personage was neither a worldly man nor a Man of this world.

Further Accounts of Joshua's Distribution of the Land of Canaan to the Twelve Tribes of Israel

The written accounts in the Old Testament (Old Covenant) are often vague or ambiguous and can lead to false conclusions since some accounts are considered to be *apocryphal midrash*, a term used to describe a story, interpretation, or statement of doubtful authenticity though it be widely circulated as being true. One such statement pertains to the distribution of land to the tribe of Simeon. According to one such interpretation (an apocryphal midrash) the tribe of Simeon was deported by the Babylonians to the Kingdom of Aksum (in what is now Ethiopia), a place referred to as being *behind the dark mountains.* The tribe of Reuben is identified as "a member of the Northern Kingdom of Israel, and the tribe of Levi had no land appropriation but had six cities of refuge and the temple of Jerusalem under its administration. Accordingly, to this day, Joshua's distribution of land to these contending twelve tribes remains the singular cause of continual disputes over the land of Israel and brings to the fore the issue that is considered by Baha'is of the world "the Most Challenging Issue --- racism. Although the full delineation of the remaining tribes in terms of their land distribution is available for anyone interested, in the interest of brevity, they are not under consideration here.

The Tribes of Gad, Asher and Naphtali are known interchangeably as Ethiopian Jews and Beta Israel and claim descent from the tribe of Dan. These tribes migrated into the Kingdom of Kush (now Sudan) during the destruction of the First Temple. The Tribe of Simeon was also deported to the Kingdom of Aksum (now Ethiopia). According to R. David Kimchi in Chronicles 9:1, the Tribe of Issachar remained composed from the tribes of Ephraim, Manasseh, Issachar, and Zebulun in the territory of Judah after the exile of the ten tribes. This remnant returned with the tribe of Judah after the Babylonian Exile. The Tribe of Zebulun was part of the Kingdom of Israel and was conquered and exiled by the Assyrian. The manner of their exile led to their history being lost.

Ayoob Kara, Israeli Knesset member speculates that the Druze are descended from one of the Lost Tribes of Israel, probably Zebulun. Kara stated that the Druze share many of the same beliefs as Jews, and that he has genetic evidence to prove that the Druze were descended from Jews. In biblical tradition, because Ephraim and Manasseh constitute the Tribe of Joseph it is called the "two-half-tribes of Joseph." Since it was often called the "two half-tribes of Joseph," it was often not listed as a single tribe among the other tribes. This situation occurred when Joseph's tribe split into the two separate tribes mentioned, each with its own unique tribal symbol. Additionally, these two tribes, although recognized individually as the tribes of Manasseh and Ephraim were often referred to as the House of Joseph in an effort to avoid the use of the singular term *tribe*. Even though Ephraim and Manasseh were Joseph's sons, they were considered heads of two of the twelve tribes of Israel because Joseph's father, Jacob (renamed in later life by God as "Israel"), adopted Ephraim and Manasseh as his own sons (Genesis 48:1-16). And finally, the Tribe of Benjamin simply, and without fanfare, became part of the Tribe of Judah.

There were obvious linguistic differences between at least one portion of the tribe of Joseph and the other Israelite tribes. At the time when Ephraim was at war with the Israelites of Gilead lead Jephthah to pronounce a single word --- shibboleth, as sibboleth (without pronouncing the first *h*). This was sufficient evidence to single out individuals from Ephraim, and subject them to immediate death by the Israelites of Gilead.

Israeli Jewry Today

Nearly 70 years after the founding of the modern State of Israel, its Jewish population remains united behind the idea that Israel is a homeland for the Jewish people and a necessary refuge from rising anti-Semitism around the globe. But alongside these sources of unity, a major new survey by Pew Research Center also finds deep divisions in Israeli society – not only between Israeli Jews and the country's Arab minority, but also among the religious subgroups that make up Israeli Jewry. In addition, nearly all Israeli Jews identify with one of four categories: "ultra-Orthodox", "religious", "traditional" or "secular". Although they live in the same small country and share many of the same traditions, highly religious and secular Jews live with relatively few close friends and little intermarriage outside their own subgroups in two completely separate social and political worlds.

The concept that the Jews are the "chosen people" is believed by two-thirds of Israeli Jews. According to this belief, the Jews have been selected *exclusively* by God to be in a covenant with Him. This concept that the Israelites were chosen by God is found most directly in the Book of Deuteronomy and is upheld by three of the largest Jewish denominations --- Reform, Orthodox and Conservative Judaism. Each maintains the belief that the Jews have been chosen by God for a purpose. This covenant makes the Jewish people responsible in achieving one goal --- and that is to be a "light unto the nations." However, many non-Jews equate the idea of one people being "chosen" to mean and therefore justify the idea of ethnic supremacy, which, no matter how one tries to avoid the term race, is essentially the same idea of white supremacy. However, the term ethnicity and the term race, no matter how one parses them are, when examined under the glaring light of biological reality, indistinguishable. Modern science regards the division of human beings into races more as a necessity of economics, socio-political power, and as an ethnic contract of superficial identity and loyalty which, like gender, class, and status, is assigned at birth and is based on trends and rules which are conceived as norms by an influential social and political *hegemony.* While partly based on physical similarities within groups, race does not have an inherent physical or biological meaning. The concept of race is essential to the functioning and foundational structure of racism. It is the mindset that divides human beings according to the notion of one group of people being superior to others. And because race is not a biological reality but rather a matrix of cultural, social, economic, and political ideas, religion has been used to codify and justify its continual existence even among those who have been victimized by it and lives on --- originally used to justify slavery. Instead of the term race, modern geneticists now prefer the term genetic ancestry. Given the history of the twelve tribes of Israel that we've already examined, it doesn't take much to see how this religious concept --- "the chosen people" was later co-opted by Germanic tribes to support their own concept of ethnic supremacy in the 19th century.

However, we must keep in mind that within the Faith of Judaism, the status as a "chosen people" does not preclude a belief that God has a relationship with peoples other than Jews —rather, the scriptures of Judaism holds that God had entered into a covenant with *all* humankind, and that Jews and non-Jews alike have a relationship with God. Biblical references as well as rabbinic literature support this view noting that the name Moses itself refers to the title "God of the spirits of all flesh." The Hebrew Bible also identifies prophets other than those recognized within the community of Israel, and the prophet Jonah is explicitly told to go prophesize to the non-Jewish people of Nineveh. Just based upon these statements, many rabbis held, in the words of a Jewish theologian of the 12th century in Yemen, that "God permitted to every people something he forbade to others, and that *God sends a prophet to every people according to their own language.*" Finally, in the words of one citation from the Mishnah which is the first major written collection of Jewish oral traditions the traditions are known as the *Oral Torah.* This oral tradition is similar if not identical to the griots of sub-Saharan African tribes. Accordingly, Jewish oral tradition preceded the written word. Mishnah states that "Righteous people of all nations have a share in the *world to come.*" [57]

The Baha'i World Faith

In a masterwork of prose, Bahá'u'lláh's <u>Epistle to the Son of the Wolf</u>, contains the following counsel: "The Divine Messengers have been sent down, and their Books were revealed, for the purpose of promoting the knowledge of God, and of furthering unity and fellowship amongst men. But now behold, how they have made the Law of God a cause and pretext for perversity and hatred." [58]

This last statement is a telling one for it pinpoints the specific text in Genesis in the Old Testament that was purposed to justify the transatlantic slave trade and to create racial hatred specifically against black people. Its racist agenda teaches that Canaan, son of Ham; grandson of Noah, and all his descendants, were cursed by

God. This false proposition is a clear confirmation how the Law of God, that is the furtherance of unity and fellowship amongst men was corrupted to be a cause and pretext for that same perversity and hatred of which Bahá'u'lláh spoke.

Throughout the past 2,000 years of the Adamic Cycle, all religious leaders of the three Abrahamic religions have, perhaps unwittingly, contributed to fueling the racist environment in which mankind now finds itself. Firstly, by refusing to ignore their own religious timetable and not recognizing the 500 to 1000-year cyclic nature of divine revelation. Mankind's collective refusal to acknowledge the connecting spiritual essence, the spiritual tissue that connects the entire body of humanity to the Source of their beings; and that, with a pure heart when reading any of the ancient sacred scriptures --- any one of them, to link them all as the one eternal religion of God. Bahá'u'lláh coined this spiritual principle as *"Progressive Revelation."* And now, we have arrived at a precipice unlike any in the history of civilization where religion itself has become the cause of so much human conflict and misery. Secondly, the concept of supremacy itself is reserved for none but the Author of Creation --- the Supreme Being. Without any doubt, the ideology of white supremacy has ensnared many in its fanatical efforts to enshrine a race of people as *gods* has created an atmosphere of self-worship with no end in sight. The dangers are clear. The stage has been set for either perpetual conflict between individuals and between nations, incessant circular firing squads parading as debates that only end in confusion and refutations; a world-wide gang turf war, with nothing to offer but promises of mutual destruction, human degradation, and self-inflicted violence. To my mind, xenophobia is at least comprehensible because of the history of our past immature encounters between classes, tribes, religious sects, genders, secret societies … politics. For example, to dislike or fear people from other countries or cultures seems to have more to do with one's lack of experience with them than from any real involvement. In Western countries, antipathy towards foreigners and strangers seems directed almost exclusively toward immigrants and even tourists in one's home country. The same holds true for feelings about different customs, foods, and religions. Perhaps, this xenophobia is based upon a tribal *flat earth* concept where the earth sits at the center of the universe filtered down over time into all aspects of one's life where even their religion is the center of God's revelations round which all things, including the revelations of non-Abrahamic religions, revolve. A bit childish, I know, but, in many ways, humankind has been and still is just that …. childish. To believe that one religion is the *only* way to God is the same as believing that only one path is the only way to any destination. With each of the Abrahamic religions clinging to the belief that their religion is the *conclusive revelation* (notably, Islam), or that theirs is the *only* Word of God (as in Judaism and Christianity), or that theirs is the *chosen religion of God* and its adherents the *chosen* people of God, there's no wonder none seem capable of *practicing the most basic tenent of* their faith which is to *love thy neighbor as thyself.* Given the 6,000 years of religious practice of any faith that appeared during that time span, what remains as elusive today as it did then is what should now be at the very least *a spirit of coexistence.* Perhaps a magnanimous spirit with a generous dose of humility could fix that standoff. But it is as it is for the path was never said to be easy; and despite the multiple "wars and rumor of wars" between tribes and religious sects, the collective yet has been fully tested. However, should we achieve even a tiny step upon this path it may be possible to at least make comparisons with that initial step in favor of the existing impasse in the political sphere. Perhaps, that is what is needed to release the power to reshape both our individual and collective consciousness and to take even greater steps. This recognition demands careful examination of reality by way of both scientific and spiritual self-examinations. Let us open up all sacred scriptures and examine their contents word by word, metaphor by metaphor, parable by parable, law by law, and broaden the discourse on science and religion and rigorously examine the attributes of each that may contribute to a unified and harmonious conception of reality:

"O SON OF MAN! Wert thou to speed through the immensity of space and traverse the expanse of heaven, yet thou wouldst find no rest save in submission to Our command and humbleness before Our Face." [59]

The Expansion of Human Consciousness

A perfect illustration of how difficult it is for the Prophet of God to expand human consciousness can be found in Genesis, the chapter on Exodus, as told in the Old Testament. The narrative demonstrates the difficulty Moses encountered in transitioning His Hebrew followers during the decline of the previous religious cycle as the emergence of the formative years of the new cycle began. During Moses' ministry, the Hebrews were described by Him as contentious rebels. Even though He had successfully led them out from Egyptian slavery into the desert, they continued to wrestle with Him constantly not only on practical material matters like food and water, but most especially over His role as a divine Prophet.

"And Miriam and Aaron spake against Moses because of the Ethiopian woman whom he married: for he had married a Kushite woman. They said, "Has the Lord indeed spoken only through Moses? Has He not spoken through us also? And the Lord heard it." [60]

Christ, too, who never put His Teachings in writing, faced unrelenting condemnation by Jewish Pharisees. Christ's teachings, penned as *narratives and parables* by Matthew, Mark, Luke, and John in the New Testament; and His *sayings* in the Gnostic Bible allegedly written by Mary of Magdalene, Phillip, Judas, and other disciples of Jesus, were all written between the year 30 CE and 110 CE within a single generation. Given the level of humanity's brutal hostilities within the twelve tribes of Israel and toward gentile tribes; and given the level of spiritual evolution at the time, it helps to keep in mind that the level of scientific inquiry of the time and the non-existence of both anthropological and archaeological explorations placed grave limitations upon both high and low alike. The probability that xenophobia was as much a part of ancient cultures as conspiracy theories are today, rampant and without merit, should serve as a reminder that in every ancient culture and religion, there have been attempts to hold hostage the *Word of God* by powerful religious leaders who imposed their own dogmatic and autocratic agendas upon the faithful when all else failed to garner public support. Their once exclusive and direct access to that which has been enshrined in the sacred teachings has come to an end. For true faith is sanctified above human conception. Fanaticism rather than independent investigation of the truth cannot endure. The percentage of adult and youth who can read for themselves has significantly increased. The global adult literacy rate was 86% in 2016, while the youth literacy was 91%.

Perhaps, when we consider how many stages of evolution humanity has undergone since our long crawl out of the primordial muck --- the dirt and waste matter of creation which was essentially the *womb of humanity's nascent understandings of divinity* --- by the time mankind arrived at the Abrahamic Cycle six thousand years ago, humanity was being forced to learn new navigation skills as they faced new perils they hadn't anticipated while still behaving like children on a school playground ride with perils. Toddlers and young children tend to disparage easily. Rather than engaging in debate and rational discourse, cliques and gangs are formed to bully and fight until a single dominant force rules the schoolyard. And though fighting and bullying may have once been the most *expedient* means of defending a belief system, in our age it just doesn't work. Perhaps, too, this, and only this, is what led those who should have known better to dismiss all indigenous people's religions as being "polytheistic" rather than a belief in multiple although forgotten or unknown messengers and prophets of God. Non-Europeans and non-Semites appear to have been completely left out of the loop when it came to explaining their ancient religious beliefs. This led me, non-semitic Afro-Choctaw-French-German-Cherokee

Creole-American, to ask many, many unorthodox questions which this chapter will attempt to present and explore without prejudice. I think it's time to stop bullying and begin to enquire. Hold on to your seatbelts.

Polytheism was practiced in just about every far-flung or nearby nook and cranny of the world, except in West and Sub-Saharan Africa. Surprised? Me too! The condemnation of the notion of multiple gods seemed to me to be a bit too harsh for a people who considered themselves to be superior in every way to those who professed belief in "multiple gods", an idea that received fierce condemnation apparently based in religious zealotry rather than scientific examination. How then, can we explain its ubiquity without investigating its relevance to human social evolution? Was there a willful coordination of purpose to marginalize non-Christian and non-Jewish ethnic groups from the dominiant mainstream religious belief systems? Which would be what, Christianity or Judaism? And, given the general antipathy between Christians and Jews as generations have seen played out from ancient to modern times, neither of the mainstream religions have yet to offer a reasoned, rational explanation either for or against having a belief in a single God or in multiple gods --- though the Old Testament clearly states that the twelve newly freed Hebrew tribes, impatiently waiting at the foot of Mount Sinai for Moses' return, engaged in a feast of revelry, worshipping the iconic idol of the 'golden calf'. And even after Joshua had led them to Canaan and had destroyed the city of Jericho, the uninitiated, understandably disoriented, perhaps even confused followers of the new Faith of Judaism continued to struggle with the concept of a single God. According to the narrative depicted in the Old Testament, this rebelliousness and ignorance led them having to wander in the desert for 40 years until they had learned to obey the Mosaic laws and to strive to follow its divine teachings. Yet, many conflicts remained which had lingered among the twelve tribes. Many held conflicting views about the new religion and continued to worship various gods (as recounted in the narratives about King Solomon). Centuries later, other major religious and secular differences kept the tribes at odds with one another. One in particular was a significant difference that still festers between the Samaritans and the Jews. The Samaritans believe that God had chosen Mouth Gerizim near Shechem for his dwelling place while the Jews hold that God chose Mount Zion in Jerusalem. These and other differences have endured for thousands of centuries long after the proverbial 'Promised Land' had been settled by the Hebrews who now called themselves Israelites.

What is the real lesson here? That human beings get bored? That people get bored and get impatient? That people get bored, impatient and then start killing one another? Or is it something else? I just want to know why one religious group is willing to destroy another religious group of people --- entire families, innocent children, old women and men, be they sincere worshippers of God or not. Perhaps, it is this aspect of reality --- that even religion is subject to the 'law of decline and decay' which is most disturbing to the "faithful". Perhaps, it is this uncertainty that *"God is no respecter of persons"* (Acts 10:34 and Romans 2:11), signifying that God shows neither partiality nor favoritism to *anyone* --- for, by the appearance of the Manifestation of God, and in accordance with natural law, every religion and every atom of creation is cyclically renewed. Perhaps, this is what humanity finds so difficult to comprehend; yet, can neither resist nor impede.

So, in my prayers, I have started putting the question to God Himself. Of course, He gave no direct audible answer, but I didn't feel that He had either written me off or abandoned me either. In fact, I felt that I was being guided as many seemingly inexplicable coincidences soon followed --- a book falling from a shelf and landing at my feet in a public or school library. The aloneness was liberating, and the silence suggested that I had to figure it out for myself --- all by myself. There was no one to even have this discussion with. I was on my own. This has led me to consider a rather unorthodox take on how religious fanaticism dovetails with white supremacy which has clearly impacted European Christian thought at the highest levels -- its rulers, its scientists, its scholars and philosophers, and its religious leaders, and how, perhaps, that intersection of white supremacy and religious dogmas led to perhaps the misrepresentation that Ancient civilizations such as India and Egypt believed in 'multiple gods' --- aka polytheism.

The Egyptian Symbolism of the Sun as God

One of the most well-known religious symbols found in ancient Egyptian iconography is the symbol of the sun representing the 'Aten' or 'God'. 19th century western archaeologists steeped in Christian iconography concluded that this representation of God indicated that the ancient Kemetians (Egyptians) literally worshipped the sun as a 'god'. However, this short-sighted conclusion is more a reflection of what Christians in general think of as Christian exceptionalism rather than an awareness of its true significance as the eternal symbol of the relationship between the one God and the abundant number of divine revelations (symbolized by the physical rays of the sun) that flow from Him (symbolized by the physical sun); without which there can be no life. This awareness of the eternal nature of divine revelation, that is, that is continual and progressive, and represents the successive staves of Divine Intervention upon the elevation of human consciousness and that it has streamed forth from the Source of all life according to humanity's spiritual and intellectual capacity to receive and comprehend it since the beginning of time.

> "The term "suns" hath many a time been applied in the writings of the "Immaculate Souls" unto the Prophets of God, those luminous Emblems of Detachment. Among those writings are the following words recorded in the "Prayer of Nudbih": "Whither are gone the resplendent Suns? Whereunto have departed those shining Moons and sparkling Stars? Thus, it hath become evident that the terms "sun," "moon," and "stars" primarily signify the Prophets of God, the saints, and their companions, those Luminaries, the light of Whose knowledge hath shed illumination upon the worlds of the visible and the invisible." [61]

Prehistorical and Historical Religious Faith in an Ever-Changing, Ever-Advancing World

There must've been the same inclination to dominate other primordial tribes and ancient peoples when they discovered that other's particular understanding of divinity was either different from or even more advanced than their own. It seems possible that polytheism, *the belief in many gods,* began, at the very least, as a means to coexist, to get along, to exercise some form of albeit primitive diplomacy. At first glance, that possibility may seem far-fetched. But wait. Humans have always been human, and, apart from ever-increasing technologies from the discovery of how to make use of fire to space exploration to space travel, all of which are particular to a given stage of humanity's capacities; affecting from what can be eaten and digested, to how our social and economic systems distribute resources, to how we consider human exceptionalism in a vast cosmos filled with massive planets and, perhaps, multi-universes. Yet, in the past 6,000 years, human beings really haven't functionally changed all that much. What has changed, however, is our thoughts, our understandings, and our capacity to learn even more. And for this reason, Bahá'u'lláh tells us, Prophets of God are commissioned to renew, to educate, and to uplift a continually evolving humanity giving birth to a new religious cycle. We will always cherish life, family, and friends. We will still mourn the death of our loved ones. If these basic human characteristics and nature have not changed, that is, self-preservation, then why would the religious hierarchy which is made up of fallible human beings who are the trustees of those belief systems, be any different from high priests of previous and subsequent Ages when confronted with the continuum and succession of divine revelations? Each of these revelations have appeared at different times, were delivered by different prophets, and had their birth in different and distant locations of the world.

I Am God

In many religions, the station of the Prophets of God are said to be equivalent to being God Himself. In fact, generally speaking, the human concept of God is expressed exclusively by what the faithful call the attributes of God. However, attributes are not the essence of the Reality of God. For example, the attributes of a tree are its branches, its leaves, its fruit and the seed(s) lying dormant within the fruit. However, the essence of the tree is not visible to the naked eye for it precedes and is the cause of its attributes. From this supernal reality the branches, the leaves, the fruit and the seed(s) appear and are made manifest to the naked eye. This Singular Reality (the Essence of God) has never been attributed to the 'Revealers' of religions, but rather it is His attributes, 'the Unknowable, 'the Almighty', 'the All-Powerful', the 'All-Wise', the All-Glorious' which are (among other things) comprehensible, sensorial, visual and have form. As it is said, "All human beings have been created in the image of God"; not in form but in spirit. It is, therefore, the spirit that returns from Age to Age, not the form. The attribute is the thing itself, and the essence is that which emanates from within the attribute such as kindness, love, resilience, thoughtfulness. Abdu'l-Baha, eldest son of Bahá'u'lláh further explains that:

> "In man five outer powers exist, which are the agents of perception, that is to say, through these five powers man perceives material beings. These are sight, which perceives visible forms; hearing, which perceives audible sounds; smell, which perceives odors; taste, which perceives foods; and feeling, which is in all parts of the body, and perceives tangible things. These five powers perceive outward existences. Man has also spiritual powers: imagination, which conceives things; thought, which reflects upon realities; comprehension, which comprehends realities, memory, which retains whatever man imagines, thinks, and comprehends. The intermediary between the five outward powers and the inward powers, is the sense which they possess in common, that is to say, the sense which acts between the outer and inner powers, conveys to the inward powers whatever the outer powers discern. It is termed the common faculty, because it communicates between the outward and inward powers, and thus is common to the outward and inward powers."

In order to be able to at least attempt to wrap our minds around this spiritual reality, one must be willing to step back a bit and consider what is the essence of God's promise to 'never leave *mankind* alone' --- not one tribe or race, but all humankind. If we are able to recalibrate our thinking to fully consider what the essence of these words means, we may even apply this promise to our own social media-twenty-four-hour-cable-news-instantaneous-microwavable-fast-foods-easy-gratification-over-technologized-over-saturated existence. To put all this into a digestible context, a recap of the list of the number of the minor prophets of Israel (aka messengers) is helpful, especially considering that those who believed in them during their religious cycles considered them to be *gods*: Húd, Ṣáliḥ, Abraham, Isaac, Jacob, Moses, Aaron, Joshua, Phinehas, Eli, Elkanah, Samuel, Gad, Natan, David, Ahijah, Solomon, Shemaiah, Iddo, Jehu, Oded, Azariah, Hanani, Jahaziel, Eliezar, Elijah, Elisha, Micaiah, Jonah, Amos, Hosea, Amoz, Isaiah, Micah, Joel, Zephaniah, Nahum, Habakuk, Urijah, Jeremiah, Mehseiah, Neriah, Baruch ben Neriah, Seraiah, Haggai, Zechariah, Mordechai Bilshan, Malachi, Balaam, Beor, Job, Eliphaz, Bildad, Zophar, Elihu, Ezekiel, Obadiah.

The following is a list of the Manifestations of God, all of Whom are considered to be *God* by those who believe in Them. The following list of major prophets of the Adamic Cycle and where appropriate the spiritual principle each came to establish in the hearts of men are listed according to titles and not by birth names out of respect for their Divine Station:

Adam - Man' and 'Son of the Crimson Earth' - (Family)

Abraham - 'The Father of Nations' – (Tribe)

Noah - 'The He who Reposed or Rested.'

Zoroaster - 'A Golden Star'.

Krishna - 'The All-Attractive'.

Moses - 'He Who was Drawn from Water'.

Buddha - 'The Enlightened One'.

Christ - 'The Anointed One' – (Love of God)

Muhammad - 'The Seal of the Prophets'(Submission to the Will of God)

The Báb, whose title means 'The Gate' (The Primal Point).

Next, we shall consider the overarching title 'Manifestation of God'. It should become clear that it is a title to distinguish the divine station of each of these Holy Souls, that a Manifestation of God occupies an immensely superlative Station to that of the station of a Prophet, a messenger or a holy one of God. The reason for this is that, according to the Prophet, The Báb, His brief dispensation ended the Age of Prophecy which included the dispensation of His Holiness Muhammad. The religious cycle of Muhammad is known among Muslims as the *Seal of the Prophets.* However, as brief a ministry as the Báb's ministry was (six years), it signaled an entirely new and revolutionary trajectory in religious history --- a trajectory that in the annals of religious history has never been conceived or ever occurred. For humanity this trajectory is a steep, expansive surge forward as unpredictable as it is ever-accelerating. Metaphorically speaking, the Báb's ministry represents the final senior class exam before entering the next level of education (humanity's university studies). Bahá'u'lláh Himself refers to the sacred writings of the Báb in a prayer where He states, "His Book is the Mother Book, did ye but know?" (63)

Anyone who reads the Writings of the Báb, soon comes to realize that the His revelation is the pure distillation (without human commentary or interpretation) of all the spiritual teachings and spiritual knowledge of all the religious teachings of the past in one holy book --- the Bayan, written in His Own Words. He is referred to as the Primal Point ... the point, as in basketball, where the Will of God suddenly and without warning shifts direction which is both a test for believers and a warning to His enemies. The Báb is also known as the Precursor of "He Whom God Shall make Manifest," a reference to Bahá'u'lláh, which is Arabic for the "'Glory' or 'Light' of God." As Precursor to the Baha'i Revelation, the Bab is to Bahá'u'lláh what John the Baptist is to Christ. In addition to calling the people to prepare for the advent of the new Revelation, His mission included protecting Bahá'u'lláh's identity from those who would seek to do Him harm, that is, the violence that has been meted out to all divine Prophets by ambitious, envious and depraved Muslim clerics. Keeping in mind that the specific divine revelations delivered during the cycle of Prophecy (also known as the Cycle of Promise) is the period in human history whereby each prophet delivered not only a new layer and spiritual direction to fulfill God's ever-unfolding Plan with a new message, but also served to gradually shift the religion towards its final outcome of the Religion of God itself --- *the establishment of the Kingdom of God on Earth.* They alone were invested by the Divine Will to achieve that goal. They alone had the power to reveal God's Word as it is revealed to Them in real time. Each a fulfillment and continuance of all previous dispensations. Thus, Christ was authorized to change the Law of Moses and to put humankind upon a totally different path in fulfilling God's irrevocable Covenant despite any and all resistance to it. This is attested to in Matthew 5:17 where Christ stated, "Think not that I am come to destroy the law, or the prophets: I am not come to destroy it, but to fulfill it." It was the Mosaic Law, the Old Covenant that Christ was replacing with the New Covenant. These obsolete laws included all of the rules about animal sacrifices, the role of priests, the temple, and the tabernacle; how foods were to be prepared, foods to avoid, and foods that could be consumed, as well as forms of capital punishment, and how to handle disease. The fundamental change that Christ made to the Mosaic Laws was placing emphasis on the inner *spirit of the law* rather than just the outward *letter of the law.* The martyrdom of Jesus signaled the end of the Old Covenant with Moses --- the Old-World Order --- which was replaced by the New Covenant with Christ --- the prelude to the New World Order. Jesus Christ eliminated of the Mosaic laws and commandments according to the timeline preordained by the 1,000- years cycle. And because religious cycles are engravened (figuratively) into the very DNA of the very purpose of revelation, the old commandments, and laws --- no matter how relevant it was to the needs of that cycle --- could no longer serve the ever-unfolding purpose of God --- to raise the consciousness of all faithful human souls. This is why the revelation of Jesus Christ was deemed heretical and was condemned by the high priests for they viewed themselves as the sole arbiters of that declining cycle. It was for this reason that Christ was put to death. In effect, Hebrews 8 is a chronicle of God's Will *that the Old Covenant, that is, the Mosaic Law, was prophesied to replace the Old Covenant (Agreement).* In this light we can reason why these Holy Souls willingly acquiesced to sacrificing Their lives, assured that Their martyrdom would be the means by which the sanctification of their divine station and the purification of the hearts and souls of all who believed in Them was destined to occur. From time immemorable, this is what makes divine revelations irresistible! This is the Power of God! Indeed, this cyclic divine process applies not only to every primordial and ancient religious dispensation, but to all dispensations yet to be revealed. It therefore becomes obvious why contentions arise: attachments to human titles and the prestige it engenders, to authority and power, self-righteousness, and a sense of being "chosen" by God over other Faiths believing *their prophet is the only prophet.* This last attachment is the veil that keeps otherwise rational human beings from recognizing that the spirit within each of these holy messengers is the reflection of the Essence of God; the animating force which sustains all prophets of God whom He has "chosen", and will continue to do so from the beginning that has no beginning and the end that has no end --- and that spirit is the *Spirit of Truth.*

What each of these religions have in common is the tenet that God is *One, that His Prophets are His Messengers,* and that *His Word is a blessing for all humankind regardless of its dawning place of revelation.* In a single summation it is *Progressive Revelation.*

It doesn't take much to realize that the notion of race supremacy of any hue is the cause of religious conflicts. What we are witnessing today is the same that has plagued humankind for millennia: whose prophet is to be revered *above* the others.

Long before the 'Law of Discovery' was enshrined as the new cornerstone of Christianity in 1452, the ubiquity of polytheism throughout the world was a known fact. By the very terms of its decrees, the Papal Bulls essentially condemned non-Christian deities, referring to them as false gods and their prophets as inconsequential beings unworthy of investigation despite the beauty and order that had emerged as ancient kingdoms and civilizations --- all founded upon ancient sacred teachings, the Papacy dealt itself a fatal blow. Their ignorance and greed ultimately led them to conflate paganism, idolatry, and polytheism in order to justify the desecration and sacking of sacred lands, reducing entire populations to perpetual slavery, and thereby establishing new expressions of Christian faith --- the exploitation and genocide of indigenous peoples as the modus operandi of Western Europe. This exploitation exploded! Though not specifically identified as such, the very core principle of the Papal Bulls that turned faith into fanaticism and emerged as the quintessential holocaust of indigenous peoples everywhere --- colonialism.

Polytheism itself was not the target of Pope Nicholas V's decrees and the Abrahamic religions were not founded upon the condemnation of the worship of different *gods, but rather upon idol worship.* The condemnation was founded upon the worship of images of the divine be they made of stone, paintings, or contemporary photographs. This injunction still holds true to this day. Abraham had condemned idol worship, and it was this condemnation that forced him to leave Syria; again, for the land that God was to show him. As acknowledged by Christian and Muslim religious leaders of the 15th century and onward, and later, anthropologists, and archaeologists, it was only possible to observe this ubiquitous practice among non-Abrahamic religions only because of the seafaring circumnavigation of the entire earth which the Vikings, who had crossed the north Atlantic to the new world, were unable to do. It was only because of the innovations in shipbuilding that this was made possible, enabling later generations of explorers to dare go beyond the horizon which previous generations had believed to be the edge of a flat earth. For this new, younger generation of seafarers the supposedly unchartered lands and riches could be theirs for the taking. Without a doubt, the importance of the circumnavigation of the earth must have been seen as not only opening up the entire planet to exploration but was unwittingly as important to the 15th century and the unification of humankind as the fervor for space exploration was to the mid-20th century world … the 'one small step for mankind' adage. Only, this step was not viewed by theses seafarers so much for mankind but rather for one people --- white people. It was because of this new exploration tool that they were enabled to encounter the polytheism as other peoples of the world practiced it. Unfortunately, without knowing anything more than that whoever they encountered were to them strange and unfamiliar people on these lands, their first encounters clearly led them to believe that they either had no religion or that the religious beliefs and practices they did have were neither rooted in monotheism beliefs and Christianity. And, with hearts and minds poisoned by both ignorance of these ancient religious practices, and with greed for gold, land, and unlimited material resources as their essential moral compass, these same explorers were put to the test whereby it is stated:

> *"O Son of Being! Busy not thyself with this world, for with fire We test the gold, and with gold We test Our servant."* [64]

However one may view the many first encounters between European and indigenous peoples, clearly, underlying this encounter was the cyclical overlap of the 500- to 1,000-years cycle of one religion (e.g., the Mayan religion) with the rise of the other. By the mid-15th century, the teachings of Christ were now either being reshaped, re-interpreted, refashioned and repurposed to accommodate the decree of the Papal Bulls' 'Law of Discovery'. Whatever misunderstandings mortal men may have had at the time, the urgency to put the Papal decrees in place reveals not a noble intent to spread the teachings of Christ but an expedient way to justify the genocide and sacking of lands that was needed to achieve material goals --- in other words, greed. This urgency to rewrite and impose human interpretations of scripture, to ignore the many undeniable signs of the nobility of ancient indigenous civilizations, and the repeated issuances of the Papal Bulls to which the 'Law of Discovery' owed its very existence, served only to shut the door to the unification of humanity beneath the umbrella of Christianity for centuries thereafter. Spiritual progress had come to a screeching halt. And although polytheism had been practiced by every culture on the European continent for well over 1500 years, the high priests of Christendom ignored the teaching "to love thy neighbor as oneself" and fervently replaced it with the vanquishing, the domination, the enslavement, and genocide of non-Christian peoples --- all natural outcomes of a declining and obsolete theology.

What Does the term Religion even Mean?

The very origin of the word religion comes from the Latin word 'ligare' meaning: to join, to unite or link together, classically understood to mean the linking of humans with the divine. Therefore. It appears there is a need to re-think the word 're-ligion' as the act of re-joining, of re-uniting, and of re-linking humanity with God. It seems this is what our duty to God is today … not condemning but re-uniting humanity.

I would submit that such ubiquitous religious practices as polytheism were vestiges of other more ancient divine revelations that, like so many other religions, have fallen into obsolescence and superstition. And that with the ensuing confusion that followed then fell prey to a religious hierarchy desperate to hold onto its prestige, their influence, and their control and sway over the unsuspecting and more than likely illiterate, simple masses of people, who, like today, were primarily preoccupied with their own day-to-day survival in even more inhospitable and violent environments. Was it a coincidence that so many cultures throughout the world practiced some form of polytheism? Was this practice due to some random primordial event which separated tribal peoples one from the other and due to this separation, that which had unified them became lost and was forgotten. Or was it some human tendency which, when left to themselves, as was the case with the Hebrews when waiting for Moses at the foot of Mt. Sinai to return to them approached Aaron of Moses, and asked of him that which was prohibited by Moses saying:

> "… make us gods who shall go before us. As for this Moses, the man who brought us up out of the land of Egypt, we do know what has become of him. Aaron then instructed the people to remove their gold jewelry and bring it to him. They did so, and he 'fashioned it with a graving tool and made a golden calf. And they said, 'These are your gods, O Israel, who brough you out of the land of Egypt!'" Aaron built an altar in front of it and declared a feast the following day. [65]

So here, we have a clear analogy to our own times. It demonstrates how because of jealousy (Cain and his brother Abel, Joseph and his ten brothers, Quetzalcoatl and his brother Tezcatlipoca, Christ, the Judean and Caiaphas, the Levite) religious truth becomes corrupted by humans who grow impatient and come to doubt the Revealer of the Divine Will (Moses) even while He is in their midst. The Hebrew's impatience led to the return to idol worship. This corruption of divine law, that is, admonishing Moses during the exodus for not returning quickly enough from the top of Mt.Sinai, is as much a lesson to us all, illustrating the Divine Will in fulfilling His promise to free the Hebrews from bondage. The real bondage was not just slavery, but selfish disobedience. The story serves to demonstrate the fickleness and unfaithfulness of human beings even in the light of the authority of divine revelation. How many of the world's cultures have been guilty of this form of apostasy? Many. This may all seem to be common sense, but common sense doesn't always prevail especially when people are caught up in the crucible of unimaginable and difficult tests of faith. However, to arrive at a more rational conclusion we can look elsewhere. Let's begin with an explanation of the *1,000 Years Religious Cycles* and *500,000-Years Universal Cycles*.

Religious Cycles and Universal Cycle

According to Abdu'l-Baha, *"A Universal Cycle signifies a long duration of time, with innumerable periods and epochs, with a Supreme Manifestation bringing the world to maturity ..."* [66]

Bahá'u'lláh is the Supreme Talisman of the Universal Cycle, and we are at the precipice of the old cycle's end with humanity's new cycle of spiritual evolution before us. One need not be told that the world we once knew is slowly declining. We all feel it in our very bones. We are indeed living at the inception of something far greater than humanity has ever known. Abdu'l-Baha elaborates further writing, *"After His Dispensation of 1,000 years or so "... other Manifestations will arise under His shadow, Who, according to the needs of the time, will renew certain commandments relating to material questions and affairs, while remaining under His shadow. He further states that "there is no record in history, or in the teachings, of a Prophet similar in station to Bahá'u'lláh having lived 500,000 years ago. There will, however, be one similar to Him in greatness after the lapse of 500,000 years..."* [66]

Universal Cycles & the Duration of Civilizations

Abdu'l-Baha, the son of the Founder of the Baha'i Faith (His Holiness Bahá'u'lláh) explains Cycles and Universal Cycles of Revelation and why they are central to the unfoldment of God's Plan for humanity. Hopefully we will come to understand 'how' and 'why' that during the past 6,000 years all of the world's primordial and ancient civilizations rose to such great heights and then fell so completely as to be erased from memory; particularly, ancient indigenous kingdoms everywhere throughout the globe. With consideration of the theme of this presentation, that is, white supremacy and racism, we will focus primarily upon African kingdoms; but all such kingdoms and civilizations have undergone the same process of rise and fall. Without the knowledge of the pattern of divine revelations as they pertain to Universal Cycles, we have been solely reliant upon archaeological and scientific discoveries that have relatively only recently been made since the late-19th century. We must also acknowledge these early scientists brought to their study of these civilizations a material attachment and racial bias that has clearly obscured any spiritual insight they might have had, obviously ignoring what was apparent and leading them instead to create an entire body of false information known today as "scientific racism". Here I defer to Abdu'l-Baha's explanation because it offers new insights into how civilizations flower suggesting that it is due to the singular perfecting agent to human progress --- divine revelation. In other words, civilizations are the outcomes of the application of divine teachings that have been brought by numerous Prophetic (Teachers) Who are the Founders of great religions named after Them which has occurred throughout each passing Age (Cycle). Their Holy Teachings have always animated human beings to strive to live increasingly enlightened lives, to organize societies accordingly, and to elevate the conditions across all spheres of social, economic, educational, political, spiritual endeavors, through measures both scientific and in the arts, and is the cause of new inventions and new thoughts that has led to the rise of each civilization of the Adamic Cycle. Each civilization, therefore, is the manifest "fruit" and is the definitive proof of their divinity which Christ spoke of when asked by His disciples … How shall we know them (i.e., prophets)? The answer is: the fruit of their teachings. It is the civilizations that arise from those teachings, that is how we shall know them.

If we consider the above statements as worthy of investigation, then that is what any critical thinking person would do. It is possible to evaluate the past primordial, ancient, and even modern religions with both a pure heart and a rational soul --- dispassionate and non-condemnatory, with an attitude free of prejudice. That alone allows the lights of guidance to radiate the true nature and purpose of religion --- the unification of humanity into one human family. For it suggests that all human institutions (secular or religious) have been erected upon both the sacred and the social teachings of divine Founders, Souls who not only spoke truth but lived and sacrificed their own lives for the elevation of human consciousness stage by stage, paso a paso, step by step until it was consistent with the needs of the times as both institutions and mature human beings. Even so, all such institutions are subject to the immutable law of change and deterioration and without exception they eventually fall; and thus, this law of change and decay is both a curse and a blessing for it ensures that the advancement of civilization proceeds unencumbered by whatever contention arises in its efforts to circumvent the natural order with hastily formulated moribund interpretations intended to serve only the needs of a few. Human interpretations inevitably lead to sectarian divisions in religion and disunity within a nation, which, because they are neither authoritative nor stable, degenerate into often fanatical beliefs which in turn suck the very life of what once was the mystical and vibrant spirit of the original sacred teachings and the unity of a people. All we end up with are the dead and intolerant dogmas which only hastens both fanaticism and disunity while the one continues to bear the name of its Divine Founders and the other strives to regain its glory as a nation. Again, history shows us that this degeneration inexorably leads to disputes, wars, and the corruption of religious text in order to justify whatever violent actions are taken. Such was the case with the transatlantic slave trade; engendered by the Papal Bulls of the 15th century to spread the teachings of Jesus Christ and to curb the spread of Islam.

In a book entitled The Book of Certitude, Bahá'u'lláh writes: "Consider the past. How many, both high and low, have, at all times, yearningly awaited the advent of the Manifestations of God in the sanctified persons of His chosen Ones. How often have they expected His coming, how frequently have they prayed that the breeze of divine mercy might blow, and the promised Beauty step forth from behind the veil of concealment and be made manifest to all the world. And whensoever the portals of grace did open, and the clouds of divine bounty did rain upon mankind, and the light of the Unseen did shine above the horizon of celestial might, they all denied Him, and turned away from His face -- the face of God Himself. Refer ye, to verify this truth, to that which hath been recorded in every sacred Book. Ponder for a moment and reflect upon that which hath been the cause of such denial on the part of those who have searched with such earnestness and longing. Their attack hath been fiercer than tongue or pen can describe. Not one single Manifestation of Holiness hath appeared but He was afflicted by the denials, the repudiation, and the vehement opposition of the people around Him. Thus, it hath been revealed: "O the misery of men! No Messenger cometh unto them but they laugh Him to scorn." Again, He saith: "Each nation hath plotted darkly against their Messenger to lay violent hold on Him and disputed with vain words to invalidate the truth."

But Who are these Divine Prophets and Messengers?

In the pantheon of the major and minor Old Testament prophets of Israel there are at least sixty-one such illumined Figures listed below. Some names are familiar to us all, others are not. Here is a list of just a few of them: Noah, Húd, Ṣáliḥ, Abraham, Isaac, Jacob, Moses, Aaron, Joshua, Phinehas, Eli, Elkanah, Samuel, Gad, Natan, David, Ahijah, Solomon, Shemaiah, Iddo, Jehu, Oded, Azariah, Hanani, Jahaziel, Eliezar, Elijah, Elisha, Micaiah, Jonah, Amos, Hosea, Amoz, Isaiah, Micah, Joel, Zephaniah, Nahum, Habakuk, Urijah, Jeremiah, Mehseiah, Neriah, Baruch ben Neriah, Seraiah, Haggai, Zechariah, Mordechai Bilshan, Malachi, Balaam, Beor, Job, Eliphaz, Bildad, Zophar, Elihu, Ezekiel, and Obadiah. Apart from the above minor and major prophets listed, there have been nine major global prophets of the 6,000-years Adamic Cycle (also known as the Cycle of Promise). The nine prophets of the Adamic Cycle are Abraham, Zoroaster, Moses, the Buddha, Krishna, Jesus Christ, Muhammad, the Báb, and Bahá'u'lláh.

Divine Titles

We are all accustomed to titles that are used to distinguish a person's status within a particular institution or religious organization. One of the ways in which we distinguish Holy Personages who are founders of a religious system is by the title they assume. Historically, such titles tell us what purpose or measure of knowledge they have come to bring to humanity. Most impressively, these Founders of divine religions take upon themselves a specific spiritual title to distinguish their dispensation and station as the *Word of God* rather than a philosopher, a king or queen, a president, a doctor, or scholar. This is because their mission is infused with what is termed the *Holy Spirit* which is the medium between the Source of Creation and His Manifestations, who in turn is the Divine Repository of Divine Revelation. And, given the 500 to 1,000-years length of a religious cycle, it is delivered, received, and will endure throughout the cycle in which their dispensation occurs until its divinely ordained duration has reached completion.

The spiritual titles any of the given Sources of Divine Revelations assume are now generally familiar to everyone be they believers or not. For instance, the dual title for the prophet *Adam* is 'Man' and 'Son of the Crimson Earth' which, one can say, illustrates what His mission was, that is, to teach others the spiritual path to becoming more human. The singular title for the prophet *Abram (Abraham)* according to the Torah is 'Father of a multitude of nations' which illustrates his mission as dispersing and spreading His seed throughout the lands of the world which of course later became the diverse nations that we know today. The singular title for the prophet *Noah* is 'He who Reposed'; the prophet *Zoroaster's* title is 'A Golden Star'; the prophet Krishna's title is 'the All-Attractive'; the prophet *Moses* (a title disputed to have been given to Him by the sister of Pharoah. It is disputed because several medieval commentators suggest that Yocheved, the mother of Moses, rather than Pharaoh's daughter, gave Him the name which in Hebrew means 'He who was drawn from water'. The prophet *Buddha's* title is 'The Enlightened One'; the name Jesus means 'The 'Deliverer' or 'Savior'; the Greek title *Christ* means 'The Anointed One'. Additionally, the title *Muhammad* means 'The Praiseworthy One', the title *'The Báb'* means 'the Gate'; and, in our own cycle, the Cycle of Fulfillment, the Arabic title, *Bahá'u'lláh*, means the 'Glory of God'.

From the Very Beginning, the Eternal Creator, God, Has Always Guided Humanity

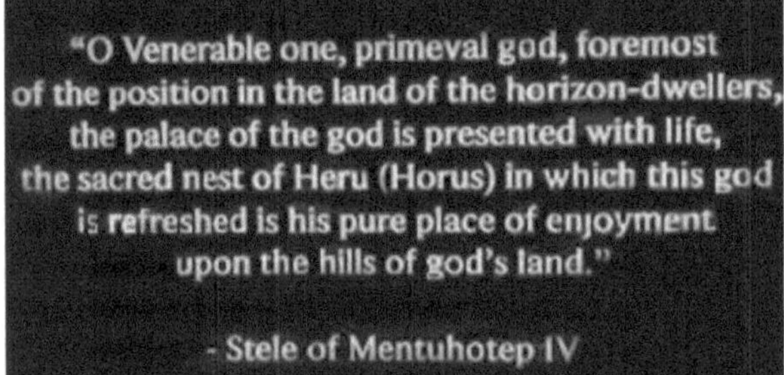

Mentuhotep IV

Primordial and Ancient African Prophets and Religions

For over 10,000 years, so-called gods & goddesses guided the Pharaohs, Kings and Queens of the African continent. Nebtawyre Mentuhotep IV was the last king of the 11th Dynasty in the Middle Kingdom. His father, Mentuhotep II, was an Egyptian pharaoh and the sixth ruler of the 11th Dynasty. Mentuhotep II is credited with reuniting and ending the turbulent First Intermediate Period which made him the first pharaoh of the Middle Kingdom. According to the Turin King List, his reign lasted fifty-one years.

The Yoruba, Dogon, and Kuba peoples of Africa worshipped many Orishas. According to African theology, Orishas are holy souls (Messengers, prophets and saints) sent to earth by the Supreme Creator to assist humanity and to teach them to be successful while on earth. They are complex, multidimensional unities linking people, nature, and metaphysical powers. The Orisha religions of Trinidad and Recife is a complex system of beliefs and practices drawn from a number of ancient African cultural and religious traditions.

Some of the Names of the African Orishas

- **Ajé Shaluga** – god of Stability & Prosperity
- **Babalú Ayé** – god of Healing
- **Bumba** – god of Creation
- **Eshu** – god of Protection and Benevolence
- **Nana Buluku** – goddess of Motherhood
- **Oba** – goddess of Pure Water
- **Obatala** – god of Compassion
- **Oduduwa** – god of Creator
- **Ogo** – god of Chaos
- **Ogun** – god of War and Iron
- **Oko** – god of Agriculture
- **Osanyin** – god of Nature

These Orishas are some of the most powerful and well-respected among the different West African cultural groups. Each culture has a different creator god or goddess, which explains the creation of humans and the lands. These orishas also rule over various elements and are part of all Africa's indigenous religious and cultural beliefs. Orisha refers to Sacred Divine Beings in the Yoruba religion of West Africa. These Sacred Beings are actually emanations or manifestations of the One Supreme Creator Olodumare. Orishas are venerated in several religions of the African diaspora that derive from it. They are any of numerous gods or spirits worshiped by the Yoruba people of southern Nigeria, also figuring in folk religions such as Candomblé in Brazil, and Santeria of South America and the Caribbean, namely Cuba, the Dominican Republic, Haiti, and Puerto Rico.

Unumbotte, the Creator God of the African Bassari people.

The creation story of **Unumbotte** is an ancient African narrative of the Senegalese, Gambian, Ghanaian, Guineans, and Guineans-Bissau peoples of West Africa. The narrative is reminiscent but predates the Old Testament Hebrew story of the Garden of Eden in Genesis that we will examine in the next chapter. In this narrative, "**Unumbotte** creates a man, then the animals, including an antelope and a snake, and later a woman. He gave the humans seeds, from which trees and plants emerged, including one bearing red fruit. **Unumbotte** would eat from the tree every seven days, but the humans would not. Eventually, the snake persuaded the humans to eat from the tree, giving the excuse to **Unumbotte** that they were hungry. Hearing this, **Unumbotte** gave each creature a different food to eat; to humans who had cultivated plants, he gave them plants; to the antelope he gave them grass; and to the snake he gave poison with the desire to attack humans." [67]

Earthworms

When me and my brother were children, we would dig into the soil to collect earthworms as bait for fishing. As everybody knows, fish love earthworms. Our neighbor, a girl who was the same age, was terrified of earthworms, and whenever we felt naughty, we'd hold up a large, squiggly earthworm in front of her face and chase her around the yard as she screamed for dear life. Of course, we always got into trouble with both parents and would vow never to do that to her ever again. (Not!) At the time, we didn't know that earthworms eat soil! We didn't know that their nutrition comes from decaying roots and leaves that fall upon and in the soil, and that animal manures are also an important food source for earthworms. There was so much to learn about earthworms. Did you know that earthworms help to increase the amount of air and water that gets into the soil that nurtures young fruit trees and vegetables that we depend upon for our own health and survival? They break down the organic matter of leaves and grass into all kinds of foliage that can be used by animals and human beings. When earthworms eat, they leave behind castings that are a very valuable type of fertilizer. Earthworms are the farm helpers that keeps humanity alive.

I share that story to illustrate how racism and white supremacy are like the earthworm in many, many ways. They are pervasive, they are everywhere --- in every land and on every continent, they squirm and squiggle. They prefer to remain hidden beneath the ground because they cannot withstand the heat of the sun. It's too hot. And because they have no protection from the sun's intense heat, they shun the light and all the beauty that sunlight reveals. They may look scary but that is an illusion. In the scheme of things, they are merely fangless, venom less and harmless miniature snakes by which air is circulated through soil and used as bait for catching fish. In the end, they are the scared ones --- for both humans, soil and fish have all been created to thrive and give life in the warmth of the sun.

When Jesus returns, will His Name still be Jesus?

Among all the questions a person may ask about one's religion, this, perhaps, is one of the most asked questions among Christians. At first glance it may appear to be a question that a child might ask his mother when confronted with the idea of 'return'. I asked a similar question when I was a four-year-old in kindergarten, though it had nothing to do with Jesus. I had come home for lunch and much to my surprise, there was a framed photo on the kitchen counter of a man that I'd never seen before. I asked my mother who the man was. She smiled and told me that it was the man she would have married had she not met my father. After thinking about her answer for a moment or two, I had asked her … "Would I be the same person if you had married him?" I don't remember her answer, but I'm pretty sure she gave me an age-appropriate answer to a question which was essentially a question of genetics. In religion, such questions abound when one is faced with their own common sense and dogma. Will Jesus have the same name? What do you think His surname would be? Would arrive as an adult or as a newborn babe wrapped in swaddling clothes or kingly regalia? Just how does one answer such questions?

The New Jerusalem - Revelation 3:12

In Revelation 3:12, John gives an account of an extraordinary vision attributed to His Holiness, Jesus Christ. The vision was associated with His promise that he would return with a *new name*. [66]

Unlike many of his literary images used in the Revelation of John the following statement is clear and straightforward and avoids the use of any imagery that appeals or terrifies the developing mind of a two-year-old. In this passage taken directly from Revelation 3:12 he seems to have toned down his own emotional or psychic reaction to the visions he had and chose to relate them as fascination, awe, beauty, and tranquility. In other words, his metaphors are used to inspire faith within the individual rather than to entertain or to instill fear and terror. Here is the heart of his vision:

> "Him that overcomes will I make a pillar in the temple
> of *My God*, and he shall go no more out: and I will write
> on him the name of My God, and the name of the city of
> *My God,* which is *new Jerusalem*, which comes down
> out of heaven from *My God*: and I will write on him *My*
> *new name.*" (68)

As we have witnessed in the foregoing excerpt from Revelations, John clarified and specified both the amorphous literary symbol 'new name' as well as the *"new Jerusalem."* Simply put, he did not identify the new name as being Jesus Christ which would negate its newness; nor as the new Jerusalem as being Jerusalem which too would negate anything new about the ancient city that we all know so well. Also, I find it interesting how the symbolic phrase "new Jerusalem" resembles Moses' symbolic phrase "the Promised Land," and how the coming "Kingdom of God" which Jesus spoke to His disciples about resembles 'the Promised Land'. And so, it is with *the new Jerusalem.* After being enslaved for 430 years in Egypt, it would be unreasonable to believe that the average, illiterate, impoverished and enslaved Hebrew would remember or know anything about the location of the patriarch Jacob's homeland or which direction to take to get there. There was no iPhone with GPS, no WhatsApp, and no maps. In addition, most doubted safe passage and wanted to return to Egypt, preferring slavery in Egypt to wandering in the desert with a Man who had neither shared their enslavement nor their religion. The fact was that neither the Promised Land nor the Kingdom of God were phrases that any previous prophets had ever used; and that included the patriarch of monotheism, Abraham. It would be reasonable to suggest that when the mass of Hebrews heard Moses refer to the "Promised Land" that they had no idea what land He was talking about. This was certainly true of Christ's followers for not only did He attempt to explain His message in easy-to-understand parables, more often than not, He expressed Himself in such profound esoteric language that many remained clueless, preferring to see miracles to hearing the Word of God, especially when speaking of "the Kingdom of God." Symbolism works that way. It serves simultaneously *to inspire with the Word of God*, to *test one's faith in the Word of God*, and *to shield the Word of God from charlatans, hypocrites, and wolves in sheep's clothing* (another metaphor); all necessary to protect a nascent and vulnerable Faith. Today, in the Age of Fulfillment, the fact is that these symbolic biblical terms which were unheard of at the time, indicated specific geographical locations which GPS can quickly identify.

Based upon the biblical description of the Hebrew's attitude and rebelliousness against Moses during the exodus from Egypt, I suspect that among the reasons the twelve tribes (descendants of the twelve sons of Jacob) were forced to wander in the desert for forty years (that's a long time to be walking) was due to among other things their lack of faith in Moses's return as illustrated in their impatience at the foot Mt. Sinai. But again, when thirst brought them to their knees and they pleaded for a miracle from God to quench their thirst. This is not a condemnation of the Hebrews. This is an illustration of how God has always separated the wheat from the chaff: "Do men think when they say, "We believe" they shall be let alone and not be put to proof?" --- Bahá'u'lláh, Book of Certitude, pp. 8-9

The "city" referred to in Revelation 3:12 is also associated with the name of Bahá'u'lláh, the Prophet-Founder of the Baha'i Faith which is the new name mentioned in the Revelation of John. The translation of the Arabic title, Bahá'u'lláh, is "the Glory of God." This symbolism of the holy city (My God) passage from the Baha'i teachings is explained thusly:

> "… what the Sacred Scriptures most often mean by the Holy City or divine Jerusalem is the *religion of God*, which name changes according to the name of the Divine Founder of that religion. Thus, it "has at times been likened to a bride, or called "Jerusalem", or depicted

> as the *new heaven* and the *new earth* ... Clearly, the
> New Jerusalem which descends from heaven is not a
> city of stone and lime, of brick and mortar, but is rather
> the religion of God which descends from heaven and is
> described as new. For it is obvious that the Jerusalem
> which is built of stone and mortar does not descend from
> heaven and is not renewed, *but that which is renewed is
> the religion of God.*" [68]

In the only other verse that refers to a new Jerusalem descending out of heaven, God shows John that great city and discloses its sacred name: "And he carried me away in the Spirit to a great and high mountain, and showed me the great city, the holy Jerusalem, descending out of heaven from God, having *the glory of God.*" [68]

The biblical phrase, 'the glory of God' is a clear and direct reference to the *new name* mentioned in Revelation 21:10 --- the Arabic title, *Bahá'u'lláh,* means *"the Glory of God"*.

The Proclamation of Bahá'u'lláh

Napoleon III,
France

Czar Alexander II,
Russia

Queen Victoria,
England

Kaiser Wilhelm I
Germany

Emp. Francis Joseph
Austria

Sultan 'Addu'l-' Aziz,
Turkey

Naesrer al-Din Shah
Persia

Pope Pius IX
Vatican, Rome

Andrew Johnson
President USA

'The Proclamation of Bahá'u'lláh is a compilation of the Tablets delivered to the heads of state of Europe and the Americas. Each Tablet is written by Bahá'u'lláh, the Founder of the Baha'i Faith, beginning in early 1867 to 1868 addressed to the kings and leaders of the world. He tells them, among other things, that they must cease spending their money on wars and spend it on what will bring happiness to mankind. He addressed the rulers of the world and the Pope. All either ignored or rejected His Tablets and all lost their power. The only one who responded was Queen Victoria. The Tablet that was delivered to the Queen is currently in the British Library. Bahá'u'lláh criticized and rebuked all of the monarchs and religious leaders for their wars, their unjust practices, and their greed. However, Bahá'u'lláh's tablet to the British Queen praised the British Empire for abolishing the slave trade and giving democracy to her country. Here is an excerpt from the official document entitled 'Summons to the Kings and Rulers of the World Collectively:

"O Kings of the earth! He Who is the sovereign Lord of all is come. The Kingdom is God's, the omnipotent Protector, the Self-Subsisting. Worship none but God, and, with radiant hearts, lift up your faces unto your Lord, the Lord of all names. This is a Revelation to which whatever ye possess can never be compared, could ye but know it. We see you rejoicing in that which ye have amassed for others, and shutting out yourselves from the world which naught except My Guarded Tablet can reckon. The treasures ye have laid up have drawn you far away from your ultimate objective. This ill beseemeth you, could ye but understand it. Wash your hearts from all earthly defilements, and hasten to enter the Kingdom of your Lord, the Creator of earth and heaven, Who caused the world to tremble, and all its peoples to wail, except them that have renounced all things and clung to that which the Hidden Tablet hath ordained ..." [69]

The Baha'i Cycle Is Come - The Advent of Divine Justice and Divine Civilization.

The Seat of the Universal House of Justice, Mt. Carmel, Haifa Israel

The Shrine of the Báb

According to Baha'i religious scholars, the Baha'i Cycle is also known as the *Cycle of Fulfillment* and, according to the central Figures of the Baha'i Dispensation, it will endure for the next 500,000 years. This new cycle has brought the 6,000 years Adamic Cycle, also known as the Prophetic Cycle of Promise, was a religious cycle which witnessed many periods of unimaginable wars and violence between the people of the world. It is now slowly grinding to a halt.

This Cycle of Fulfillment has been unfolding since its beginning in Persia (known today as Iran), on May 23, 1844. With over 2,100 different indigenous and ethnic groups worldwide, including China, India, Japan, Russia, and Vietnam. This fast-growing young Faith has adherents of over 7,000,000 believers and counting throughout the world, According to Baha'i scriptures, this same religious dispensation will end at God's appointed time of no less than 1,000 years. Also, according to Baha'i Sacred Writings, the Baha'i Cycle itself is a *Universal Cycle*. Universal Cycles have been and will continue to be as cyclical as the four seasons of earth. Each Universal Cycle lasts for a period of no less than *500,000 years*, each bringing humanity to fuller and fuller stages of an ever-advancing process of perfecting the human spirit. According to these sacred writings of the Faith, humanity will witness the establishment of the *oneness of humankind*, the elimination of racism, universal education, the full equality of opportunity for women, a universal auxiliary language, and will erect the foundations and establish its crowning glory --- a World Commonwealth built upon timeless spiritual values of justice, love, peace, and cooperation:

> "... a world community in which all economic barriers will have been permanently demolished and the interdependence of capital and labour definitely recognized; in which the clamour of religious fanaticism and strife will have been forever stilled; in which the flame of racial animosity will have been finally extinguished;

in which a single code of international law—the product of the considered judgement of the world's federated representatives—shall have as its sanction the instant and coercive intervention of the combined forces of the federated units; and finally a world community in which the fury of a capricious and militant nationalism will have been transmuted into an abiding consciousness of world citizenship—such indeed, appears, in its broadest outline, the Order anticipated by **Bahá'u'lláh**, an Order that shall come to be regarded as the fairest fruit of a slowly maturing age." [70]

FROM THE AUTHOR

I'd like to thank each reader for taking the time to read my book. The entire process of combing through mountains of research materials and then attempting to write a coherent presentation that is as much sympathetic as it is revelatory has been challenging. When I began putting pen to paper, coexistence was and still is upper-most in my mind. It is my hope that knowing the genesis of white supremacy as a fallacious ideology will serve to remove the cognitive dissonance that for centuries it has ravaged the soul of humankind.

Admittedly, the subject of white supremacy and racism can never be fully examined in a single book. There are so many moving parts. This is one attempt to put the topic in a context that may resonate with the majority of readers regardless of religious beliefs. Personally, I believe that all divine religions are from God, and that believers who put their Faith's Divine Teachings into practice, are truly the leaven of this world. All Holy Scriptures have spoken about this.

Finally, I wish to acknowledge that there is much to learn about ourselves as one, single human family. While the mounting turmoil threatens only to increase in intensity, the question emerges: Will this generation exemplify the stoic wisdom, the fortitude, and the courage required to put past injustices aside and replace them with meaningful service to all humanity? Or will it pursue its own selfish desires? I believe that reason, patience, and forgiveness are among the keys to connecting with others different from ourselves. Discourses on racism can take place without assumptions and accusations but with empathy; not only in the halls of governments, social media, and industry, but in classrooms, homes, synagogues and churches, temples and mosques, where informed discourses can cause the spiritual leaven to appear. This is what's so desperately needed now. Each man, each woman and each child has the capacity to be potentially that leaven that leaven; that pervasive influence that can transform our world into a colorful rose garden. With love and faithfulness this is the way that pride, oppression and hatred will be eradicated. It is my fervent wish that the information found herein can serve as a catalyst and a positive galvanizing step toward healing.

FOOTNOTES AND BIBLIOGRAPHY:

1. Series: Tree of Life, Part 1, World's Dream: A Sacred Tree, Tim Wood, March 27, 2015

2. The Promise of World Peace, the Universal House of Justice, 1985.

3. What Did Einstein Mean by Time is an Illusion? - Interesting Engineering, Jaime Trosper, Apr 06, 2023.

4. Biblehub.com, https://biblehub.com/daniel/5-25.htm

5. The Promise of World Peace, the Universal House of Justice, 1985.

6. Epistle to the Son of the Wolf, Bahá'u'lláh

7. The Promise of World Peace, The Universal House of Justice, 1987.

8. Muhammad and the Course of Islam, H.M. Balyuzi, George Ronald Publication, Oxford, Reprinted 1976.

9. Islam QA, 73 Sects in Islam, Mishkaatul Masaabih

10. Nicolas V and the Portuguese Slave Trade, The Lowcountry Digital Library, Carl Wise, and David Wheat.

11. The Promise of World Peace, the Universal House of Justice, 1985.

12. Papal Bull Dum Diversas June 18, 1452, Doctrine of Discovery, Dum Diversas, Indigenous Values Initiative

13. KJV, 'Think not that I have come …', Matthew 10:34-37

14. Extracts From the Writings of Bahá'u'lláh, Compiled by: The Research Department of the Universal House of Justice.

15. How Woodrow Wilson Tried to Reverse Black American Progress, History, Published by A&E Television Networks, Becky Little, July 14, 2020; Updated September 11, 2023

16. Center for Bioethics, University of Pennsylvania Health System, Philadelphia, PA 19104, USA, Correspondence to: A Caplan

17. Excerpt from The Tablet of Ahmad, Bahá'u'lláh, Baha'i Library Online

18. The Human Genome Project, https://www.bmj.com/content/319/7220/128

19. 'America's Forgotten History of Forced Sterilization', Santana Manjesgwar, Berkeley Political Review, 2020.

20. 10 Horrifying Facts About American Eugenics, ListVerse.com, Debra Kelly, fact checked by Jamie Frater, February 5, 2014.

21. Good Question blog, Christopher R. Smith, https://good question blog.com/author/understandingbooksbibleThisDayInHistory

22. This Day In History 1588 Spanish Armada Defeated, https://www. history.com this-day-in-history/spanish-armada-defeated#Battle

23. JSTOR Daily, Mohammed Elnaeim, June 20, 2021

24. Hidden Words of Bahá'u'lláh, #59

25. Hidden Words of Bahá'u'lláh, #68

26. How Kings from Nubia Became Pharaohs of Ancient Egypt and Ruled both Lands, Michael Eli Dokosi, November, 2019.

27. What was the Scramble for Africa? The World Atlas, https:// www.worldatlas.com/what-was-the-scramble-for-africa.html

28. Pope Innocent III and the Annulment of Magna Carts, Cambridge University Press & Assessment

29. Abdu'l-Bahá, *The Advent of Divine Justice*, p. 31

30. The Pupil of the Eye - African Americans in the World Order of Bahá'u'lláh, compiled by Bonnie J. Taylor, Palabra Publications, 1998

31. The Universal Emancipation Proclamation, Christopher Buck, January 12, 2014

32. The Hidden Words of Bahá'u'lláh, Arabic #2

33. The Hidden Words of Bahá'u'lláh, Arabic 44

34. John Locke, Racism, Slavery, and Indian Lands, Oxford Academichttps://academic.oup.com/edited-volume/28299/chapter/214977811

35. John Smith, History.com Editors, June 6, 2023, Original November 12, 2009.

36. New Fire Ceremony, Azteca Rituals, Britannica, https://www.britannica.com/topic/New-Fire-Ceremony

37. Conquistador, PBS, https://www.pbs.prg/conquistadors/cortes/cortes_e02.html

38. The Native American Government That Inspired the U.S Constitution, History News Networkhttps://historynewsnetwork.org/article/178157

39. Abdul-Baha, Some Answered Questions, newly revised edition, pp. 182-183.

40. Abdul-Baha, Excerpt from Some Answered Questions, Newly revised edition, pp. 182-3

41. Ten Oldest Civilizations in the World (Updated 2023), https://www.oldest.org/culture/civilizations

42. The Same Spirit Gives Eternal Life. – Abdu'l-Baha, *Paris Talks*, p. 82.

43. Holy Bible, King James Version, Genesis 11:4

44. Adam and the Age of Prophecy, BahaiTeachings.org, https://bahaiteachings.org/adam-age-prophecy/

45. Memories of the Sojourn of Abdul-Baha in Paris, Lady Blomfield, The Baha'i Faith, https://www.bahai.org/documents.essays/ladyblomfield

46. *Holy Trinity,* Written and fact checked by The Editors of Encyclopaedia Britannica, Last Updated: Jan 2, 2024

47. Bahá'u'lláh, The Manifestation of God, Baha'i International Community and Published by the Baha'i Reference Library

48. Some Answered Questions, Abdu'l-Baha, pp. 182-183.

49.The Promulgation of Universal Peace.

50. Abdu'l-Baha, <u>Selections from the Writings of Abdu'l-Baha</u>:

51. Abdul-Baha, <u>The Secret of Divine Civilization</u>

52. The Faith of **Bahá'u'lláh**: A World Religion, Shoghi Effendi, Haifa, Israel, 1947

53. Joshua 13-21 of the Old Testament

54. Genesis 37:7, Bible Hub, https://biblehub.com/genesis/37-7htm

55. Jewish Virtual Library, https://www.jewishvirtuallibrary.org/the-twelve-tribes-of-Israel

56. Vicar of Christ - Wikipedia

57. Tosefta/Sefaria, https://www.sefaria.org/texts/Tosefta

58. Epistle to the Son of the Wolf, **Bahá'u'lláh**

59. Hidden Words of **Bahá'u'lláh**, #40

60. Numbers 12:1, Bible Hub, https://biblehub.com/numbers/12-1.htm

61. The Kitáb-i-Íqán (The Book of Certitude), The Baha'i Faith, https://www.bahai.org/library/authoritative-texts/. | Bahá'í Reference Library

62. *Some Answered Questions*, Abdul-Baha, Part Four -- On the Origin, Powers, and Conditions of Man

63. The Tablet of Ahmad, Prayer by **Bahá'u'lláh**, https://www.bahaiprayers.org/ahmad.htm

64. The Hidden Words of **Bahá'u'lláh**, #55

65. Exodus 32:23, Bible Hub, https://biblehub.com/exodus/32:23/htm

66. Some Answered Questions, Baha'i Reference Library, The Baha'i Faith, https://www.baha'i.org/library/authoritative text

67. Unumbotte and the Origin of Languages, Oxford Reference, https://www.oxfordreference.com/display/10.1093/oi/

68. Revelation 3:12, KJV

69. *The Proclamation of Bahá'u'lláh*, Summons to the Kings and Rulers of the World

70. Abdul-Baha, Some Answered Questions, Newly Revised Edition, p 76-77

71. The Promise of World Peace, Section II, The Baha'i Faith, The Official Website of the Worldwide Baha'i Community, 1985.